A MURDER ON CAMPUS

THE PROFESSOR, THE COP, AND NORTH CAROLINA'S MOST NOTORIOUS COLD CASE

BRIAN SANTANA
CAMERON SANTANA

WildBluePress.com

A MURDER ON CAMPUS published by:
WILDBLUE PRESS
P.O. Box 102440
Denver, Colorado 80250

Publisher Disclaimer: Any opinions, statements of fact or fiction, descriptions, dialogue, and citations found in this book were provided by the author, and are solely those of the authors. The publisher makes no claim as to their veracity or accuracy, and assumes no liability for the content.

ISBN 978-1-964730-28-8 Hardcover
ISBN 978-1-964730-29-5 Trade Paperback
ISBN 978-1-964730-27-1 eBook

Interior Formatting and Book Cover Design by Elijah Toten
www.totencreative.com

A MURDER ON CAMPUS

This book is dedicated to all those who tirelessly work to preserve the memory of Virginia Olson. Your unwavering dedication keeps her legacy alive.

Table of Contents

Acknowledgments

Working on this book has been an incredibly fulfilling endeavor that would not have been possible without the help of far more people than we can thank in these acknowledgments. First and foremost, we want to thank our wives, Erin and Jenna. They offered unqualified support for this project and endured hearing pieces of our daily phone conversations during the research and writing phases. Even with these secondhand conversations, they probably heard more about terrible crimes than they anticipated or wanted when we first announced this project.

Ashley Whittle and the entire Special Collections and Archives staff at UNCA's Ramsey Library were the most professional archive staff we've ever worked with. Ashley is the unsung hero of this project. She promptly responded to our near-daily requests for university administrative files and ultimately did invaluable research legwork. We are forever grateful for the time and support she provided.

Equally generous were the many individuals who knew and loved Virginia Olson and who agreed to share their memories, letters, and pictures with us. When we first started this project, we never expected the outpouring of support we would receive from Olson's friends from her days at McLean High School and at UNCA. Jeff Doyle, one of Olson's closest friends, offered support, kind words, and candid memories that we had no right to expect but were humbled to receive. Many individuals from Olson's days at McLean High School came forward and sent us pictures and shared details of personal correspondence with her. Others reached out to friends of friends to help us track down classmates who emerged from our research.

Special thanks go to the following individuals from McLean and UNCA: Patricia "Patti" Pedigo-Dunn, who helped us track down members of the 1971 McLean High School graduating class. Others who contributed pictures or memories include Ken Sargent, Raye Anne Harris, and Alex Woo.

Arnold Wengrow, Rob Bowen, and Rob Storrs provided helpful support and information about the atmosphere at UNCA in the 1970s.

The faculty director of UNCA's student newspaper, *The Blue Banner*, Michael Gouge, offered encouragement and always picked up our phone calls when questions arose. If you search for "Virginia Marie Olson," the first page of results will be student-authored articles produced under his supervision. Gouge wrote about this case while an undergraduate at UNCA in the 1980s and is single-handedly responsible for keeping each incoming class of students aware of its existence. Since most media coverage surrounding this case is only available through paid digital newspaper archives, Gouge's work has ensured the case retains some visibility for general audiences.

Renee Roberson, the host of *Missing in the Carolinas*, offered early support for this project. She also cares about this case and continues to cover it on her podcast and website. She has been generous with her time and resources.

Chris Barbuschak, the Virginia Room Archivist for the City of Fairfax Regional Library, guided us through locating copies of McLean High School yearbooks from the 1970s. He also generously searched the physical microfilm collection of the McLean-based *Providence Journal* and other resources associated with the Virginia Chronicle Database for materials related to Olson.

Even though we are sure the Asheville Police Department and the North Carolina SBI are glad that they are no longer getting weekly messages from us, we do appreciate the time they gave us. Capt. Silberman and Det. Kevin Taylor, in particular, offered their thoughts on this case; whenever possible, they addressed our questions to the best of their ability.

Angie Grube, the Public Information Director of the North Carolina SBI, provided helpful information concerning personnel records of agents from the 1970s. Even though the SBI's retention schedules did not permit easy access to documents that would address all of our questions, Angie was always prompt and generous. On one occasion, she sought help from other staff to locate records associated with one of our requests.

The North Carolina Medical Examiner's Office staff and the North Carolina Division of Health and Human Services staff worked tirelessly to help us locate a copy of Virginia Olson's autopsy report. This file has not been easily accessible to the public since the 1975 fire that destroyed many of their records. It is a small feat that they could retrieve a copy for us, and we appreciate their diligence. Both offices were prompt in their communications and apologetic when they couldn't fulfill a request.

Maria Martinez from the Santa Fe Police Department offered valuable insights into obtaining "agency assist" records and expressed enthusiasm for our project.

Mary Crebs, who formerly worked for a medical examiner's office in Pennsylvania, helped us to sort through the Olson autopsy report and offered clear and thorough explanations about questions related to some of the findings.

Trevor Hoyle, Ben Washburn, and Hannah Weenink offered valuable insights and expertise concerning crime scene management and contemporary forensic practices. At a critical moment in our research, they also helped us to clarify our understanding of the significant obstacles that contemporary investigators face.

Don Bardes provided legal research assistance and advice during a crucial part of our work related to Buncombe County search warrants and the North Carolina Archives.

Finally, Steve Jackson, Jennifer Tedford, and the staff of WildBlue offered consistent support and enthusiasm for this project. This encouragement made the entire process much easier than we anticipated. A kind word of support can go a long way, and we received more than a few during this process.

Part I:

The Cop, The Professor, and the 51-year-old Unsolved Murder

Prologue: "The Harvard on the Hill"

"It was the Harvard on the hill. The outside world didn't impose on it...."—Michael Gouge, Class of 1990

But evil things, in robes of sorrow,
Assailed the monarch's high estate;
(Ah, let us mourn!—for never morrow
Shall dawn upon him, desolate!)
And round about his home the glory
That blushed and bloomed
Is but a dim-remembered story
Of the old time entombed.

—Edgar Allan Poe, "The Haunted Palace"

On April 12th, 1973, the UNCA faculty senate assembled at 3:15 p.m. in the school's Administrative Conference room to discuss a report released by the Committee on Academic Policies. Dr. Browning, the committee chair, called the meeting into order, and senators quickly approved past minutes before turning their attention to proposed changes in the Sociology Department's course offerings. The day's most animated conversations involved the merits of a math placement exam that roughly 40% of incoming students failed. It was the last significant meeting of the university's leadership for the 1972-1973 academic year.

These discussions, even contentious ones, were part of the routine bureaucracy of university-level administration that existed then and persists today. Pundits sometimes imagine universities as hotbeds for political activism and radical thought, but employees granted lifetime tenures rarely feel the same pressures as those in the private sector. Universities thrive on monotony and are often distrustful of change. Instead, they place their faith in the bureaucratic rules, motions, votes, and the tabling of discussions for another time. While it might be tempting to imagine this as unhealthy stagnation, this predictability creates structure and stability for those who live within it. Students can discover new ideas and experiment with ways to understand themselves and the outside world. At the same time, the university infrastructure serves as a counterbalance for youthful inclinations that demand wholesale change.

The spring 1973 semester was winding down, and as the faculty senate adjourned, seniors filled the library, cramming for finals. Finals week meant it was okay to start anticipating graduation and what came next. The year passed quickly for everyone on campus. In September, new students had moved in and heard welcoming remarks from Chancellor William Highsmith. Soccer games, peace rallies, and dances were among the events held during the fall and winter terms. Students overwhelmingly voted Karen Head as "Ms. UNCA" in October, and a Black Arts Festival hosted a soon-to-be-famous poet named Nikki Giovanni. By April, graduation and end-of-year festivities were starting. The mood on campus was celebratory. Bands like Grass Roots and Sugar Creek were scheduled to play concerts on UNCA's central quad on April 14th, which promised a welcome distraction from the stress of final exams.

The campus was also safe. P. Thomas Deason, the Dean of Students, liked to brag that UNCA, unlike some other schools in the UNC system, lacked a police presence. This was true. In 1973, the campus only had a handful of security guards who were unarmed and unable to make arrests. Not that arrests were needed. Chaos might have reigned on college campuses throughout the country as protests of Vietnam and Watergate raged, but life at UNCA provided a protective bubble from any immediate threats. As Michael Gouge told us, it was a "city on the hill" capable of recognizing the outside world but not fully touched by it.

The leisured movements of the spring semester and these widespread presumptions of safety were violently disrupted on April 15th at 3:30 p.m. when two local high school students discovered the bound and gagged body of Virginia Marie Olson, a 19-year-old drama major whose family and classmates affectionately called "Ginger," in the campus Botanical Gardens. Her death certificate, signed by Buncombe County Medical Examiner Ray Hampton, would list the immediate cause of death as a "stab wound to the chest" and would cite a "laceration" to the "left neck" as a secondary significant injury. It was a brutal scene with no campus precedent, then or now.

A cacophony of shock, fear, confusion, and blame ensued in the days that followed as police struggled to contain the investigation and quell community anxieties. Rumors and gossip quickly flowed through the campus of UNCA and the wider Buncombe County community. It soon became clear there was no shortage of suspects, from whispers about the professor who was navigating a messy divorce and sexual relationships with students to gossip about the son of a prominent business owner who knew more than he told authorities.

This book is the first to examine the 1973 murder of Virginia Marie Olson. It is the story of the people changed by the events of April 15th; it is a story about a school that has struggled to narrate the tragedy within its history; and it is also a chronicle of the tireless work of three generations of police investigators who continue to seek justice for Olson, her family, and the Asheville community.

Chapter 1: "My First Real Dead Body:" From Police Investigations to True Crime Investigations

Until I became a police officer, I never had the experience of seeing a real dead body. Sure, I had been to funeral homes and seen dead people, but by the time I saw them, they had thick layers of makeup. The only one I can recall in detail was a distant cousin. I still can't remember how we were related, but I remember the vague parental warning that it was my duty, as a 9-year-old, to obediently attend with my parents and brother to "show my respect." The viewing was in the rural eastern North Carolina town of Goldsboro, where going to funerals is a pastime. My grandmother regularly attended so many funerals that it was common to call and ask about her plans for a day or week, and she would only need to say "funeralizing."

My brother Brian and I wore church clothes to this wake, and when we arrived, we took our place in a short receiving line. It was like Disney World—if those rides culminated with you confronting your mortality and then casually moving on to the next experience. Once inside, I could see an old barber's pole, and upon further inspection, I noticed that the corpse of this distant cousin had his barber's uniform on. Of course, you can't cut hair in the afterlife without scissors, so those were also added. As I mentioned earlier, this wasn't my first dead body, but it is the only one that made much of an impression.

As a cop, I've seen a lot of people die, and, at this point, I've seen more dead bodies than I can remember. You get used to it, and when you arrive at a crime scene, you go to autopilot. You secure the crime scene, lock down the area with tape, get someone to be a crime scene recorder who documents everyone in and out of the scene, and canvas for witnesses and cameras. Everything is documented in detail.

I first saw this documentation up close while in the Raleigh Police Academy. One of our more frequent assignments was to take paper records to the old records building to file. At the time, the main headquarters for the police department was at 110 S McDowell St. The department had another building that stored old police files on Hillsborough St, which was about five blocks away. Seven of us from the academy would take a handful of files and walk them over to the Hillsborough Street location. Now, this task would not take long, maybe an hour max. The goal for the department was to keep us employed, busy, and out of people's way.

So what would we do for the rest of the seven hours? Besides taking a long lunch, we would read all of the old case files. These were not recent cases; many were from the 60s and 70s. For us, it was not as much reading as looking at the 8 x10 crime scene photos. The victims did not seem real—bloody crime scenes of lifeless bodies. We looked at these images, knowing we would soon be police officers, and, in whatever way we could, we tried to prepare for the reality of being at a murder scene.

Corpses dressed as barbers and gruesome black-and-white photos were one thing, but I will never forget the first violent crime scene I experienced as a rookie cop with the Raleigh Police Department. It occurred during a midnight shift on our first weekend of training. In Raleigh, after an extensive academy that teaches you all the policies and laws you should not break, you go on "field training," which is 30 weeks long and includes a two-week evaluation. It is during this time that you become a real cop. Luckily, I was assigned a great training officer who shared my brother's name, Brian. I remember driving around southeast Raleigh and not knowing where I was going. Back then, we did not have GPS or smartphones. Instead, we had a "map book." Some training officers made their rookies use only the book and did not give them directions.

That night, while we drove around Martin Luther King Blvd, dispatch played a tone signifying that a major crime just occurred in the city. The dispatcher followed it up with "103 at Bragg and East." 103 was the code for someone shot and killed. We were less than a mile away. Brian tells me to turn on the lights and siren and to "go go go!"

He called out directions, and we got there in about a minute. Dispatch advised us that the suspect was a "black male wearing all-black clothing." When we arrived, the street was flooded with people, and the community we arrived in was predominantly African American. To make it even more complicated, wearing plain black T-shirts at the time was popular.

I jumped out of the car and asked Brian what to do, and he yelled at me to stop someone. Now, remember, I am right out of the academy; I don't know what the fuck I am supposed to do, and it just so happens that the only other white guys on this street are two police officers. So, I go full-blown rookie cop and chase after the first person I see. It's a young black male with a black t-shirt and black pants. I am sure I yelled at him to "stop" and probably some other bullshit line they taught in the academy. I catch up to him rather quickly and tackle him to the ground.

I grab his arm and say, "Why are you running?" He exclaims, "Because there are two dead people back there!" After realizing he had a good point, I helped him up and took his statement.

I was then given the job of guarding the dead body. EMS had decided to take one of the other victims. In all reality, the guy they took should have stayed at the scene. He had a bullet in his head, but someone thought they were going to save him. I again asked my training officer what to do, and he said, "Simple. You stand next to the body and make sure no one gets near the scene."

At this point, I am standing in the dirt yard of a low-income housing development, and I don't know if I am supposed to look at the corpse or if I should avoid eye contact. Then, I hear a phone in the corpse's pocket ringing. Back then, it was popular to have a ringtone. This guy had a rap song I did not recognize. All I knew was it kept ringing and ringing. What do you do in that situation? Eventually, homicide detectives arrived; I loaded back into the patrol car and went to the next call.

That story captures the life of a beat cop. You go to the craziest call of your life, then move on to the next one. In 2022, I decided to move on from being a cop full-time. My life was complicated. I had been a cop for over 18 years, but after having my daughter, who was born with special needs, on top of having a son with my ex-wife and wanting to have a family life, the rotating shifts and being called in for protest after protest were taking too much of a toll.

I became a stay-at-home dad and helped take care of my daughter. I had lots of time, and my brother called me about a true crime class he taught. The class would investigate murders and missing persons cases. They would use the Freedom of Information Act (FOIA) and human sources for information. He told me about some of the cases, and I started to get the urge to do police work again. I found myself watching true crime shows and researching the cases. One day, Brian called me and told me about Virginia Marie Olson. He gave me the basics of the case and said that not a lot had been written about the murder. He suggested that we should write a book or an article.

The idea of being an author still has not sunk in. When my 11-year-old son learned about the project, he said, “So you are going to be an author?” I had to think about it, but I responded, “I guess so.” I always saw myself as a cop, which I did for over 18 years. I proceeded in that mindset when writing this book. I reviewed articles, contacted sources, and kept an open mind to suspects.

The following pages are a joint effort by Brian and me to bring light to this case and all the possible suspects. We will give you our perspectives and thoughts on the case and offer who we think was likely responsible. We hope that the book will stir up new leads and information that can help the police to close this case officially.

This book is also about sharing a passion of mine with my brother. Together, hopefully, we can bring Virginia justice. This may seem impossible, but we will not quit until this case is officially closed. The best lesson I learned in the academy is no matter how hard it gets you, “Stay in the fight!”

Chapter 2: The Professor Who Became an Unlikely True Crime Investigator

My introduction to "true crime" occurred when I was still in elementary school. My parents occasionally took me and my brother Cameron to my grandmother's house for monthly weekend visits, and when I was around ten years old, they informed us that we would be staying with our "Aunt Minnie" for a night. "Aunt" Minnie was an aunt in name only. Minnie was my grandmother's longtime friend and she interacted with us like family. She was a short and wiry woman in her late 70s with cropped white hair who wore oversized glasses and tended to squint when she smiled. She drove a tiny yellow car with barely enough room for three people, and she was kind and gentle and enjoyed taking us to the local Big Lots to buy toys.

On this visit, Aunt Minnie introduced me to the terrifying world of *Unsolved Mysteries*. The experience remains vivid. For dinner, she had picked us up some takeout from McDonalds, and when we returned to her house, she ushered us into her tiny living room, turned the T.V. on, and then motioned for us to sit on the sofa. She scurried around between the living room and the kitchen and retrieved the kind of aged, metal, T.V. dinner trays that were popularized in the 50s when television sets first became a staple of the suburban living room.

The purple graphics of *Unsolved Mysteries*, accompanied by the show's ominous prelude music, began, and I wasn't sure what I was watching, but I glanced over at Aunt Minnie and her strong focus was enough to make any interruption seem rude. She sat motionless except for small gestures that allowed her to quietly nibble on her food. Even though I was young, I understood that our visit had coincided with one of her rituals that could not be disturbed.

As the episode began, the show's host Robert Stack emerged from a misty background wearing a suit and open trench coat. He deliberately walked towards the camera and in his famous baritone voice intoned, "Welcome to Unsolved Mysteries." At this point, it's worth noting that for Aunt Minnie, my grandmother, and even my parents, Robert Stack was most associated with his work on the popular ABC television show *The Untouchables*, which ran from 1959-1963. Stack played Treasury Department agent Eliot Ness, who in real life was most famous for taking down mobster Al Capone for tax evasion. *Unsolved Mysteries* played to these associations to help emphasize the "crime-solving" participatory element of the show. Just as the show blurred the boundary between Robert Stack, "the host," and Robert Stack, the "actor who played Eliot Ness," it also blurred the boundaries between fiction and non-fiction in dramatic re-enactments of unsolved cases. *Unsolved Mysteries* wasn't the first show to seamlessly blend actors, real-life investigators, witnesses, and victims through a combination of documentary reporting and fictional, speculative reenactment. Still, it was the first instance of this treatment that I remember, and the boundary for me was non-existent. Everything felt very real.

What especially bothered my ten-year-old self was the grave, humorless stare and the monotonous quality of Stack's voice, which conferred an eerie quality on everything recounted over the 60-minute episode. There was a quiet intensity to his perfunctory introductions to each mystery that seemed out of place and threatening, almost like part of his job was to convey the deeply disturbing news that no story had a happy ending or even a clear resolution. While audiences might have associated him with crime-fighting, for me, he appeared scarier than some of the criminals profiled in the show.

The only case from that first experience with *Unsolved Mysteries* I recall focused on an unsolved murder that the show hypothesized could be connected to a local satanic cult. Pardon the pun, but the episode scared the hell out of me. That night, even the sound of Aunt Minnie's old air conditioner woke me up and kept me on edge. I'm not even sure what specifically bothered me since I wasn't having nightmares about being murdered by a satanic cult or anything like that. It was more the strange combination of fact and fiction, entertaining and disturbing, and repulsion coupled with a morbid curiosity that the show awakened in me. I didn't sleep well that night but was already looking forward to watching it again the next day.

I couldn't articulate it then, but this was the start of my lifelong fascination with true crime, and also the earliest indication of my complicated relationship with the genre. *Unsolved Mysteries* soon gave way to the more taboo "true crime" section of Waldenbooks at our local mall. These books introduced me to the underbelly of society and to the dark side of the human psyche that felt far from my everyday sheltered assumptions about people and the world. The stories were dark, but reading them as a child felt worldly because they made me realize the precariousness of the things I often counted on and assumed to be unchanging about my life. These stories were a stark reminder that life can change for the worse very quickly, but I also saw in them a kind of optimism that my wife Erin, to this day, finds a bit disingenuous. It is hard to articulate, but since a young age, I've viewed true crime stories as disturbing but also strangely optimistic. Even though the stories often depict people at their worst, there is also something affirming to me in the genre's insistence that crimes can be explained and people can be understood and the world can be ordered with the right approach.

Despite my interest in true crime, I'm skeptical about why I have spent (and continue to spend) so much time with this genre. My friends don't participate in true crime communities, and my wife of 15 years actively dislikes the entire genre. At home, I am generally banned from discussing anything true crime-related because even a single story can disrupt my wife's sleep for a day or two. Michelle McNamara, the brilliant bestselling author of *I'll Be Gone in the Dark,* articulates a kind of conflict I've felt and heard others describe when she reflects, "I love reading true crime, but I've always been aware of the fact that, as a reader, I am actively choosing to be a consumer of someone else's tragedy. So, like any responsible consumer, I try to be careful in the choices I make. I read only the best: writers who are dogged, insightful, and humane."

The ethical implication of actively consuming someone else's pain is one that genuinely weighs on me. Unlike my brother Cameron, who has seen the worst of humanity many times while working as a member of law enforcement, I've always been more comfortable observing it from afar. Perhaps it is even worse that I prefer to keep it all at arm's distance since this buffer provides a level of emotional protection that law enforcement and victims don't possess. For much of my life as a consumer of true crime, I've thought about these questions, but articulating them is hard because they can easily come across as petty, abstract, or worse, pretentious.

While my brother graduated from Western Carolina University and went to the police academy in Raleigh, NC, to start a career in law enforcement, I finished my undergraduate degree down the road at UNCA. I went to graduate school to study English and then American

Studies. I completed a Master's degree in English and I eventually finished a PhD from The George Washington University in Washington, D.C. I ultimately landed a tenure-track academic job teaching in the English Department at Shepherd University, a small liberal arts college nestled in the Eastern Panhandle region of West Virginia.

Even though my interest in true crime has persisted since childhood, it was Sarah Koenig's podcast *Serial*, which became a cultural phenomenon in 2014, that transformed my interest in true crime into a socially acceptable hobby. My wife even listened to *Serial*, *S-Town*, and a few others. The genre's growth continued with Netflix documentary series like *Making a Murderer*, *The Keepers*, and *The Disappearance of Madeline McCain*, and many others. The days of slyly migrating from the young adult section of the bookstore to the more lurid "true crime" section to sneak peeks of book descriptions and crime scene photos were over.

The true crime boom of the 2000s not only increased the popularity of the genre, but it also changed who produced work in this genre, what stories they told, and their rationale for telling them. These new true crime stories became less associated with sensationalism and more about social justice. When I was growing up, the kind of character that Robert Stack played as host of *Unsolved Mysteries* played a powerful role in shaping how I thought about the people who told these stories. They were men who wore trench coats, and fedoras that possessed a world-weariness observable in their gait and stare. They traveled through dangerous places so the reader or viewer didn't have to, and they gave consumers permission to confront their deepest fears and dark curiosities.

By the time I started teaching, the true crime author and producer looked more like Tina Fey than Robert Stack, and the audience looked more like my mom than my youthful playmates. As the people who produced true crime changed, so did the stories. Podcasts like *The Vanished* tackled tough stories dealing with substance abuse and suicide, while documentaries like *Murder in Big Horn* spotlighted the impact of crime on marginalized communities. As national conversations about policing and equity were taking place, these creators viewed stories about crime and society as making a positive societal contribution.

Something else happened during this time: I'd always made small talk with my students before the start of class, but I noticed that for the first time in my career, my students were casually chatting about the latest podcast episode of *Crime Junkie* or the latest true crime documentary that aired or was about to air. Students became actively engaged and invested when I interjected myself into these conversations. In fact, students would increasingly show up to class early just to have a conversation with me or their classmates about a case that had caught their attention.

This led to an idea: what if I restructured my freshmen writing class to focus on true crime? The main goal of these types of classes is to introduce students to the principles of professional research. Students learn to navigate different types of digital and physical databases. This typically means conversations about locating and reading different primary and secondary sources and using them to create academically sound arguments. The idea sounded wild to some of my peers, but I moved forward anyway. My initial conception of the class was this: I would divide the class into four research teams. Each group would be assigned an actual unsolved murder or mysterious disappearance.

Each week, students would complete different research activities, and I would teach them how to navigate various types of information. For instance, I taught students how to analyze media coverage for their cases and asked them to compare local, state, and national coverage. Students also learned how to file FOIA requests and obtain public records like death certificates, search warrants, and medical examiner reports. They gathered census data and crime statistics tracked by the FBI. Finally, students also practiced interviewing sources. My students interviewed medical examiners, police investigators, and, in some cases, friends and families of victims.

The first year I taught this course, I was genuinely shocked by the number of people directly associated with cases who agreed to sit down for interviews with my students. The whole experience taught me that sincere interest can go a long way. I also came to appreciate the scope of crime's impact on individuals and people far removed from the actual incident.

When I teach true crime, I encourage students to find a case that matters to them. When I decided to finally work on a case myself, the answer to this question had been obvious for 23 years. I first heard about Virginia Olson in 1999 during my first semester at UNCA. Like Olson, I studied drama at UNCA. In fact, when I started in 1999, Arnold Wengrow, who was Olson's drama professor in 1973, had only recently retired. Similarly, Rob Storrs, one of Olson's co-stars and dance partners in *U.S.A.*, her last college production, was still an adjunct acting professor in the department.

The first time I walked into Carol Belk Theater, I saw a whimsical photograph of a beautiful woman painting scenery from a past era. I first learned her name when a classmate walked up behind me and said, "Hey, that's Ginger Olson. She died in Carol Belk, and her spirit haunts the theater." Later, I learned she had been murdered, not at the theater, but in the Biltmore Botanical Gardens across the street from the university. Still later, I was told she was "raped and murdered near the Botanical Gardens." It seemed like the story changed slightly each year, but the result always remained tragic. At the time, I couldn't quite place why her story fascinated me so much. I would ask other faculty and students for information but no one seemed to know very much and I consistently received conflicting information.

Even though the answers I received didn't help me learn much about Olson, I felt a kinship with this person who, like me, arrived at UNCA, found a home and friends, and began to think for the first time about her place in the world. I was privileged to grow up, have a family, and find my niche. She will always be a 19-year-old girl on the brink of "becoming."

UNCA was where I became who I am today, and understanding what happened to Virginia Olson is one way of understanding the real person and events behind the image that played a central role in how I relate to some of the most critical years of my life.

When I started this book, I realized it was a project I wanted to work on with my brother. Cameron and I are very different, and our busy lives have caused us to grow more distant over the years. We live in different states, we both have young children, and we both navigate jobs that are not traditional 9 a.m.-5 p.m. work hours. However, so much of the way I relate to this genre traces back to those shared childhood experiences with true crime, and if this was going to be a difficult experience, I wanted to go through it with someone I could trust. As a police officer, Cameron possessed the language and connections to members of the law enforcement community in North Carolina that would be necessary for this case.

Investigating this case also became a way for us to connect our shared history to a shared purpose. From tracking down leads to checking in at the end of a long day, we talked more while researching this book than we had in the previous five years before it.

This book occurred at a crossroads in our lives, and what we found proved stranger than anything we could have imagined when we started.

Chapter 3: "Unrealized Hopes and Plans": Searching for Virginia Olson

In 1973, members of the Asheville Police Department hung Virginia Olson's picture on the long, barren wall of their detective's bureau. Today, that picture resides in a case file with numbers so old they are barely legible. The original placement of the photograph captured the department's earliest commitment to solving her case, and its home today serves as a painful reminder of the three generations of detectives who have failed to do so.

Over the past 51 years, the levels of media coverage, community awareness, and drive to solve Olson's murder have dwindled; many of the detectives associated with investigating it have passed away, retired, or now work on the case part-time. Names like Hall, Maxey, Chambers, Matthews, Annarino, Gilchrist, Taylor, and others have become part of a once-infamous case that has faded into obscurity. The name "Virginia Olson" is still widely known throughout western North Carolina; a clear understanding of what happened to her, what occurred in the original investigations, and why this case remains unsolved is far less clear. It is far more likely that the experiences of others are similar to the explanations I received at UNCA, which were often conflicting, unclear, and sometimes downright bizarre.

We talked about these issues during our trip to find a young woman we had never met and who had been dead for 51 years, whose story we had come to care about.

Today, Virginia Olson resides in Prospect Cemetery, the primary burial site in northwestern Decatur County, Tennessee. It sits just off the rural Prospect Road, which divides the roughly 650 graves into two parts, with the oldest dating back to the 19th century. As the road branched, we studied our map and notes to confirm that our intended location was in the "South of Prospect Road" section of the property. We were here to find Virginia Marie Olson. While Olson grew up in Northern Virginia and spent her last years in North Carolina, her family tree traces back to this part of Tennessee.

We have spent virtually every day of the past year searching for Virginia Olson, and on this unseasonably warm fall day, we were about to "find" her. By this point, we had already discovered that the circumstances of the original investigations into her death were filled with many twists. Still, this task felt different because it had a definite ending.

"You will probably see a double marker for Ava Elsie Quinn and Herlett Chaffee Woods first… who had a daughter Lurodine. You should find her beside them," explained a caretaker who was walking around carefully arranging flowers on the day of our visit.

A few minutes later, we found her. Her raised headstone was simple and emblazoned with the family surname "OLSON" in all capital letters. In smaller letters, "Virginia Marie (Ginger)" announced we had reached our destination. Beneath her name was a Biblical verse that cryptically promised that "it is not far to Jerusalem if you know the way."

"There she is," was the only exchange that passed between the two of us.

In this terse acknowledgment was a recognition that after spending months interviewing law enforcement, people in Olson's life, and debating aspects of her murder investigation, finding her grave brought us back to memories we didn't experience directly—stories we heard vividly recounted by those who knew and loved her. We took this trip because we wanted to remind ourselves that Virginia Olson was a real person who lived and loved and was trying to figure out what she wanted her life to look like when it was taken away.

When you research a murder, it is easy for victims to become pieces of a puzzle. For people in the Buncombe County Clerk's office and the Asheville Police Department, Olson is officially known as 73-0972, the case number assigned to her criminal investigation records. However, this record and the person attached are no longer commonly recognized. Initially, the criminal investigation slowly overtook the person. Eventually, the case itself faded from public consciousness, only to be replaced by 51 years of innuendo and gossip that obscured the most basic facts about her murder and distanced contemporary audiences from her humanity.

It is strange to think that an event that transformed many people's lives could be lost.

"It appears the records you request we no longer have in our possession as the retention schedule for personnel files is 30 years," wrote one member of the North Carolina SBI's Public Information Office in response to an early personnel records request to confirm the dates of active employment for two agents associated with the Olson investigation in 1974.

And it isn't just the investigators who have been forgotten; it is the institution Virginia Olson called home for two years. An event that shook the campus of UNCA in 1973 and forever impacted those who were Olson's peers has become an urban legend and ghost story today.

We interviewed many current UNCA students and faculty to gauge how much awareness they possess about this crime, and we were surprised to learn that many have little or no knowledge of it. One professor recalled that talk of a "ghost" occasionally occurred in first-year students' discussions. This professor acknowledged that she assumed the story was an urban legend passed down to students as a rite of passage, and she expressed surprise to learn it was grounded in an actual event: "I remember hearing students speak of the ghost named Virginia who lived in the Belk Theater. I never knew Virginia was a real person who died in such a terrible manner."

Another current student voiced a similar sentiment when he observed, "I'm sure there is some truth to it... maybe there was a girl named Virginia who died in some kind of accident a long time ago, but I would be surprised if anything like a murder happened around here."

This book begins and ends with Virginia "Ginger" Olson; however, we want to give a disclaimer that it is still a kind of "ghost story" since the real Virginia Olson will remain elusive despite our best efforts to find her. How does one go about recreating a person who has been dead for 51 years? Perhaps the best place to start is with a disclaimer that it is impossible.

What traces of her that remain are a combination of fragmented reports regarding her murder and the fading memories of those who knew and loved her. These pieces make it challenging to create a coherent image of a person with aspirations, fears, uncertainties, and imperfections like the rest of us.

Over the last year, we talked to many people who knew Ginger Olson, and they shared stories that captured how they remembered her. However, despite collecting fragments of experiences people had with her, we were constantly reminded how inadequate and potentially strange memories taken out of context can seem.

For instance, one of Olson's friends at McLean High School recounted a story about Olson's time working at a fast-food place called Gino's with her friend Laura Bond. As he attempted to describe the "silly outfits" the two girls wore and their "not too serious attitudes" about elements of their job, it became clear that these intensely personal memories didn't provide much insight for those who didn't share that original experience.

Another classmate from McLean High School, who was more of an acquaintance, attempted to describe the kindness that Olson showed him when he considered running away from home. This story was offered without significant commentary or explanation. Still, it was obvious that it meant something to the person who enthusiastically shared it with us: "My favorite memory of Ginger was that when I decided to "run away from home" as a freshman; (this would have been 1969) she gave me $20. She was a truly kind gal."

One thing that became apparent is that people are very protective of Virginia Olson's memory. Getting former classmates, friends, and acquaintances to talk about her was not hard. Their comments consistently demonstrated that she made a lasting impact in many people's lives—even those she only knew for a short time. There were at least eight individuals we talked with who were little more than Olson's acquaintances, but they spoke movingly about the impact of her kindness on their lives and how her death had never been forgotten. One of these individuals remarked, "At some point in the early 80's, our gang got together around Christmastime and she was remembered as the sweet, kind soul she truly was."

Writing about Virginia Olson is tricky because the more conversations we had with people who interacted with her, the more elusive she started to feel. Following her death, many people attempted to put forth their memories of her and assign them meaning. Some described the way that she taught them the meaning of love, compassion, selfless kindness, "how to avoid taking life too seriously," "what it means to love God," "she taught me what it means to love another person," and many descriptions that indicated her life, while cut short, still had meaning.

Some attempted to claim her death and story for darker purposes. Rob Storrs, one of Olson's classmates and theater colleagues at UNCA, described attending a Christian revival a year after her death and hearing the preacher invoke Olson's death as an example of the penalty for sin:

> While I was researching the character Preacher Haggler in "Dark of the Moon," I went to a tent revival off Riverside Drive down by the French Broad. I wanted to hear the preacher's cadence, and inflections. It was an actual tent with white painted crude chairs, alter and a red cross painted on the pulpit podium. I sat in the back, my note pad mashed against my inner thigh, so I could discretely record any impressions of the evening that I might find useful. As the congregation filed in and sat down, they glanced back at me, immediately knowing that I wasn't one of them.
>
> The service started, and after a few perfunctory salutations and invocations, the preacher started talking about "that murdered girl at the college." With seeming "inside," perhaps divine knowledge, he proceeded to claim that she got what she deserved. He went on to say that, though she wore clothes that were appropriate for college students in the '70's, her scant attire invited the attack. I couldn't bear any more, so I quietly got up and headed for the rear tent flap. Before I got outside, I heard the preacher proclaim that the devil had been banished from the service, the loud murmurs of the congregation in agreement.

The paradox true crime writers face when reconstructing a life is similar to the one that historians navigate when excavating the past. There is a particular danger in imagining people of the past as entirely different from you, and there is an equally present danger in imagining those who lived in the past as sharing many of your core attributes, beliefs, and assumptions. Both approaches ultimately erase the individual.

In true crime, this tension gets amplified. The examples we discussed above demonstrate that even the best memories might not help us to understand actual lives. Bereaved friends and relatives are vested in preserving the best possible version of an individual because they know that any public narration threatens to enshrine how other people will first encounter and come to think about their loved one.

We appreciate the stakes that many feel because this book is the first to attempt to write Olson back into the story, and we also want to capture something that approximates her. Yet, to imagine someone as "purely good" deprives them of the complexities that make them human, just as focusing solely on a person's faults or, even worse, ignoring the victim entirely, threatens to undermine the incalculable loss that occurs in any murder.

More than anything, these well-intentioned reminisces invoke that sensation that Australian novelist Christina Stead wrote to a friend in the 70s following the death of her husband when she thoughtfully observed, "There was the ghost story ("every love story is a ghost story")." Later, other novelists like David Foster Wallace would borrow this phrase and use it to capture the sensation of someone superimposing their image or ideas onto another. In doing so, the traces of the original person matter less except insofar as they remind of something lost.

In one light, some of the comments made about Virginia Olson might sound odd, but we think her life (and death) still matter to so many people because it reminds them of a moment when their perception of the world changed. Many individuals mentioned that Olson was the first peer they knew who died. When they remember the tragedy of her death, they are also remembering that moment in which their perception of the world changed.

Ghostly associations surround Olson, and even former police investigators attached to the case were not immune to similar sentiments.

"Have you seen the picture of her they published in the 1973 yearbook? It's haunting and captures what a sweet kid she was," observed one former Asheville detective who worked on the case when we asked him about Olson.

The picture he referenced *is* haunting, capturing many of the ethereal qualities that others abstractly described through their stories. It depicts a young woman painting theatrical scenery. She seems focused but also slightly aware of the camera's presence. Her body is relaxed and balanced- her pose is reminiscent of a dancer or someone trained in ballet or movement. She looks elegant, and her graceful posture contrasts with her casual attire. She wears a short-sleeved t-shirt neatly tucked into jeans and a single sock; her left foot is bare. She is in the middle of extending her right arm, and she holds a paintbrush in it. It seems like a staged moment meant for a picture. The setting of the photograph is the drama department's scene shop; there are no paint stains, the background is slightly out of focus and bright white, and all of this has the general effect of conferring an angelic look that aligns with the way many relate to her today: the person who "lit up" a room but whose light was extinguished far too early.

After weeding through a supply of memories and fragmentary anecdotes that arrived on a near-daily basis, we think it is only appropriate to attempt something more coherent.

Who Was Virginia Olson?

Virginia Marie Olson was born on September 13, 1953, in Washington, D.C., to C. Doswell Olson and Lurodine Woods. She grew up in a quietly devout religious family with two siblings, Karen and Carl. Her family attended Lewinsville Presbyterian Church in McLean, Virginia, and her journal entries, poetry, and the reminisces of others often invoke her religious beliefs in one way or another. One close high school friend would describe her religious faith this way: "She was quietly passionate and utterly sincere, yet never in a heavy, judgmental way." Another former classmate described her religious faith as manifested in small ways when she remarked, "I don't think I ever heard her preach to me, but her investment in her beliefs was obvious. She was kind."

Patti Russell was a classmate of Olson's at McLean High School, and she shared a panoramic class photo with us that captured an unassuming quality that many of her friends at UNCA would later stress. Those who didn't know her would often describe her as shy and soft-spoken; her roommate even said she might have come across as "awkward" to those who didn't know her. In Russell's picture, Olson is barely recognizable in the large group. Russell had to circle Olson's image for us and noted that, unlike her classmates, she is looking askance from the camera towards the ground.

One of the fascinating things about the memories shared with us is how friends and acquaintances stress her introverted and quiet personality while simultaneously describing something hypnotic about her. Olson made an impression on virtually everyone she came in contact with in a way that is difficult to explain without descending into the kind of cliché that we discussed earlier.

"Even after all these years, Ginger stands out because of her incredible kindness, sweetness, and shy smile. Even though we were only classmates, I remember Ginger as one of the most genuinely kind people I have ever met. Never once did I ever see a frown on her face or hear her speak a harsh word," Russell recounted as she tried to find the right words to describe why this person, who was merely a classmate and not a friend, had made such a deep impression on her life.

Despite navigating several childhood moves due to her father's employment, Olson maintained this publicly positive attitude. She was described as an easygoing child who made friends quickly in elementary school while maintaining a quietness that others might interpret as introversion. During her elementary school years, her family moved to Great Bend, Kansas, and they remained there until she completed junior high school.

When the family relocated back to North Virginia, Olson started at McLean High School and discovered her passion for the arts. At McLean, she took drawing and painting classes and was active in theater and performing arts. She eventually joined the National Thespian Society at McLean and even placed first in their forensics competition before she graduated. One McLean classmate who took drawing with her shared this memory: "Ginger sat in front of me. She had long, strawberry blonde hair (a light reddish color), and during one boring class, I sketched her hair from behind, and the drawing turned out great. Unfortunately, I have lost track of it after all these years, which breaks my heart."

During her senior year, she became widely associated with the school drama productions. She appeared in Kaufman and Hart's *Once in a Lifetime* as one of the "Foolish Virgins" singing group. She was also a member of McLean's Yearbook staff. Members of the yearbook staff would remember her as "lovely, funny, kind, quirky."

During her final two years of high school, she developed a close friendship with Jeff Doyle, who worked with her on the school yearbook, and they soon became inseparably close. Theirs would be a friendship that would last the rest of her life. She taught Doyle how to play James Taylor songs on her Yamaha guitar, and they both discovered a shared love of nature. Doyle explained it this way: "Both of us loved nature, and I was taking the botany class that ended up shaping my future career, so we spent a lot of time walking together in the woods, me taking pictures of flowers with my macro lens."

After graduating from high school, members of Olson's circle of friends went to different schools. Jeff Doyle planned to attend William and Mary, another friend planned to attend the University of Virginia, and Olson decided to apply to the University of North Carolina at Asheville. Her general artistic leanings made UNCA an ideal choice. Asheville, North Carolina, was home to some of the oldest writing groups in the South, and the area had a reputation as a haven for creative people. Olson saw herself as a creative person who always wrote, but she also enjoyed dance, journaling, painting, reading poetry, and performing in theater. She expressed some sadness about leaving her friends, but she also expressed excitement about starting over in a new place.

In 1971, during the summer before her first year in college, Olson's family moved from the DC-VA area to Lexington, North Carolina, in Davidson County; this move played a role in her decision to attend UNCA. The move was part of another transfer for her father, who worked for the United States Department of Agriculture and had taken on a project working on rural telephone cooperatives.

In Lexington, she quickly befriended Jennie Mills, who lived across the street from her family. Mills described her as someone who enjoyed as much time in nature as possible. She said, "We'd ride bicycles together. She liked to be outdoors a lot. Sometimes, we would ride up to the pony pasture and just sit around and talk."

Even though Olson moved to North Carolina, she committed to maintaining her friendships in Virginia. Whenever she could travel, she would visit high school friends like Robin McHugh. She also consistently wrote letters to keep everyone updated about her life in North Carolina. In one of her letters, she described teaching a Lexington girl how to swim and expressed interest in getting a job as a lifeguard at a local pool.

While many people loved Olson, understanding her dating life is complicated. Those around her tended to think about Doyle as her boyfriend during these years because it was clear they were very close. Doyle offered us one story that we believe summed up their close bond: "We saw each other a few times during breaks, and in the summer after freshman year, I visited her in Lexington and painted a logo of intertwined 'G' and 'J' runes from *Lord of the Rings* on her basement wall with the motto, 'An eternity is too short a time" in elven script.'

The interest that Olson expressed in becoming a lifeguard in a letter to one of her high school friends would come to fruition when, shortly after arriving in Lexington, she landed a job as a lifeguard at Brookside Swimming Pool. Her coworkers at Brookside tended to describe her as "bookish and introverted," but Richard Sink, her boss at the pool, added that she was also a "deep thinker and a real sweet person." Her passion for finding ways to help others emerged when she began volunteering for a group that recorded works of literature on tape for people who were blind.

She wasn't sure what she ultimately wanted to do with her life, but she told many friends that she wanted to find ways to use her creative talents to help others. When we gently pressed one of her friends from UNCA about specifics she might have voiced about her future plans, she reminded us that she and Olson were young: "I don't know how important career plans were for us."

It is tempting to imagine that an unfinished life had a clear trajectory, but at the time of her death, Olson was only 19 years old and imagined she had plenty of time to figure it all out. This theme repeatedly emerged in conversations with people who knew Olson in college.

When Olson started college, she did so as an undeclared major. However, when she returned to campus for the Fall 1972 semester and the start of her sophomore year, she confidently walked into Drama Department Chair Arnold Wengrow's office to declare a drama major. After declaring a drama major, she was prominently featured in the Drama Department's fall production of *U.S.A.* by John Dos Passos. Rob Storrs, one of Olson's Drama Department colleagues and co-stars in this *U.S.A.* production, described her: "We were dance partners in the big 'chorus line' at the end of an act. I think we learned the Black Bottom. I knew little about her except that she was very religious, attending daily prayer meetings on campus and keeping a journal of her soulful life." Others in the *U.S.A.* cast offered us similar remarks.

A few months after this show closed, she placed in a speech competition at Catawba College.

By her sophomore year, she had formed close bonds with the other residents of Craig Dormitory, her campus residence. They had warmed to the reserved Olson and had become accustomed to seeing her studying on the university quad or heading out for walks in the nearby Botanical Gardens. In 2017, Dee James, Olson's dormitory proctor, would tell UNCA's student newspaper, *The Blue Banner*, that Olson "was quiet, she was not a big effusive kind of personality, but just sweet, nice kind of person." There were even close friendships with a few other boys in her classes, including at least one who expressed interest in dating her.

However, as the spring semester of 1973 began to wind down, Olson's main focus was landing a summer stock acting job. She also confided to friends that she was considering a transfer to UNC-Greensboro the following year. She loved Asheville, but a transfer to Greensboro would put her only 40 minutes away from her family.

As she pondered these immediate questions, her life seemed to be taking shape, and then it was taken from her on April 15, 1973, in an act that stunned the entire campus community. We will address the circumstances of her murder in detail later, but for now, we want to focus on the impact of her death on the campus community. Rob Storrs, her dance partner from the fall *U.S.A.* production, described the campus mood after Olson's death:

> At the time, there were only 800 students at UNCA, and 80% were commuters. The news of Ginger's death flattened the energy on campus, eliminating the academic and social partitions that kept us apart from one another. This happened to all of us, not just those who knew Ginger. Roy Riggs [the Vice Chancellor of Academic Affairs in 1973] could walk across the quad and address every student he passed by their first name. After Ginger, every student may not have known other people's names, but they made eye contact with everyone they met on the quad — long, horrible eye contact. It may have made some of us late for our next class, but no one was marked late.

Jennie Mills, one of Olson's new friends from Lexington, would express her shock at why anyone would commit this act when she told the *Greensboro Daily News* that Olson "was the sort of person who trusted everyone, but if she found out she was wrong she still wouldn't hate them."

A campus-wide memorial service was held soon after Olson's death, and four days later, her body was transported to New Prospect Baptist Church Cemetery in Parson, Tennessee, for a funeral service and burial. It was a sad and surreal affair for all of Olson's closest friends from UNCA who made the trip to Tennessee.

Some of these individuals are haunted to this day by the image of seeing Olson in her open casket. One classmate reported feeling deeply troubled by details like the make-up that the mortician used that left traces of a wound on her neck visible. Others, like Jeff Doyle, were dazed and struggled to reconcile the connection between the body in front them with the vibrant person they knew: "I remember the open casket, and thinking that this wasn't really Ginger, just a remnant that looked a bit like her, but was missing the important parts, the vitality."

When the service concluded, the dark clouds outside finally gave way to rain, which intensified as mourners walked in dazed unison toward the final burial plot. A group of pallbearers, composed of Olson's friends, carried her casket to her burial plot. The rain quickened, and pallbearers slipped on the wet grass as they struggled to grasp the casket. Everything felt off. One pallbearer later recalled the maddening sounds of graveside mourners attempting to sing hymns of hopeful expectation against this grim backdrop: "I remember everyone singing 'Amazing Grace' horribly off-key, but it didn't matter." The graveside service swiftly concluded and Virginia Olson, who just a week earlier had her entire life in front of her, had now been laid to rest.

Today, Olson's haunting picture remains in the Carol Belk Theater. Without context, it resembles images of other productions from a bygone era that adorn the theater's lobby and hallways. These photos remind current drama students that people have "come before" without asking them to think about the person behind the moment captured in time.

"I imagine that Ginger is mostly a mythical figure at UNCA at this point…more like a ghost than like the wonderful, warm human being that she was," mused Jeffrey Doyle on the 44th anniversary of her death.

The repeated emphasis on ephemeral ghost imagery here is simultaneously profound and sad. Olson was buried on April 19, 1973, in the New Prospect Baptist Church cemetery in Parson, Tennessee. Yet, her story and fragmentary traces continue to haunt UNCA and those who knew her to this day. She is a permanent part of the memory and geography of the university, regardless of the location of her physical body.

While we can never fully locate Virginia Olson, we can at least allow "Ginger" to have the last word in this brief chapter about her life. Among her possessions that police found at the murder scene was the notebook that she always carried to journal her thoughts and write poetry in. We think one of her poems offers the best insight into the person she was and who she aspired to be before her life was cut short:

I will be happy
Adjust myself to what is
Exercise, care for and nourish my body
Strengthen my mind
Do somebody a good turn and not get found out
Do two things I don't want to
I will be agreeable, dress becomingly, talk low,
Act courteously, praise others, and not try to
Regulate or improve anyone,
Deal with today
Have a program
Quiet time, four times of prayer, Bible read
Try to relax and not worry

Just for today I will be unafraid, especially,
I will not be afraid to be happy, to enjoy
What is beautiful to love—to believe
Those I love, love me.

Part II:

A Murder and a City of Suspects

Chapter 4:
A Murder on Campus

"If I had thought about what my reaction would be to the person I loved most in the world being harmed—let alone murdered—by someone, I would have said that I would hunt that person down and kill him as slowly and painfully as I could. But when the unthinkable happened, I could feel nothing but pity—pity that someone so obviously twisted and tortured took a knife and killed a person who could have really helped him had he simply said, 'I need help, please talk to me.'"—Jeffrey Doyle, Interview, 2024

In April of 1973, UNCA was finishing another year. Graduation was approaching, and the campus buzzed with final events. A music festival on the school's main quad would feature bands like Grass Roots. Meanwhile, Theater-UNCA was beginning final rehearsals for a production of Moliere's bawdy comedy *Tartuffe*, about a lecherous monk who preys on aristocratic women but whose true predatory motives are somehow unseen by the story's male characters. The play was scheduled to open on April 26th at Lipinsky Auditorium and run through the 28th. Drama Department Chair Arnold Wengrow directed the play for the Drama Department, and it featured a cast that included students like Donna Glick, Dee Grier, Scott Cumbaugh, and Rob Storrs. In retrospect, the play offered a chilling foreshadowing of events that were about to happen.

As the last full month of the spring semester started, Virginia Olson's main concern was not the final Drama Department production of the year. She had already distinguished herself in a well-received rendition of *U.S.A.*, which Wengrow also directed. The play ran from October 12-14th. A review published in the *Native Stone* on October 19, 1972, singled out a series of scenes that prominently featured Olson, and the reviewer observed that "the Janey-Joe-Alex scenes (Ginger Olson, Lachie MacLachlan, and, again, Kim English) attained true sentiment and pathos without mawkishness."

U.S.A. was the first significant role Olson landed since declaring a drama major during the Fall 1972 semester. That same semester she had also placed in a speech competition at Catawba College, and some of the upper-classmen in the Drama Department expressed admiration for her enthusiasm and commitment to honing her craft. During the spring semester, she would add the debate team to her growing list of activities; in late March, she would travel to a competition at Pfeiffer College with classmates Lynn Hyde, Betsy Davidson, and Janie Fishburn. Olson would once again place in this competition in interpretive reading and drama.

All of this success validated her longstanding passion for theater and the arts. As summer approached, she told friends she was considering a transfer to UNC-Greensboro. She loved Asheville, but the campus was close to 144 miles away from her parents' home in Lexington, NC.

"I do love it here, but I can't help but feel homesick," she wrote to one high school friend, in a letter dated 3 months before her death.

She tried to get home whenever she could, and she saw Greensboro, which was only 33 miles away from her family's new residence, as an opportunity to pursue her dreams while maintaining regular familial contact. While some of her friends excitedly described taking road trips to out-of-state concerts or finding summer internships across the country, Olson was content to spend her summers lifeguarding and in the company of friends and family. She wasn't worried about missing out on potential opportunities. She seemed to create opportunities wherever she went. More than anything, she thrived on her familial support system, and Greensboro felt like a good balance between her competing loves and passions.

Olson's focus on family as her most important priority was something she had learned from her father, Charles. She had become involved with recording works of literature for the hearing impaired because her father had lost most of his hearing while fighting in World War II. Her father was also an accomplished baseball player who played exhibition games against some baseball legends like Joe DiMaggio. When the war ended, he was offered a spot on the Chicago Cubs but declined.

Olson was similar in this respect; while some of her classmates pursued opportunities in New York or California, she dreamed about these potentials but ultimately prioritized her family.

She sometimes came across as shy and introverted to others, but she quickly made friends and developed close relationships at UNCA. She also worked hard to preserve longstanding friendships from McLean High School, and by April of 1973, she continued to visit friends back in Northern Virginia; she and Jeff Doyle planned to see one another whenever they could.

In interviews for this book, Doyle stated that they were not officially dating, but he was undoubtedly in love with her and had begun allowing himself to envision a future with her. That winter, Olson had driven from North Carolina to Virginia to surprise her old high school friends. Doyle was ecstatic to receive "Ginger" in this surprise visit: "She visited McLean at Christmas, knocked on our door unexpectedly … she had gained weight, and some of her friends made a point of that, but I didn't care, I was so happy to see her. Somehow, things fell into place."

In early April 1973, Doyle and Olson met to spend their Spring Breaks together. They passed their days taking leisurely walks in the woods, taking pictures of plants, and listening to music. Doyle had recently discovered botany, and Olson was interested in and amused by his preoccupation with shooting images of plants during their outings. In the evenings, they spent time with friends and extended family, listened to music, and discussed summer plans. Spring Break passed too soon, and while they were sad to part, the start of summer recess was only a few weeks away. Doyle drove Olson to the bus station a few days before the end of break and bade her farewell. It is a memory that haunts him to this day. He recalled: "I put her on the bus that took her back to Asheville and her death, got in my car, and drove south to visit my parents in Montgomery, Alabama."

Olson arrived back on the campus of UNCA on Friday, April 13th, and immediately checked in with her friends in Craig Dormitory. She was pleasantly surprised to learn that her parents decided to make the 2.5-hour drive from Lexington, NC, to spend the day with her. They were starting an Easter vacation and took advantage of a route taking them through Asheville. She had a great time visiting her high school friends, but seeing her parents was always a cause for celebration. According to Jane Nicholson, Olson's roommate, when she learned of her parents' detour through Asheville, she gleefully remarked, "Something good always happens to me on Friday the 13th." Olson's parents spent a few hours with her that Friday, hugged and kissed her, and told her they would "see her again when they returned home." There was a lot of work to complete to prepare for final exams, but she always welcomed these surprise visits.

Around noon on Sunday, April 15th, 1973, Olson told Nicholson that she wanted to take her books to the Biltmore Botanical Gardens adjacent to UNCA's campus to enjoy the nice weather and study. She spent a few minutes grabbing her Spanish textbook and notes and grumbled, in a half-serious way, about her desire to do better on this exam than her midterm. Nicholson would later tell police and reporters that this kind of thing was routine for Olson: "It was not unusual for her to go by herself and study." In an interview with the *Winston-Salem Journal,* she elaborated: "She liked to be out and take hikes and look at the different flowers. One of her favorite spots to be was the Biltmore Botanical Gardens."

Olson exited Craig Dormitory and almost immediately ran into some of her peers from the Drama Department in the parking lot. They spent 10-15 minutes exchanging stories of spring break adventures and filling Olson in on the progress of *Tartuffe* rehearsals. By 12:45, Olson excused herself from the conversation with an apology and a disclaimer that she was heading out to study. With a smile, she waved goodbye and playfully promised to finish their conversation in the dining hall that evening. These students observed Olson walking to the Botanical Gardens entrance and turned their attention back to their conversation as she entered. According to the *Asheville Citizen-Times*, at least 100 students had the same idea as Olson and took to the Botanical Gardens to enjoy the nice weather.

There are ambiguities in the timeline concerning Olson's movements between 1:45 and 3:30 p.m. What we do know is that at 3:30 p.m., two South French Broad High School students named Thomas Guthrie, age 14, and Larry O'Kelly, age 17, discovered Olson's body in the middle of a trail of a secluded hilltop spot overlooking Weaver Boulevard and the UNCA campus.

Guthrie and O'Kelly told police that they had been in the area since 1:30 p.m. cooking hot dogs (or "weenies," as they called them in their official statement) with two other boys and three girls from their school. The picnic concluded around 3:15 p.m., and they began returning down the path from their picnic area. Guthrie explained the moments preceding their discovery of Olson's body when he said, "We had been up there for a picnic and were coming down the path when we saw her lying there." They discovered the body around 3:30 p.m., two hours after they entered the woods for the picnic. Their group's 1:30 p.m. arrival followed Olson's entrance into the Botanical Gardens by around 30 minutes.

The scene the two young boys encountered was horrific and left them struggling to catch their breaths. As they walked down what authorities would later describe as a "well-worn path," they saw a young woman, face up, directly in front of them. Her hands were tied behind her back, her mouth gagged, and her feet were tightly bound. The girl Guthrie and O'Kelly saw appeared to be wearing a green shirt, but it was shredded, and she had been gagged and bound with the strands of her clothes. Her body was half naked, and her dungarees were soaked in blood and pulled down towards her knees.

"I saw two young boys running, white as ghosts, yelling that someone was hurt…I initially thought it was some kind of joke…The kind of thing that boys that age do," reported one witness we interviewed who was in the gardens that day.

Initial police reports described a single visible stab wound to Olson's chest, and officers noted her throat had also been slashed. Her notebook and glasses were neatly arranged a few feet from her body, and no apparent murder weapon was visible in the surrounding areas. The majority of the blood at the scene appeared to originate from Olson's chest. The laceration across her neck was deep, but police told reporters that very little blood appeared to emanate from it, which led some to speculate that this wound might have been inflicted post-mortem.

By 4:00 p.m., police cars and ambulances flooded the Botanical Gardens. At least four squad cars arrived minutes after Guthrie and O'Kelly's urgent emergency call.

"I was only a child, but I remember my mama telling me it was time to go. The whole situation…the sirens, and people running…it was quite frightening…a day at the park became a frightening experience that I will never forget," recalled one young witness.

Around this time, Jane Nicholson returned to her dorm and noticed that Olson had not yet returned. When word started to spread around campus of a murder, she immediately feared the worst: "I suspected right then it must have been Ginger because there were no signs that she had returned to her room after she left…Afterward, I returned to the dorms and sent some friends down to the Garden with a picture of Ginger." Within 30 minutes of arriving with Olson's picture, the pathologist on the scene would confirm that the woman in the photo was the victim.

It was a chaotic scene with police, medical personnel, students, and Botanical Gardens visitors attempting to see what was happening. Police had blocked off access to the main path, but that didn't stop *Asheville Citizen-Times* reporters from taking pictures documenting the chaos. The next day, the paper would publish a photo of officers and medics carrying Olson's body, ominously covered with a white sheet, down the steep pathway.

Meanwhile, chaos was also developing on UNCA's campus as administrators received frantic phone calls from campus community members asking for clarification about what was happening across the street. One former student told us the shock was palpable because the school had always prided itself on its safety. When news of Olson's death surfaced, Associate Dean of Students Alice Wutschel told police that it was not surprising that students would leave the main Botanical Garden area in favor of more secluded spots on days when the grounds were crowded.

This statement sounds strange, but administrators had difficulty knowing what to say early on because things were moving fast. Within two hours, the medical examiner took Olson's body away, and officers descended on the campus to begin questioning students. At this point, the university could not strategically plan a coherent response to the quickly unfolding event.

Meanwhile, Olson's parents, who had just left their daughter less than 48 hours before, were finally located by nightfall at their vacation spot in Missouri and informed that their daughter had been murdered. Hours later, Jeffrey Doyle had just returned to his dorm room at William and Mary, and a friend came to get him to say there was a call for him on the hall's public phone. When he picked up the receiver, he was surprised to hear the noticeably distraught voice of Olson's father, Charles Doswell. He struggled to speak but finally got out, "Ginger has had an accident." This revelation startled Doyle, and he quickly asked, "Is she okay?" His gut told him this was more serious than an "accident." It was unusual to receive a call from her father like this, but he still hoped for the best. Those hopes quickly faded when the truth finally emerged: "She's dead."

Charles Doswell Olson and Lurodine Woods have never given public interviews about their daughter's murder, but the news of Olson's death shocked everyone who knew her. Following Doyle's conversation with Olson's father about her death, he staggered around William and Mary's campus in shock. While many details of that evening remain vivid for him, there are many gaps. He explained what he remembers this way:

> After that phone call I walked, and walked, and walked, all around campus, well into the night. My friends learned what had happened; I may have told one of them, but I don't recall. Someone among my friends called the Catholic priest and told him; when

I stopped in to talk with my friends late that night they told me he wanted to talk to me, so I went to see him. I ended up comforting him.

The news also shocked Nicholson, who explained that it was hard to imagine the motive anyone might have to harm Olson. She described her as "introverted" and "a loner who kept to herself." For Nicholson, like many who knew her, it was hard to reconcile the publicly soft-spoken Olson with the extreme act of violence directed towards her.

The rest of the campus community was equally shocked and struggled to process the event. Chancellor William Highsmith recalled, "By Monday the entire institution was paralyzed. On Tuesday, all classes were canceled and a memorial service was held. There was not an empty seat in the house." After the memorial service, Highsmith called all department chairs into an emergency meeting to discuss options. No productive learning was taking place, and "every male without an ironclad alibi was considered a suspect." Ultimately, they decided to close the university for a few days and send all dormitory students home. They hoped that by the time students returned from this additional break, "the murderer might be identified and apprehended."

The world suddenly felt strange and surreal, and these feelings were amplified by letters several friends received in the mail days after Olson's death. Olson was a prolific writer, and some of her final letters were postmarked on Saturday, April 14th, and they arrived the day after her funeral. We spoke to Jeff Doyle about these letters, and while he didn't feel comfortable sharing the actual letter, he remembered his first impressions of reading it. His words echoed the thoughts and sentiments of others who also received these haunting messages from the now-deceased Olson: "The letter from her came after we'd buried her. Yes, a strange experience to read of hopes and plans never to be realized."

Olson was dead, and while family and friends struggled to reconcile this terrible turn of events, the Asheville Police Department began their investigation. Little did anyone know how bizarre this case was about to get.

Chapter 5: The First Investigation, 1973-1974

"Some of you out there have been murdering people... and getting away with it. The police want to catch you and charge you, but they either don't know who you are, or they do know but can't prove you did it...yet."—Billy Pritchard, *The Asheville Times*, Oct. 28, 1973

The investigation into the murder of Virginia Olson began in earnest on April 15th, 1973, amid a wave of shock, confusion, and panic on campus and in the Asheville community. After finding the body at approximately 3:30 p.m., local high school students Thomas Guthrie and Larry O'Kelly promptly called the police, and a cacophony of ambulances and squad cars descended on the Asheville-Biltmore Botanical Gardens.

The first responders to the Botanical Gardens quickly realized the gravity of the situation before them. They tried to dissuade the growing crowds of onlookers approaching the scene by telling them to "stay back." They were accustomed to the occasional Botanical Gardens call to respond to underage drinking or perhaps some teenagers becoming a little too cozy in the secluded spot in which they now stood, but murder was different.

"There was a lot of blood," one officer would grimly recall of the scene.

The first Asheville Police officers arrived two minutes after the ambulances and noticed that Olson had been stabbed in the chest and that her throat appeared to be slashed. There was little blood emanating from the throat, but there was a lot of blood in the immediate vicinity of where her body was found—a hilltop that overlooked Weaver Blvd. Even before the medical examiner would issue his report, officers on the scene theorized to the press that the neck laceration might have been inflicted postmortem since there was noticeably less blood concentrated around that part of her body.

This was, undoubtedly, a stabbing death, but no murder weapon immediately presented itself. Between 4:00 p.m. and 6:00 p.m., officers on the scene looked for the murder weapon. Meanwhile, other officers began interviewing male UNCA students.

"I remember the officers seemed flustered and stressed. They barked orders and, in retrospect, it seems like they were struggling to control a situation they realized could easily slip away from them," recalled one former UNCA faculty member, who was in his office working when he first heard the commotion.

Despite police orders, crowds of UNCA students continued to migrate towards the Botanical Gardens to discover what was going on.

Police were able to identify the victim before the medical examiner made an official announcement because Jane Nicholson, Olson's roommate, sent a friend to the Botanical Gardens with a picture of her roommate when she heard a student had been injured. She suspected the worst, and officers were able to use the picture to confirm their victim's identity.

While officers directed the crowds to keep back, they began collecting evidence from the crime scene. There wasn't much: there was a wool sweater a few feet from the body that Olson liked to wear as a coat. There was also her pair of glasses that sat next to her Spanish textbook and her journals. There was also a piece of "fatty tissue" that officers bagged even though they weren't sure if it was connected to Olson and the crime scene or not. The most valuable forensic evidence for police in 1973 was the blood that covered Olson's clothes. These would be sent to the SBI lab for testing, and so would fingernail scrapings, which were generally taken in murder investigations.

As police worked to contain the crime scene and begin their investigation, UNCA's administration put out a statement that attempted to distance the school from the murder. A spokesman met with the *Asheville Citizen Times* and explained that the Botanical Gardens section where Guthrie and O'Kelly found Olson was technically not on campus but on "unimproved" land. Representatives from the school explained that "many paths" from land owned by others intersect with the garden space. Police on the crime scene would also offer their take on the property when they told the same paper that it was an area known to be frequented by "winos and lovers."

It is hard to explain the UNCA administration and the Asheville Police Department's initial responses to Olson's murder. Whether or not Olson was "technically" murdered on UNCA property or government land seemed to miss the larger point—a student who lived on campus across the street from the crime scene, in an area frequented by students, had been brutally murdered in broad daylight. Similarly, the Asheville Police Department's characterization of the scene in the immediate aftermath of the murder seems to imply that there was something seedy about the crime scene area when, in fact, it was a highly trafficked park. Nevertheless, we tend to interpret these earliest statements as expressing the depth of the community's shock. After all, this was a campus that didn't even have a police force. It was a safe community, and there weren't many points of reference to help understand this crime.

By Sunday night, the State Bureau of Investigation arrived to assist the Asheville Police Department, and a press release was issued stating that no suspects had been identified. SBI investigators immediately noticed parallels between Olson's case and that of slain VISTA civil rights worker Nancy Morgan in Madison County, NC, in 1970. Like Olson, Morgan had been bound and gagged and stabbed to death. Other parallels presented themselves: Olson was partially unclothed, and her shirt was shredded. It seemed probable that she had been sexually assaulted, but that would be a determination that only the medical examiner could make. At a minimum, officers noted that "evidence on the scene indicated that she had been molested."

The North Carolina Medical Examiner's Autopsy and Findings

The investigation into the specific circumstances of Virginia Olson's death began when Dr. Ray Hampton, the Medical Examiner for Buncombe County, arrived at the Botanical Gardens crime scene at approximately 4:45 p.m. At that point, roughly one hour had elapsed since the Asheville Police Department began securing the scene. Hampton conducted an initial cursory examination, and then, at 5:30 p.m., he called in orders for an autopsy of Olson's body. Curiously, while the initial response from UNCA involved an attempt to distance the school from the location of the crime scene, the NC Medical Examiner's report listed the official location of Olson's body as "UNCA campus."

Dr. John A. McLeod of the NC Medical Examiner's Office was assigned to conduct the autopsy and the official report notes that it occurred on April 15, 1973, at 8:00 p.m. When we first read the report, we were surprised by the speed at which authorities acted in this case. This timing means that Olson's autopsy occurred within 4 hours of her death and around 1-2 hours after her parents were notified of her passing. This turnaround is remarkably fast even by today's standards.

McLeod's autopsy report begins with a note that, "there is no rigor mortis evident." The nature of the wounds on Olson's body began to offer clues that this murder involved a sexual assault. McLeod notes that Olson's body was "clothed in a pair of faded blue denim dungarees and a brassiere. There are no underpants. There is blood on the brassiere, blood over the face, in the hair, and around the neck."

The coroner's conclusions mirror those of the initial officers on the scene: that the primary cause of death occurred as a result of the stab wound to the heart and that the laceration to the neck, while significant, likely occurred postmortem. McLeod writes that the stab wound to the heart "penetrated the left ventricle...with massive intrapleural hemorrhage and some external hemorrhage." All told, the 2.4 cm stab wound to the heart caused Olson to lose around 2400 ccs of blood, which is the equivalent of 2.4 liters of blood. It is important to remember this figure because it comes back into our analysis later in the book when we discuss our theory about the murder. At this point, it is enough to say there was a massive amount of blood at the scene, and it would have been hard, based on the trajectory of the stab wound, for the murderer to avoid getting a substantial amount of blood on himself. In addition, Olson's elbows and knees contained small gravel abrasions, and the coroner notes that the laceration on the left side of her neck, which began around her thyroid, was around 8 cm deep.

Towards the end of the report, McLeod confirms that Olson had been raped. He notes that there were "active and inactive" sperm in her vaginal canal. There were also pubic hairs inconsistent with Olson's own near the vaginal area. In 1973, there wasn't much that coroners could do with sperm and hair evidence. They could confirm the presence of sperm or compare the similarities of hair samples, but they often did so through a very simple forensic examination. In this case, the confirmation was made through a visual examination of the body. However, it is worth noting that the coroner did save these samples. In the very last sentence of the report, he writes, "smears from the vagina and fornices show abundant spermatozoa, some of which are still motile in the wet preparation."

The Medical Examiner's Report Sparks Public Outrage and Fear

The lingering question of whether Olson had been sexually assaulted was publicly addressed 24 hours later when the NC Medical Examiner informed the police and the North Carolina public that Olson had been raped. By Tuesday, April 17th, news of the assault appeared on the front pages of papers across North Carolina. The *Winston-Salem Journal* led with a headline titled, "UNC-A Student Had Been Molested," and this language mirrored much of the news released that week. This development seemed to galvanize the UNCA community and the broader state to action.

The morning these headlines appeared, Pete Gilpin, the public information liaison at UNCA, announced that the Student Government Association would offer a $300 reward for any information about the circumstances of Olson's death. With 48 hours to prepare a better statement, the administration sought to describe Olson favorably. The earlier statement seemed out of place now, but that was due to the initial shock of the news. The Dean of Students now described Olson as "a good student with a good sense of humor and a very Christian girl." Such descriptions, which emphasized Olson's quiet, unassuming virtuousness, only accentuated the violence of her death and accelerated the public call to action.

At the state level, NC Governor James E. Holshouser stepped in and offered a reward of $5,000 for information leading to an arrest in the case. Gov. Holshouser was only three months into his term and his office seemed to take a personal interest in the Olson case. While the governor was known as a moderate Republican who focused on state-level policy, in private, he voiced support for Nixon's Vietnam policies and saw Olson's murder at UNCA as related to a more general lack of "law and order" on college campuses nationwide. Therefore, solving this case took on a level of greater political importance.

"The First Suspect"–April 17th, 1973

Police often tell you that the first 48 hours are critical in any criminal investigation. If too much time passes, evidence can deteriorate, witnesses' memories can fade, and suspects could have time to craft an alibi or dispose of evidence that might link them to a victim. As a result, interviews and evidence collecting are typically aggressive during the first few days. While police in the 1970s didn't have the benefits of our contemporary forensic technological advancement, a fact that will later come to haunt this case, this truism about the importance of getting a good start applied then just as much as it does now. In this case, those clamoring for justice in Asheville and the rest of the state wouldn't have to wait long for a significant development.

By the time the *Winston-Salem Journal* ran their April 17th article that announced the medical examiner's confirmation that Olson had been raped, the Asheville Police officially took their first suspect in the murder of Virginia Olson into custody. On the morning of Tuesday, April 17th, Asheville Police Chief J.C. Hall announced that a young man "in his early 20s" had been brought in for questioning. Hall also announced that physical evidence related to the case had been collected from the suspect and sent to the State Bureau of Investigation's Crime Lab for analysis. The evidence the police were most interested in involved some small blood stains on the suspect's shoes. In 1973, blood tests were fairly primitive compared to the later DNA tests that emerges in the late 1990s. At this moment in time, blood tests typically helped to confirm blood type and secretor status (which we will discuss more later). In other words, blood evidence alone was not indicative of guilt, but it could be used as another piece of corroborating evidence.

Aside from Hall's description in his April 17th statement, little is known about this first suspect. However, by Wednesday, April 18th, public records show that this suspect was charged with breaking and entering in an unrelated case, and he remained detained for questioning related to Olson's death. He would be arraigned on these initial charges and held on a $1,000 bond. These charges were likely filed to buy the investigators time to explore his connection to the Olson case.

Without any evidence connecting him to Olson's murder, they were not able to detain him indefinitely because there wasn't anything concrete. He was arrested for breaking into a building near the crime scene, and he had some blood on his shoes that he couldn't explain, and he was clearly suffering from some form of mental health issue. Some of the arresting officers would later describe him as "agitated" and "nervous." This immediately raised suspicions at a time when community tensions were very high.

As Thursday, April 19th rolled around, the suspect remained in police custody as newspapers around the region ran stories with headlines like "Suspect Still Questioned in Rape Death." During this time, it seemed like the police might have solved the case rapidly. The reports of some news outlets had already begun praising the police for making quick work of this case.

By the weekend, no charges were filed against the suspect, and he was released from police custody. Little was said then, and less is known today, about this first suspect or his subsequent release except that there was no evidence specifically linking him to Olson's death. The only significant piece of identifying information about him is that he had escaped from a mental health hospital in Richmond, Virginia. Following his release from police custody, he returned to this hospital.

This suspect was the first, but not last, to have strong ties to mental health facilities in this case.

SBI Involvement and the Escalation of Investigative Resources–1974

Following the release of the unidentified suspect in April of 1973, leads would go cold in the Olson investigation for the next eight months. As 1974 began with no new leads or arrests, the North Carolina SBI announced that two agents would be assigned to work the Olson case full-time. This announcement was made on February 16th, 1974, by J.N. Minter, who oversaw SBI investigations in 16 counties in western North Carolina. In his official statement, Minter named Special Agents James Thomas Maxey and Billy C. Matthews as the SBI investigators "relieved of all other duties indefinitely so that they may concentrate on the cases without distraction." He said their main goal was to "follow up any unsolved leads or leads that haven't been run out to the end." According to SBI personnel records, Maxey and Matthews represented a pairing of an experienced veteran and a newer agent. Maxey's years of active duty with the SBI began in 1962, and by the time he was assigned to the Olson case, he had close to 12 years of experience working on major crimes in western North Carolina. In contrast, Matthews had worked for the SBI for less than 2 years when he received the assignment to help with the case.

By 1973, the North Carolina State Bureau of Investigation had existed for roughly 36 years. According to the North Carolina general statutes that established this agency, their goal was "to secure a more effective administration of criminal laws of the state, to prevent crime, and to procure the speedy apprehension and identification of criminals." The SBI received its formal name in 1939 and quickly distinguished itself nationwide. The North Carolina SBI's crime lab was one of the first in the United States. In many ways, the SBI was ahead of its time. They published guides in the 1940s for smaller law enforcement agencies concerning crime scene management when no statewide standardized practices existed. By 1969, they also created the Police Information Network, an early attempt to place state criminal records and information on computer networks. The year Olson was murdered, they also swore in an agent named Karen C. McDaniel, who became the first woman to work as a criminal investigator for the agency. Most significantly, the SBI brought coherent organization, methodology, and technical prowess to investigations.

We can glean a few things from the SBI's involvement in this case in early 1974. First, this case would require a significant amount of technical resources. The SBI did not automatically have jurisdiction over any cases in Western North Carolina. Their jurisdiction began with an invitation from the local agency that took the investigative lead. Throughout the early investigation, the Asheville Police Department allegedly collected considerable "materials" or physical evidence. As early as April 17th, 1973, the *Gastonia Gazette* reported that the SBI had taken over forensic analysis of these "materials." While the specific nature of these materials was not revealed, it is reasonable to assume that many of these items related to Olson's clothes and bodily fluids (like blood and semen) since police conceded that they could not locate a murder weapon at the crime scene. Second, the decision to allocate agents to focus on the Olson case was not without controversy. Minter conceded that assigning two agents to this case "would strain SBI manpower." The fact that the SBI chose to allocate resources when the western North Carolina region was understaffed helps to underline the pressure law enforcement agencies felt to generate new leads. While Minter would publicly stress that SBI involvement was not meant to supplant the local law enforcement investigation, it is hard to avoid the conclusion that their presence was meant to expedite the process.

"A Lead in Florida": A Second Suspect Emerges, 1974

By 1974, the SBI had joined the hunt for Olson's killer, and they would point the Asheville Police Department towards a new potential suspect seven months later who resided in the state of Florida. At times, it felt like the two agencies were running separate investigations. Within the SBI, there were lingering resentments that Matthews and Maxey were asked to focus all of their attention on the Olson case. Some argued this deprived an agency already stretched thin of two skilled investigators. The SBI publicly stressed that Matthews and Maxey "would not replace or interfere with investigations by local law enforcement agencies" already working on the case. Undeniably, the presence of the SBI began to open up the scope of the Olson investigation. The second significant lead produced in this case emerged from Matthews and Maxey and was passed to Asheville Police Chief J.C. Hall.

On September 6th, 1974, Hall told reporters from the *Asheville Citizen-Times* that police were going to Florida to interview a new potential suspect in the murder of Virginia Olson. Florida police had already charged this suspect with several rapes in that region. Agents Matthews and Maxey first took note of him when they realized the man, who was initially only described as someone in his "late 20s," previously attended UNCA in 1969 and lived near the Botanical Gardens for some time after leaving the college. He had been arrested several times in Asheville on burglary charges since his college days and spent a few nights in the Buncombe County jail.

When Hall and two other members of the Asheville Police Department arrived in Jacksonville, Florida later that month, their goal was to establish a more precise timeline of the suspect's movements. In this pre-digital era, something as seemingly simple as establishing an alibi concerning one's whereabouts could require a significant amount of investigation.

On one hand, this new person seemed like a strong potential suspect. He had ties to the city of Asheville and the UNCA campus community. His criminal activities in Florida suggested that he was a predator motivated by sexual desires. Florida police stated the man was charged with "a series of rapes." However, at the time the Asheville Police arrived, their Florida colleagues were still unsure about the total number of victims. Many of these victims were violently beaten during their assaults, and some had been threatened at knifepoint to subdue their cooperation.

Furthermore, Asheville police and the SBI were not sure about the last time he resided in Asheville. They knew he attended UNCA in 1969, but he did not complete his degree. They knew that after leaving UNCA, he maintained a residence close to campus for a yet-to-be-determined amount of time. They also knew the suspect transferred some credits from UNCA to a Florida college, but it was unclear when the suspect moved to the Sunshine State to begin his spree of sexual assaults.

The SBI and Asheville P.D. were trying to discover any connection. In their announcement concerning this new Florida lead, there was also an emphasis on the fact that thousands of dollars of reward money (including money the governor pledged) had not been claimed.

By that weekend, detectives held press conferences where they announced that no arrest connecting this Florida suspect to Olson's murder would be made. Lt. Fred Hensley, speaking for the Asheville Police Department, told the public that a man named Glen Allen Carlson was the person who inspired the police trip to the Sunshine State. Hensley reported that they confirmed Carlson's alibi that at the time of Olson's death, he had been in Florida delivering the *Florida Times-Union* newspaper. Hensley also revealed that what made Carlson particularly interesting was that he had been charged with 34 different counts of burglaries in 1969 by the Asheville Police Department. This information, when coupled with the fact that Carlson was about to be charged with the rape of 40 different women in Florida, attracted the attention of Matthews and Maxey, especially given the sexual nature of the crimes against Olson.

It is important to note that Carlson's alibi meant he was not the same man that Asheville Police detained during the first days following Olson's death. That suspect was held for questioning based on a "breaking and entering" charge near campus, and we've seen some online discussions that seem to conflate these two different suspects. In some true crime communities, the "breaking and entering" charge connected to the Asheville suspect becomes conflated with the Florida "burglary" charges and the "Florida suspect;" the gaps in time between the two becomes proof of guilt—an effort to flee the state. While there are some superficial similarities between the two men, they are different people, and conflating the two obscures the scope of this investigation. Detectives constantly worked to track new leads and find connections, even if that meant exploring information that took them to other states. The SBI's investigation would eventually take them beyond Florida. Future leads would take them to Georgia, Alabama, New Mexico, and other places.

What was the ultimate fate of Glen Carlson, this second suspect in the historical investigation? He would eventually spend his days in the Florida State Hospital for the criminally insane. Today, he is an uncanny historical footnote of a moment when investigators looked hard to find possible connections.

Chapter 6: A "Frightening Coincidence": The 1974 Disappearance of UNCA Student Karen McDonald on the Anniversary of Virginia Olson's Murder

"I just wonder how many more people like 19-year-old Virginia Olson of Lexington will be murdered before the law of our land will step in and do something about it." —Mrs. D.W. Johnson

"Although there is no apparent link between the two incidents, other than the dates involved, it was a frightening coincidence."—Billy Pritchard, *Asheville Citizen-Times,* April 16th, 1974

On Friday, April 12th, 1974, the UNCA campus community prepared to remember the first anniversary of Virginia Olson's murder. In the year since Olson's shocking death, the Student Government Association had helped set up the Virginia Olson Memorial Fund. Olson's roommate Jane Nicholson spearheaded fundraising for the memorial with events like a used book sale that spring. The investigation to find Olson's murderer had not yet resulted in an arrest. However, the state continued to investigate her death, and Bill Matthews and J.T. Maxey of the NC State Bureau of

Investigation and Det. Sgts. C. R. Rhew and Ralph Cook of the Asheville Police Department worked on the case full-time.

As the Olson criminal investigation continued, the university took measures to put the trauma of the previous year's events behind them, and a sense of normalcy slowly began to return to campus life. One former student described the complexity of juggling her mixed feelings of wanting to forget the incident but also remembering how the previous semester's events had changed her life. She expressed these feelings: "We wanted things to be normal. Desperately wanted them to be normal and didn't want to go through anything like what happened to Ginger again. It was a growing-up moment for many of us."

As the fall semester passed without incident, students focused on things like creating a free student press and involving the Student Government Association in debates about serving beer at the campus coffeehouse. The fall semester following Olson's death, Becky Waechter was named Homecoming Queen, and students playfully described Drama Department Chair Arnold Wengrow as the "David Merrick of UNC-A." Olson's peers in the Drama Department had most acutely felt her death, and the 1973-1974 year was difficult, but it was also a time in which they pulled together and supported one another. As one member of the 1974 Drama Department told us, "We were all hurting but felt like we were in it together."

Other public measures sought to provide incoming students with assurances of campus safety. In the wake of Olson's death, the UNCA campus and the NC state legislature decided to allocate funding to give the school its first professional police force and, hopefully, an added sense of security that might come with this new law enforcement presence. Officers who can make legal arrests would be on campus for the first time.

At the start of the fall semester, UNCA's Dean of Students, Thomas Deason, proudly proclaimed that campus security would be "much, much better this year." Deason spoke about the heightened precautions at UNCA but refused to name Virginia Olson directly, preferring to refer to "the incident." He would reference "*the incident* that triggered changes in college security." He would continue by alluding to how "*it* made the students more aware of the need for security." Deason and other administrators struggled to address Olson's murder throughout this first year. It was almost as if uttering her name became taboo unless the utterance occurred in the context of a memorial or a past tense event that would not and could not be repeated.

A law enforcement officer named Eugene L. Ray became the head of the new campus police force that fall, and he began implementing policies to provide students with a renewed sense of safety. In interviews with the *Asheville Citizen-Times*, Ray explained that all students would receive and be expected to carry I.D. cards with photos. He also explained that law enforcement officers would regularly patrol the campus. At the start of the Fall 1973 semester, eight dormitories were on campus, and Ray placed an officer in each one to supervise people coming and going in the late evenings since some had multiple entrance points. Women's dormitories would be locked between 9 p.m. and midnight. These measures were a further reminder that even though Olson's murder occurred in the Botanical Gardens, it felt like a murder on campus.

While these new security measures differed drastically from the previous year, students responded favorably to the police presence. A senior named Jean Pry commented to *Asheville Citizen-Times* that support for these measures broadly represented the student body's desire to feel safe: "Before the incident, I felt no apprehension about going to the library at night from my dorm. Afterward, I wouldn't think of it."

The normalcy that had returned to campus following Olson's murder, the long summer break, the busy fall semester, and the added security measures was disrupted on Friday, April 12th, just days before the campus anniversary of Olson's murder, as Asheville police received reports that a UNCA student had mysteriously vanished. The *Asheville Citizen-Times* would report that on this day, an 18-year-old freshman named Karen McDonald had disappeared after last being seen at the university student center.

A weekend of planned remembrances of past tragedies became an eerily familiar nightmare. Like Olson, McDonald was young and attractive. *The Asheville Times* described her as a "slender young woman" with "long black hair, brown eyes, and a fair complexion." She was estimated to be around 5'5" tall and around 100 lbs. Law enforcement received notice of McDonald's absence when her aunt, who she lived with in the Skyland area, called to complain that she had not returned home. In the original missing person's report, McDonald's aunt expressed concern for her niece's whereabouts because she allegedly took the same city bus at the same time each day to return home. When she disappeared, she was allegedly wearing a flower-printed blouse and sandals. McDonald's absence was especially concerning to her parents because they had just arrived in Asheville to pick her up for a family vacation. This was a trip that McDonald had been excited about participating in. Part of the reason why police acted so quickly in this case was because the idea that McDonald had wandered off seemed highly unlikely.

The Asheville Police Department also wondered if McDonald's disappearance could be related to Olson's murder or whether it was merely a bizarre "coincidence." It is highly revealing that when Asheville Police Chief J.C. Hall first learned about the disappearance of the 18-year-old McDonald, he immediately ordered a full search of the

Botanical Gardens across from UNCA, which was the site of Olson's murder.

The memory of Olson's murder was fresh on everyone's mind, and McDonald's disappearance instantly resurfaced those feelings of campus insecurity. McDonald was last seen around 1 p.m. on Friday near the university center. The concern started because McDonald was known to keep the same predictable weekly routine: she would catch the city bus each day after her classes and return home to her aunt's house. When she failed to return that Friday, the family notified the police, and with Olson's memory fresh, investigators acted quickly. They began searching the UNCA campus, the Botanical Gardens, and the surrounding areas for signs of her movements.

Days later, a strange story of abduction and rape at knifepoint would horrifically emerge when McDonald was spotted walking downtown near a construction zone cordoned off near the Asheville Civic Center. According to the *Asheville Citizen-Times*, black and blue marks covered her body, she wore torn clothes, and she struggled to walk. She moved through the city streets, screaming for help from pedestrians who gawked in shock at her appearance. Nearby construction workers finally rushed to her aid and called an ambulance, which took McDonald to Memorial Mission Hospital. Doctors at Memorial Mission soon realized the patient in front of them was the missing UNCA student, and they alerted law enforcement.

McDonald told law enforcement that on the day she went missing, a fellow UNCA student drove her downtown and dropped her off near Pritchard Park. From there, she walked along Patton Avenue towards a Woolworth's store when she encountered a young woman who claimed to work for a magazine that planned to write a feature spread on college students. She asked if McDonald would sit down for an interview and photoshoot. This young woman seemed nice enough and offered to take McDonald to a nearby studio to shoot the pictures.

Police Chief J.C. Hall would later tell reporters that once McDonald and the woman arrived back at the apartment, it quickly became apparent that this was not a photo shoot. The woman immediately pulled a knife and threatened McDonald unless she complied with her requests. At this point, her accomplice, a 25-year-old man, emerged, and the couple proceeded to take turns assaulting and threatening McDonald at knife-point for the next three days.

McDonald's eventual escape on Monday, after three days of captivity, was as dramatic as the circumstances of her abduction. During a moment in which the young man was not paying attention, McDonald bravely leaped for a dinner fork nearby, stabbed her female captor in the leg, and ran out of the sadistic couple's apartment on Cherry Street, which was just a block from downtown Asheville. She eventually approached the construction workers that would ultimately help her.

On Monday night, the Asheville Police Department obtained a search warrant for the couple's apartment at 93 Cherry Street and secured arrest warrants for its two tenants, 17-year-old Louise Bray and 25-year-old Walter Smith, on charges of rape and abduction. Bray and Smith were not at the apartment when police arrived, but they were able to collect evidence that supported the harrowing ordeal McDonald recounted at the hospital. At the crime scene, police also discovered McDonald's schoolbooks and other personal items, and a citywide hunt for the two suspects officially began.

Bray and Smith would only evade authorities for 48 hours before they were taken into custody. On Wednesday at 10:30 am, Bray approached an Asheville police officer in a shopping center and turned herself in. She initially claimed that the entire incident had been consensual and that McDonald only left after getting into a fight over Smith.

However, that story quickly fell apart with inconsistencies after Smith, a Recreation Park employee, was taken into custody and questioned later that day.

The trial for Bray and Smith started four months later, in August of 1974, just as a new fall semester at UNCA began, and it quickly concluded by Monday, August 19th, when the couple agreed to plead guilty to expedite sentencing. The cases were tried in Buncombe County Superior Court, and Judge Harry C. Martin handed down both sentences. Smith received a sentence of 40 years in prison for rape, while Bray received a 20-year sentence for kidnapping and a "crime against nature."

Although the McDonald case proved unrelated to the Olson investigation, the successful resolution of the former reminded that the Olson case remained unsolved. By the time McDonald's captors had been arrested and prosecuted, Asheville citizens wondered when Olson would receive a similar resolution.

By August of 1974, the reward for information leading to an arrest in the Olson case had climbed to $4,000. When Asheville reporters inquired about the status of the Olson investigation, they were reminded that "state and local police officers have been assigned to the Olson case on a full-time basis." Still, representatives from the Asheville Police and the SBI conceded that "no new evidence has been found."

As *Asheville Citizen-Times* writer Billy Pritchard would observe, the "McDonald incident," as some would later call it, was a "frightening coincidence." The *Asheville Citizen-Times* placed its McDonald story in a column directly adjacent to the story about Olson in their April 16th edition. Readers and investigators wanted to believe the case might be more than a coincidence. With the McDonald case solved, the same outcome was surely possible with the Olson case.

These coincidences would repeatedly haunt the Olson investigation during the first and most critical investigative years. Karen McDonald's abduction was the first crime investigators explored as possibly possessing a link to Olson's murder, but it would not be the last.

Chapter 7: "Our File is Four Inches Thick. That's a lot of reading": The 1977 "Homicide Squad" and Startling Public Revelations

Following the 1974 push to solve the Olson case, the investigation slowly went "cold" for two years. In police parlance, a "cold case" generally refers to an inquiry that stops producing new leads or information. By 1975, Matthews and Maxey would be taken off the Olson case entirely. Other cases throughout the region needed their attention, and their time on the case had not generated new information as initially hoped. When they left the case, this also coincided with a significant drop in media coverage of the investigation. To understand these trends, let's look at the number of articles produced by media within Buncombe County between 1973 and 1977. Beginning in April of 1973, there were 110 articles written about Virginia Olson or the police investigation into her murder. In 1974, when the SBI became involved, there were 59 articles—a substantial drop, but still a significant number that amounts to almost 5 articles a month close to a year after her death. However, by 1977, only four new articles were published, and the Asheville Police Department had not issued any new public statements regarding the status of the investigation.

By 1977, newspapers stopped writing about Olson on the anniversary of her murder, the police stopped releasing updates, and Olson's UNCA classmates who were driving forces in establishing her memorial fund had now graduated. Life seemed to be moving on. By 1976, even the new leadership at the SBI appeared to be less knowledgeable about or invested in the investigation. Max Bryan had become head of Special Operations for the North Carolina SBI in the years since Olson's death. When an Asheville reporter asked about current rewards offered for information in the Olson case, he told the *Asheville Citizen-Times* that he wasn't sure whether the rewards were still active. He would explain that when the government gives rewards, the offers typically only extend for three years unless lawmakers or the governor undertakes specific action to renew the offer. At the time of the interview, it is telling that specifics regarding the case were not as commonly known—especially since previous investigators, as we saw in the case of Karen McDonald, seemed acutely aware of the circumstances of Olson's case, which shaped their investigative approaches.

While new leads in the Olson case had not materialized, Bryan and other SBI investigators began to develop an interest in exploring possible overlaps between up to 50 unsolved North Carolina cases. As a result, Bryan proposed an alternate way to think about these cases. Rather than assigning agents to narrowly focus on a single case- as they did in 1974- he established a task force in August 1977 to examine the similarities between unsolved cases and to consider whether any might be connected. The task force adopted the nickname "The Homicide Squad" and was composed of special agents across North Carolina whose efforts would be supervised and directed by Bryan. He would tell the *Asheville Citizen-Times* that "there are quite a few similarities between some of these cases…we may find that some of them are connected." He was also optimistic about the group's prospects for success: "We've got a good shot at finding a solution."

By December of 1977, only four months into the task force's work, they began a review of the initial investigation into Olson's murder. When necessary, they followed up with original leads and re-interviewed investigators, witnesses, and others whose names appeared in the 1973 files. The task force's efforts to return to the original investigation signaled they were trying to create new leads from previous materials. This is one of the most challenging aspects of cold case investigations. While Olson's murder was not technically or officially labeled a "cold case" at this moment, the decision to publicly label it, along with other cases, as an "unsolved case" indicates that the investigation had stalled.

There are many benefits to reviewing an older case with fresh eyes, but getting started is a time-consuming process. This was a lesson that agents assigned to the Olson case quickly learned. Remember, between 1973 and 1974, this case generated an Asheville Police Department case number *and* a SBI case number. The two groups worked well together, but each had slightly different focuses and theories, and both generated a lot of paperwork. As one special agent on the task force said: "We are starting from scratch, and we will see what we can get. Our file is four inches thick. That's a lot of reading."

Reading was one thing, but agents on the task force had to figure out what to do with the case knowledge they now possessed. Criminal investigations often require police to be tight-lipped about specific details. Doing so allows them to verify suspect statements, confessions, and other emerging information. However, keeping these details private is not always the only way to develop new leads—especially on a cold case. Sometimes, police leak previously unreleased case details to reinvigorate public discussion or help potential witnesses remember. One current Asheville Police Department officer explained, "There is no exact playbook. We take it on a case-by-case basis."

In December of 1977, the task force finally leaked new details to the general public that were withheld from the press in 1973. As the task force began disseminating details of the original investigation, a more complicated (and chaotic) set of circumstances emerged. First, while the public was aware that the Asheville Police detained a young man in the first 48 hours following Olson's murder, they now learned for the first time about *other* suspects and potential witnesses that were not reported in the *Asheville Citizen-Times, Asheville Times,* and other regional newspapers.

The most surprising revelation the task force circulated focused on an unnamed 45-year-old man who lived in an apartment two blocks from the Botanical Gardens, near Merrimon Ave and Hillside St. He was questioned several times between April 16th and April 29th in 1973. Before 1976, few details were released about this man except that at the time of Olson's murder, he was under the care of a local Asheville psychiatrist. The task force explained that in 1973, investigators questioned known associates of the man, and one of them claimed he drove the suspect home that day. Even more shocking was his comment that they stopped at the Botanical Gardens, and when they did, his companion pointed out a young girl he had seen reading on the hill overlooking Weaver Blvd. This witness claims they spotted this unnamed girl, which investigators presumed could be Olson, around 1:00 p.m. However, what made the police incredibly skeptical of this suspect and this story was his simultaneous insistence that he saw a girl sitting "atop a bank" while also explicitly stating that they never moved close enough to approach her. The problem was that the spot he claimed to have spotted Olson would only be visible had he been atop the bank with her.

"The whole story didn't add up" is how one former investigator assigned to the case characterized the puzzling narrative that the Asheville Police were left to sort out.

Aside from this suspect's lack of a coherent alibi, there was also a more disturbing revelation that police imparted to *Asheville Citizen-Times,* reported Billy Pritchard. Police initially claimed a female neighbor of this suspect told the original investigators that she encountered him around 2:40 p.m. on April 15th—just an hour shy of the discovery of Olson's body by Guthrie and O'Kelly—and she told them that the suspect "appeared nervous and asked me to pray with him." He further complained that something was "a bloody mess." He was agitated, but this behavior did not cause any immediate alarm because news of Olson's murder had not yet been publicly leaked. This man was known to have mental health issues, and odd statements and behavior from him were not uncommon. It was only after news of Olson's murder made the front page that the neighbor reached out to police with her story.

The original investigators released this suspect due to a "lack of evidence," but between 1973 and 1976, law enforcement tracked his movements. They knew, for instance, that two days after the murder, this suspect departed Asheville to travel to Myrtle Beach, SC. He allegedly stayed in Myrtle Beach until April 28th. When he finally returned to town, police questioned him on April 29th and searched his apartment that same night. The search warrant inventory that reporter Billy Pritchard received listed gloves, boots, a white t-shirt, a yellow velour shirt, a knife, and a white handkerchief among the items seized that evening. Everything collected was then sent to the North Carolina SBI crime lab for analysis. At the time of the 1977 Task Force, this suspect was living in a Boston mental health facility.

The new details about this suspect fascinated the public and propelled many theories that circulate in town gossip to this day. Stories of wealth, privilege, and cover-ups often trace their origins to this suspect. Many of these stories contain a tiny grain of truth: from the start, there was a great deal of mystery surrounding this identity. For example, investigators continuously encountered obstacles when they attempted to learn more about the man. A spokesman for the SBI confirmed to the *Asheville Citizen-Times* in their March 28th, 1976 edition, that agents tried to obtain the suspect's Army record but were told his files "went missing." The police stated the only public arrest record this suspect appeared to have was a voyeurism (e.g., peeping tom) charge for an incident that took place in San Francisco, CA, several years before Olson's death.

The public also learned a bit more about witness statements provided to investigators from individuals in the Botanical Gardens on April 15th. For example, the task force described a statement offered by a male witness from Hendersonville who visited the Botanical Gardens that day and reported seeing Olson sitting with a man around 1:15 p.m. The two were in the spot in which her body was ultimately found. This statement is crucial because it helps to narrow the timeline a bit more. Remember, up to this point, publicly known witness statements placed Olson at the Botanical Gardens around 1:00 p.m. If this witness's statement is true, then it means that Olson was still alive at 1:15, and since her body was discovered at approximately 3:30 p.m., the window of her death starts to become a bit clearer.

We know that Guthrie and O'Kelly find Olson's body at 3:30 p.m., and her death likely occurred earlier. The Hendersonville witness stated that as he left the Botanical Gardens at 1:45 p.m., he glanced up to the hilltop where Olson and the unidentified man were previously sitting at 1:15 p.m. Neither were there at 1:45 p.m., but he did report noticing "something flapping in the winds atop the bank." He was likely referring to the pages of Olson's schoolbooks, which were found a short distance from her body. This means Olson was probably attacked or killed sometime between 1:15 p.m. and 1:45 p.m., as she was no longer holding her book. Whether she was being assaulted as the Hendersonville witness departed, which seems unlikely since he didn't hear any unusual sounds, or she was already dead, which seems more likely, this period was the probable window when the crime occurred.

The other significant takeaway the public learned from the 1977 Task Force was that the Asheville Police, very early on, narrowed their focus to two main suspects. Yes, they visited Florida in 1974 at the behest of the SBI to explore a possible link uncovered by Matthews and Maxey. However, despite these public developments, they were especially interested in two individuals. The first suspect was the man that witnesses placed with Olson around 1:15 on the hilltop on the day of her death. From the Hendersonville witnesses' vantage point, this man appeared to be wearing a "green Army fatigue jacket." It is not surprising that this lead did not generate much new information. By 1973, the campus of UNCA and the larger Buncombe County community had become home to many Vietnam Veterans who liked to wear similar clothing. It is, therefore, not surprising that the second suspect was also described as wearing Army boots and fatigues.

The second suspect also had military ties and was on leave at the time of Olson's murder and staying in a hotel on Merrimon Avenue. There was even less known about this suspect than the aforementioned one because the original investigators excluded him pretty quickly from suspicion. We know he was thoroughly questioned, and his hotel room was also searched. However, like the suspect in the nearby apartment building, police could not find any physical evidence that definitively linked this second person to Olson.

What all the witnesses of this era seemed to agree on was that the suspect "appeared" to be in his 20s (which is different from actually being this age) and that he wore boots and was around 5'10," 165 lbs, and wearing some form of sweater or some kind of "small pack" around his neck. These details were confirmed by a separate witness in town for vacation and by a local foreman of an industrial plant who parked near the gardens to listen to an auto race in his car. Both witnesses spotted an individual fitting this description entering the Botanical Gardens just after 1:00 p.m., which fits the timeline of the third witness, who described seeing Olson sitting with a young man around 1:15 p.m.

As 1977 rolled into 78 and then 79, it became apparent that no new leads in the Olson case would emerge. The task force with the ferocious name— "The Homicide Squad" had quietly disbanded by 1979, and media coverage and press conference updates altogether ceased. The task force revelations momentarily captured the public's interest, but this group ultimately came to many of the same conclusions regarding logical suspects as the original investigators. The failure to generate new leads at this juncture would profoundly impact the investigative focus in the years to come.

No press conferences or media updates surrounding this case would be provided by the Asheville Police Department again until 1984. While this investigation would pick up again in 1984, if you are looking for a place to locate the moment the case officially "went cold," the conclusion of the 1977 task force is an excellent place to start.

We framed the years 1973-1978 as the "first investigation." Still, we want to clarify that law enforcement never gave up during this first wave of investigation. This broader period produced three significant investigations by the Asheville Police Department and the North Carolina SBI. Early on, the Asheville Police Department identified and took several persons of interest into custody. In fact, by the 1980s, when Will Annarino and the Asheville Police Department reopened and revisited this case, they would identify the suspect taken into custody within 14 days of

Olson's murder as their prime murderer. In addition, the work of Bill Matthews and J.T. Maxey from the North Carolina SBI demonstrates that investigators explored every possible outside lead in this case. They helped to direct the Asheville Police Department to a plausible person of interest in Florida, and they followed up with leads in three other states. Similarly, the 1977 task force examined Olson's case in conjunction with 50 other unsolved cases from Western North Carolina. By looking for potential connections between these unsolved cases, which often involved painstakingly revisiting a voluminous case history, investigators demonstrated how much this case mattered to law enforcement.

This first investigation would not be the last, and it's important to note that no investigation is linear. This investigation occurred when many bizarre and seemingly related cases threatened the investigation's focus. The most glaring example is the 1974 abduction of a UNCA student, Karen McDonald, on the first anniversary of Olson's murder.

No investigation is undertaken in a cultural vacuum. While 1977 brought new details to the public about the crime and suspects, many more shocking details would emerge in 1984 when authorities began what we describe as the second major investigative push to bring Olson's killer to justice.

Part III:

Diversions and Public Defiance, 1978-1986

Chapter 8:
"The Body in the Botanical Garden": The Murder of Mary F. Burdette, 1978

"It was business as usual today for Will R. Annarino, an Asheville police detective who was struck twice by a car, carried on the hood of the vehicle for some 150 feet, and then slammed down onto the icy pavement."—John Campbell, Sr, *The Asheville Times,* February 20th, 1979

One of the many strange things we discovered while investigating this murder was the number of curiously unrelated cases in which Olson is mentioned as a point of reference. There was Karen McDonald's abduction on the first anniversary of Olson's murder that inspired discussion of possible parallels, and five years later, the decomposing body of a woman in her 50s or 60s was found in the university Botanical Gardens on October 11th, 1978.

For UNCA students of his era, Olson's memory hung over these disturbing cases. The possibility that they could be related repeatedly called into question feelings of security at the least opportune moments. Students tried to relegate the Olson case and the experiences of the previous graduating cohort to the past by regularly holding events that would benefit the Ginger Olson Memorial Scholarship Fund. It was easier to acknowledge tragic events of the past and to honor people who died than to consider whether they could happen again. For instance, in 1977, UNCA's Theater

Department presented "Stories: F. Scott Fitzgerald," which adapted four short stories that Fitzgerald wrote between 1916 and 1936 for theatrical productions. The show charged audience members $3 for regular admission, and each ticket included a pass to see a Fitzgerald exhibit on display at Ramey Library that examined the author's connections to Asheville and his 1936 visit to the region.

F. Scott Fitzgerald was the furthest thing from student minds during the week of October 11th, 1978. It was an election year, and the campus buzzed with anticipation from the spotlight it would receive for hosting a hotly contested political debate between Lamar Gudger and R. Curtis Ratcliff to represent the Eleventh Congressional District. The campus announced that it planned to structure the debates to mimic the televised format of the 1976 Presidential contest between Jimmy Carter and Gerald Ford. The Political Science Department organized the program, and panels of students planned to ask the questions.

In the years since Karen McDonald's abduction, the campus had begun to seem safe again, and a focus on safety was emphasized in an *Asheville Citizen-Times* "community life feature" that stressed how female students make UNCA dormitories "a home away from home." Women's section editor Mary Ellen Wolcott profiled the strong dormitory communities at UNCA and the living modifications made by students to make it feel like a cozy community. Home is, after all, associated with familiarity and safety, and emotions that are the opposite of the grief and fear that gripped the campus community five years ago.

However, that morning, as students prepared for the school's first publicly televised debate, and reveled in their "home away from home" dorms, Asheville police responded to yet another call from the Botanical Gardens with reports of a partially clothed woman's body that appeared nude from the waist down and had been stabbed to death. The body was discovered that Wednesday, October 11th, around

10:30 am by members of a Southern Bell telephone crew who were in the area setting up a new line.

The initial media reports linked the death back to UNCA with headlines like "Body of a Woman Found Near UNC-A." In 1973, the university attempted to distance itself from the Botanical Gardens by stressing the boundaries of university vs. federally owned property. However, Olson's murder transformed the Botanical Gardens into school property—at least for the public. Now, when these new violent acts occurred, it was no longer a body that was found "in" the Botanical Gardens; it was now a body found "near" or "on" UNCA property.

For university administrators, it had become a familiar ritual. These crimes would startle the campus community, inspire press coverage that compared the new case particulars to Olson's original murder, and then, privately, the school would encourage administrators to publicly stress the relatively safe campus environment. In the October 12th, 1978 edition of the *Asheville Citizen-Times*, Billy Pritchard, who extensively covered the initial Olson investigation, was the first to remind Asheville readers of Olson's symbolic presence when he wrote:

> The body was found in the vicinity where a 19-year-old UNC-A coed, Virginia Marie Olson, was found bound, gagged, and stabbed to death on a Sunday afternoon more than five years ago.
>
> Miss Olson's body, also subjected to a brutal sexual assault, was found April 15th, 1973, across the street from the Botanical Gardens in a wooded area on a hilltop overlooking W.T. Weaver Boulevard.... [near] where the older woman's body was found Wednesday.

Officer Walter Gilchrest was the first member of the Asheville Police Department who responded to the scene, and he noted that the woman was "found lying on her left side facing east with both legs together." The woman's pocketbook was recovered near the body, but it did not contain information that would allow police to make an identification. In his report, Officer Gilchrist would describe her as a "dark-skinned" woman with "dark hair, streaked with gray and small in stature."

We can only speculate about the specific possible connections that the first officers on the scene theorized between Olson's death and this new one. However, we can safely assert that such a parallel would have felt reasonable. The second major SBI task force investigating Olson's murder began in 1977, and Asheville Police were part of this work. In other words, as law enforcement officials reviewed the original 1973 investigation and followed up on old leads, they were simultaneously investigating a new murder nearly at the exact location that also involved a woman who had been sexually assaulted.

For our purposes in this book, the most notable link is the leadership bridge between the investigation of this murder in 1978 and the second wave of Olson investigations that were about to start in the mid-80s. Asheville Police Detective Will R. Annarino would lead the 1980s investigation. At this moment in 1978, Annarino was the detective in charge of the new case. However, as he began work, he collaborated closely with SBI members of the 1977 Olson task force, who meticulously reviewed the original suspects and witness statements. Within six years, Annarino would have a new title, "Chief of Detectives," and he would lead the new Olson investigation.

Identifying the Victim and Connections to Olson

By Friday, October 13th, 1978, the murder victim had been successfully identified as Mary Faye Burdette, a 60-year-old woman who lived in the Livingston Heights Apartment complex in Asheville, not far from the crime scene. Her body had been taken to the NC Medical Examiner's Office for autopsy, and later that same week, investigators were surprised to learn that the M.E. reported her cause of death to be strangulation and not "stabbing," as was initially theorized and reported. According to the M.E. report, Burdette's body, especially the area around her throat, was so badly decomposed that it outwardly appeared to result from a stabbing injury.

By this point, we want to explain to you why we are discussing this case. Unlike the Karen McDonald case, the connection to Virginia Olson here seems more tenuous. Yes, Burdette's body was found in the same area as Olson's body, but the years that separate these two cases make this fact less remarkable. For us, this case matters because it would bring Detective Will Annarino- the man who, a few years later, would publicly proclaim to know the identity of Olson's killer- into contact with investigators who were actively working on the SBI's 1977 Olson task force.

It is hard to imagine a scenario where Annarino did not consider the Olson case even during his first crime scene visit. Here, it is instructive to remember that Olson's presence strongly shaped the initial inquiry into Karen McDonald's 1974 disappearance. When Asheville Police Chief J.C. Hall learned of McDonald's disappearance, the first thing he did was send officers down to the Botanical Gardens, even though there was no evidence that McDonald had traveled in that direction. We think the same general concept applies here; yes, the Burdette case was five years removed from

Olson's murder, but virtually every press story concerning the 1978 case mentions Olson in some form.

Olson's murder frequently emerged in conversations between Asheville investigators, and the location of Burdette's body inspired a new resolve in Annarino. During the time he worked on the Burdette murder investigation, he collaborated with members of the North Carolina SBI. Many of these individuals had also worked on the 1977 task force that re-examined the Olson case and sought to explore connections between it and other unsolved cases in Western North Carolina. When Annarino first arrived at the crime scene and encountered these same SBI investigators who offered their expertise and support, it seemed almost inevitable that Olson would have come up and been fresh in their memory from this review.

All of this matters because the conclusions Annarino will ultimately double down on in public closely resemble those articulated by the 1977 task force review. It is, therefore, our view that this case, in its own way, shaped his early impressions of the Olson case in ways that would transform the trajectory of the second wave of investigations he would lead in the 1980s.

"The Body Now Has a Name": What We Know About Mary Faye Burdette

Little is known about Mary F. Burdette, and her noticeably short obituaries remind us that she was the kind of victim who doesn't typically inspire reward offers by governors or the appointment of law enforcement task forces to explore all possible leads. Burdette had few living relatives other than her biological children; she was divorced at a time when making a living as a single woman was exceedingly difficult, and she primarily subsisted on social security payments. Known associates of Burdette described her as a woman who dreamed of stability and craved meaningful romantic connections. That steadfast desire for intimacy and connection sometimes led her into unhealthy relationships and a willingness to accept offers of companionship even when they came from unsavory characters.

At the time of her death, Burdette had lived in the Asheville area for six years. Most of her life can be divided between residency periods in different parts of Georgia. She was born in Franklin County, GA, and lived in a small town called Toccoa, GA. She raised two daughters, Brenda Poole and Rosella Hunter, and five sons: Larry, Henry, Frankie, Monty, and Greg. She also had two siblings: a sister named Nancy Rothenburg and a brother named Sylvester.

Despite the size of her family, Burdette is often described in media coverage as someone without a robust support system of people close to her. Phrases like "the Burdette Body" appear throughout this case's October 1978 press coverage, which is an accurate descriptor. She is a body that reminds them of other instances, like Virginia Olson, and "her death, like the other women's, remains unsolved."

Detective Annarino's Investigation Begins

Later in his career, Annarino demonstrated a dramatic flair that conveyed a supreme level of confidence in his ability to solve cases quickly, and those skills were put on full display in the Burdette investigation. Under his direction, police promptly established that Burdette, whose body had been decomposing for several days, was last seen alive on October 4th, 1978. This was one week before the discovery of her body. A witness spotted her exiting a taxi cab near the Botanical Gardens entrance. A man, who at this early point remained unidentified, allegedly shared the taxi ride with her.

The challenges this case presented were obvious. Without any close friends or relatives in the Asheville area, with little known about the victim, and with a heavily decomposed body, the precise starting point was not so obvious. J.N. Minter, the head of the SBI's Western office, seemed to echo this sentiment during the first week of the investigation. Still, he expressed hope about other more optimistic implications of solving the Burdette case: "I would like to say if we clear this (the Burdette case), then we can clear that one (referring to Olson) too."

Within eleven days of Director Minter's pronouncement, the Asheville Police Department announced that an arrest warrant had been issued for a white, 35-year-old man named Richard Levi Jenkins. The warrant listed first-degree murder of the death of Mary Burdette as the principal charge. Jenkins was described as 5'8", 165 lbs, with medium-length blonde hair, thick glasses, and slightly crossed eyes. At the time the warrant was issued, police believed Jenkins had fled the area and asked for the public's help in locating him.

As tips started to pour into the Asheville Police Department, detectives learned that Jenkins had been spotted on a bus that left for Knoxville, Tennessee, on the day of Burdette's murder. Jenkins surrendered himself to law enforcement two days later, on October 27th, 1978.

Unlike the Olson investigation, this one seemed to be coming together quickly. Annarino was suspicious of Jenkins from the start, and some of this interest stemmed from a prior history of mental illness and rapes that Jenkins carried out in 1969. In March of 1969, he was charged with assault "with intent to rape" and spent two years in psychiatric care as part of his sentence for these crimes.

In this case, the Asheville Police and SBI worked efficiently together. Assistant Police Chief Fred Hensley was part of the investigative team that arrested Jenkins in 1969, and he agreed that Jenkins was a plausible suspect who should be considered in the Burdette case. Annarino and the SBI agents supporting the case wasted no time. Within two weeks, they had not only concluded that Jenkins was responsible for Burdette's death, but they also concluded that he was also responsible for the death of Virginia Ruth Higgins Mitchell, who was murdered on July 12th in a very similar way. Like Burdette, she had been strangled, raped, and "sexually mutilated."

The speed with which the police worked here inspired public confidence, and the fact that two disturbing cases had been solved seemed to offer a promise for the Olson case. After all, police quickly adjusted their investigation to new facts they encountered and, in doing so, solved two cases.

The Jenkins Trial

On Thursday, October 26th, 1978, Richard Jenkins was arraigned in District Court before Judge James O. Israel Jr., who immediately denied the defendant's request for bond and ordered the Public Defender's office to represent Jenkins at trial. At this initial hearing, the public discovered that Jenkins was an unemployed crop picker who spent two years at Dorthea Dix Mental Hospital in Raleigh, NC from March 1969 to October 1971.

Six days after Jenkins appeared in court, Asheville Police also arrested a 32-year-old Weaverville man named James Lee Nicholson and charged him with concealing Jenkins after the murder. Nicholson was officially charged with "accessory after the fact to the felony murder of Mary F. Burdette...by carrying Richard Levi Jenkins from the general area of the crime and concealing him at the home of James Lee Nicholson."

Scrutiny of the Asheville Police Department Investigation

The Asheville Police Department's investigation into the murder of Mary Burdette came under scrutiny early in the trial of Richard Jenkins as psychiatrists debated the defendant's mental fitness. The public defender's office called a local psychiatrist named Dr. John D. Patton, who, under oath, claimed that Jenkins was "mildly retarded" and claimed the Asheville Police Department did not take any measures to ensure Jenkins understood the charges against him before they began their line of questioning.

At issue here was a confession that Jenkins allegedly made to police when he was taken into custody. Police responded that Jenkins was given a Miranda warning. At the same time, the defense contested that even if such a warning had been given, Jenkins would have been unable to comprehend the substance of the allegations. The prosecution countered this testimony with an evaluation by their psychiatrist, Dr. James Groce, of Dorthea Dix Hospital, which was the facility where Jenkins was treated in 1969 following a rape conviction. Groce argued that Jenkins could fully understand the notion of not incriminating himself. The judge ultimately agreed with the prosecution, and Jenkins was ordered to stand trial.

Annarino Takes Center Stage for the Prosecution

A central part of the prosecution's case was the timeline and testimony offered by Detective Will Annarino. In a testimony on August 1st, 1979, Annarino demonstrated a prodigious memory by reciting specific quotes as he recounted his early interrogations of Jenkins. In his early confession, Annarino explained that Jenkins told him he wanted "to get this thing off his chest." Annarino then recounted the story he heard from Jenkins about meeting Burdette for the first time while dining at a Lexington Avenue diner on October 4th. According to Annarino's testimony, Jenkins told him they decided to leave to go someplace more private, and the suspect took her to what he knew would be a secluded spot near UNCA. Once at the Botanical Gardens, Jenkins told Annarino that he and Burdette had consensual sex and that he fell asleep soon afterward. Annarino, in a somewhat incredulous tone, then quoted a comment from Jenkins that he "put his hands on" the victim's neck, "but he did not remember squeezing… All I know is that when I woke up, Mary was dead."

Annarino's public-facing instincts were on full display during the trial when he brought enlarged color photographs of Burdette's crime scene to show the jury. The defense objected and argued that they were prejudicial, but the jury was ultimately allowed to see the images because the judge ruled they merely illustrated police testimony. Annarino used these photos to stress the horrific nature of the "mutilation" that occurred here. Jenkins not only murdered Burdette, but based on the medical examiner's report and information that came from an interrogation of a local taxi driver, Annarino argued that days after the crime, Jenkins went back to the scene of the crime by taxi with the intent to further sexually mutilate Burdette's body. The taxi driver who drove Jenkins to the crime scene the second time would also testify at the trial that Jenkins "walked out of the wooded area with blood on his shirt."

Annarino's testimony was vivid, courageous, and confident. The jury, composed of seven men and five women, was noticeably impacted by his testimony. When the jury went into deliberations, it would only take them 35 minutes to find Jenkins guilty of second-degree murder. Judge F. Fetzer Mills would then impose the maximum life sentence without parole.

The Burdette Case as Predictor of Annarino's Later Approach to Olson Investigation

The Burdette case offered valuable insights into how Detective Annarino conducted investigations. He moved swiftly, guided by his instincts, but he also proved surprisingly collaborative with outside agencies like the SBI. He took suggestions from the SBI and other members of the Asheville Police Department seriously when Jenkins came up as a possible suspect.

The case also demonstrated his relentless efforts to bring Jenkins to justice once he became convinced of a suspect's guilt. Yet, even when he was sure of a suspect's guilt, he never took shortcuts. "Thorough" was the word used most often by current members of the Asheville Police Department to fondly describe Annarino. In this case, the thoroughness of the investigation eventually led detectives to add two additional murders to the charges against Jenkins. Not only was he convicted of Mary Burdette's murder, but he was also charged with and convicted of killing Virginia Ruth Higgins Mitchell and Gloria Gosnell as well.

Annarino was highly successful here despite daunting odds and a victim that didn't automatically elicit the same public outrage as Virginia Olson. Olson had her whole life ahead of her, and the network of people she touched produced calls for action from her college campus up to the governor of North Carolina. Mary Burdette was different. She was older and poverty-stricken and had few close friends or relatives. Little is known about her as a person, and her death could have become one that inspired the bare minimum of resources and efforts from law enforcement. However, that wasn't the case; agencies worked together to solve it quickly and investigate other cases that seemed connected to their perpetrator.

When the Burdette investigation began, the consensus was that if this case could be solved, there was still hope for the Olson case. However, the reality was more complicated, and by the time Jenkins was sentenced to life in prison in 1979, the Olson case had gone completely cold. It would be another five years before any significant attention or leads would be pursued. When the case did come back into the public eye, it did so through a fresh re-investigation instigated at the insistence of Will Annarino as part of his new promotion to Chief of Detectives. As he started work on the case, he shared his belief that it was finally close to being solved.

Chapter 9: "An Arrest is Imminent": The Second Olson Investigation, 1983-1986

"That's what gripes me so much. He thinks he's got it made. He's not worrying about this case."—Lt. Will Annarino, 1983

In 1977, the Asheville Police Department convinced Buncombe County District Attorney Ron Brown to reopen the Olson investigation. At the time, the goal of these officers, working alongside the "Homicide Squad task force," was to "shed new light on old evidence." Yet, as we have already discussed, the task force's work concluded in 1979 without any fresh developments in the case. Four years would pass before investigators would make another effort to solve the case.

By September of 1983, Will Annarino had moved through the Asheville Police Department's promotion ranks and had established himself as one of the most dogged investigators in the state. Soon after cracking the Burdette case, he was promoted from detective to lieutenant by Asheville Police Chief Fred W. Hensley. Within two years, Annarino would be promoted again to captain. After his promotion, he sought out every professional development opportunity that might allow him to become a better investigator. For instance, in 1982, he completed the FBI's executive training program at their main Quantico campus.

He attended it alongside investigators from all 50 states and learned about new investigative technologies, resources, and techniques he could bring back home to North Carolina and apply to current investigations. These kinds of training opportunities were significant in the 1980s because the SBI, during this era, only tended to assist smaller departments with high-profile homicides. Their presence also had to be requested. Noted North Carolina true crime author Mark Pinsky explained that most murder cases in Buncombe County were handled entirely by the Asheville Police Department. The Buncombe County Sheriff's Office in 1981 did not have a single homicide specialist on their staff.

One of the main things on Annarino's mind in 1983 was the still unsolved Olson case. The original 1973 investigators, a pair of full-time SBI agents in 1974, and a 1977 task force had failed to result in an arrest. His swift handling of the Burdette case made him confident that Olson's murder could be solved despite the passage of an extended amount of time. He was realistic and understood the challenges that these kinds of cases brought. By 1983, the Olson investigation was ten years old and had not generated a significant lead in more than five years. He understood the case would only become more challenging to solve as time passed. Annarino would explain the complicated politics of cold cases to *Asheville Times* reporter David Nivens in 1981 when he stressed that "keeping a case active after some time has passed is hard because some investigators lose interest after (public) interest in the case dies down."

Despite the investigative difficulties of the past, Annarino's recent Quantico training taught him that these newer technologies offered fresh perspectives on previously collected evidence. These new technologies have already produced results. In 1981, the Asheville Police Department was able to use some of these forensic technologies to arrest and convict those responsible for the 1979 murder of Joseph Rosen. Forensic science advancements in the 1980s included laser identification of fingerprints and the ability to distinguish new subtypes of blood that contained unique distinguishing markers.

While investigators never give up on unsolved homicides, Annarino conceded that they could get "unofficially" placed in a deprioritized category when the central suspect dies or ends up in prison on a different charge. There is no set formula for how these "cold" investigations proceed or the resources allocated to them, but factors like the ability to interview previous witnesses or test/re-test previously connected evidence can be deciding factors. The possibilities can be dramatic when significant evidence exists, and the 80s offered hope. Annarino spoke about this issue as early as 1981 when he described the differences between current investigations and those in the 70s: "We are better organized than ever before to handle these investigations."

In 1982, the Asheville Police Department's detective bureau reopened seven unsolved murder cases, and Annarino announced that the Olson murder would receive fresh scrutiny. He sought to utilize the new technologies from the start of his investigation, realizing that the early part of his re-examination would involve "waiting for laboratory results." All original materials collected at the crime scene were sent back that same year to the North Carolina SBI's crime lab for analysis. Annarino was especially interested in Olson's blood-soaked jeans and what the new forensic tests might be able to yield.

While detectives on Annarino's team waited for the SBI's lab results, which they believed could take months, they also began reviewing the original investigation. While this was the third major review of the Olson investigation, many of Annarino's conclusions mirrored those of the 1977 task force. The task force had identified two plausible suspects for Olson's murder, even though SBI investigators in 1974 had followed up with leads in Florida, Georgia, and Alabama. At this point, we want to emphasize that Annarino worked closely with several members of the 1977 task force while he led the 1978 investigation into the murder of Mary Burdette. Given the parallels between the two crimes- both bodies were murdered in the Botanical Gardens across from UNCA, and both were sexually assaulted- we find it impossible to imagine a scenario in which these same investigators did not share their theories and thoughts about the case with Annarino.

The 1977 task force focused on two suspects, but after completing his investigative review in 1983, Annarino publicly announced a break in the Olson case. Annarino was so confident in his assessment that even before the SBI lab returned the results of their testing, he sat down with *Asheville Citizen-Times* reporter Linda McNabb, who would write an article with a bold title: "Asheville Police Nearing Arrest in 1973 Murder of UNC-A Co-ed."

Overstating the Asheville community's surprise at this provocative proclamation is impossible. By 1983, the region's major papers had not run a story about this case in almost five years. Then, seemingly out of the blue, one of the town's most respected and seasoned detectives publicly stated that an arrest was *imminent*. It was a bold move that is hard to understand from a 2024 vantage point. Was this statement meant to put the prime suspect on notice? Was it designed to get the public talking about the case again? Given Annarino's prior statements about gaining public interest, it is reasonable to assume this was part of his motive. However, we still have a hard time reconciling the bravura of a public commitment to make an arrest before receiving confirmed lab results. This is especially perplexing since Annarino, in the same interview with Linda McNabb, states that "we've got enough information. We are just waiting on one more piece to tie it together."

The trouble with such statements is that they seem to undercut the confidence of the arrest prediction. How can an arrest be imminent if other pieces are still needed to "tie it together?" Since the lab results had not yet been returned, there seems to be little substantive difference between the investigative materials that Annarino examined compared to those studied by the 1977 task force. Was this a matter of a different interpretation of the same information? Was this about Annarino's gut, or did he put something novel together? In a different interview with a reporter from the *Asheville Times*, Annarino expressed confidence in the perpetrator's identity: "We have no doubt in our minds who did this one."

Another dramatic development occurred at this stage when the Asheville Police Department released more previously unknown details about their prime suspect. As we stated in an earlier chapter, it is not unusual for departments to leak additional information to the public after a significant amount of time has passed to encourage new leads. While withholding critical pieces of evidence or information has strategic value in areas like testing, after ten or more years, there is a diminishing value in maintaining such strict observances.

The task force leaked information about the man's age and location, but Asheville Police went far beyond these details and provided a significant amount of biographical information to the press. Police told reporters that the prime suspect was questioned two weeks after the murder. Annarino confirmed that this suspect was the same man who lived in an apartment a few blocks from the location of the murder. He explained that on the day of the murder, two different residents of this apartment complex contacted the police to report the suspect's odd behavior. One witness claimed the man approached her and asked her to "pray with him." The statement from this witness was reported by the media in 1978; however, police didn't publicly disclose that another witness also described odd behavior from this suspect and allegedly told investigators that on the day of the murder, he paced around and complained about the "bloody mess." The original investigators questioned this individual that same evening, and on April 29, 1973, the SBI executed a search warrant to collect potential evidence for testing. The results of those original tests were "negative," and shortly after, the police said the suspect had left the state.

By 1983, Annarino said the prime suspect was now in his early 50s and living "west of the Mississippi River." Annarino said locating the suspect was pretty easy because he made no effort to hide. His name remained the same, and he lived a relatively normal life. He described the suspect as highly educated and from an upper-class family. The suspect's father was a partner in a northern law firm and had worked to protect his son from legal entanglements over the years that were allegedly the result of several mental health disorders. The suspect reportedly spent extended periods in mental health treatment facilities throughout adulthood. Annarino explained that the suspect had served in the U.S. Army and attained the rank of lieutenant. Despite his mental health struggles and potential ties to other crimes (including the Olson murder), he had only been formally arrested once in his life. This arrest occurred around the 1960s in San Francisco and consisted of a single voyeurism charge.

The 1984 Santa Fe Trip

The public disclosures about the prime suspect in 1983 gave way to an even bolder statement on November 23, 1984, when Annarino announced that he would travel, along with another Asheville Police detective, to Santa Fe, New Mexico, to interview the prime suspect in Olson's death. Like the prior public announcement, this one focused on soon-to-be-undertaken actions. The November 23rd *Asheville Times* title announced, "Man to be Questioned in 1973 Co-ed Slaying."

Annarino's choice to disclose info about the trip to interview the primary suspect is another decision we struggled to reconcile when researching the 1984 investigation. Publicly disseminating information about an inquiry always carries some degree of risk. Some circumstances, especially those related to enticing public interest or encouraging new tips, might be worth the risk for investigators. However, it is hard to imagine the value of letting a main suspect better prepare or simply "lawyer up" and refuse to answer questions. After all, the stated purpose of this trip was to ask the suspect questions, not to serve an arrest warrant. In these circumstances, the suspect is under no obligation to engage in any communication with investigators. Further, with an advance headline like "Man to be Questioned in 1973 Co-ed Slaying," any benefits of engaging officers seem to evaporate.

Our judgment aside, it is undeniable that these headlines represented the first significant break in the case since 1973- when the media reported that a 19-year-old man had been detained and questioned in connection with Olson's death. Other inquiries had taken place, but these primarily involved a review of the original investigation and did not lead to any public breaks in the case. The coverage during these investigations, 1974 and 1977, tended to emphasize the act of the investigation, not any new lead.

Another important context is that a year earlier, Annarino publicly announced that the police were close to making an arrest. News that a suspect would be questioned seemed to represent progress towards fulfilling his public promise. It also appeared to complete the work of the original investigators since police confirmed that the Santa Fe suspect was the same man that investigators questioned and searched on April 29, 1973.

Annarino told the *Asheville Citizen-Times* that the stated mission of the Santa Fe trip was to "bring the New Mexico man back to North Carolina to stand trial." He further pointed out that in 1983, the SBI lab had analyzed Olson's blood-soaked pants. The curious thing about this comment is that he didn't say the lab discovered anything, but placing this comment within the context of the one about bringing "the New Mexico man back to North Carolina to stand trial" subtly implies, without ever directly stating, that they have evidence to compel the suspect's return to the state.

Annarino's promise of closure at the end of November was replaced by disappointment weeks later when police announced that the Santa Fe trip had not led to an arrest. On December 3, 1984, Maj. Jim Beaver of the Asheville Police informed the media that an arrest was no longer imminent, but they also failed to disclose whether new evidence had exonerated their main suspect. Beaver stated that Annarino and another detective met with the prime suspect but could not secure a confession. Beaver would go on to express the frustration that many in the public felt about this new development when he lamented, "The case right now is in limbo. We took what we had and made another stab at it. We went there hoping to get a confession, but it didn't work out. He never was in custody; all we did was go out there and interview him."

Despite the lack of an arrest, by 1985, Annarino continued to insist that the case was essentially solved. In a wide-ranging discussion of six unsolved murders in the Asheville area, he took exception to the idea that the Olson case was still a mystery that should be grouped among the other five cases. He claimed police have known "who did it…pretty much all along." He would repeatedly reference a point he made throughout the early 1980s: the suspect has never changed his name or tried to conceal himself. Annarino almost seemed skeptical when he described the state of the investigation: "I know where he is living and where he works. The man lives out of state and has mental problems, which is one reason why police have had such a hard time getting concrete evidence against him."

Obtaining evidence against suspects and engaging in criminal investigations had changed significantly during Annarino's time investigating criminal cases, and the first and second Olson investigations offer a helpful marker of some important shifts. To his credit, Annarino tended to change his investigative methods with emerging technologies. The same month that he went to Santa Fe to question the main suspect in the Olson case, he also spearheaded the push to get the Asheville Police Department to switch to computer-based record systems. He explained that his change of heart was tied to the results he observed firsthand at FBI trainings: "Everybody's so afraid of these things. I was. Maybe we're a little resentful of them. But once you see what they can do, you appreciate them."

The new computer system Annarino installed for the Asheville Police Department focused on case management instead of suspect management. In other words, the computers allowed detectives to instantly access arrest records, court dispositions, inventories, pawn shop records, parole records, case management, intelligence, and stolen property reports in the same system. The new system also allowed Annarino to track the work of his detectives: "Most departments assign a case to a detective and forget about it until the case is closed. Here, Det. Lt. Edwards or I constantly review each case…the old-time detective managed suspects. They worked on what they wanted to. In a nutshell, there was no accountability."

While Annarino did not directly state why the primary suspect was not arrested, he repeatedly cited the "less sophisticated" way crime scene evidence was preserved and processed during the 70s. The assumption is that this same complaint also applied to the Olson investigation since materials were repeatedly sent to the SBI crime lab for new testing throughout the 1984-1986 investigation. Since no arrest resulted from these tests and the test results were never disclosed, this indicates two possibilities: either the tests did not implicate the primary suspect, *or* the original materials were too severely degraded to produce reliable results. Given Annarino's steadfast insistence- even after the failed Santa Fe trip- that he had identified the man responsible for Olson's death, it seems more likely that the original samples had deteriorated beyond the point of being useful.

As the second Olson investigation wound down, we think one statement Annarino made best captures the general sentiment of the state of the 1980s Olson investigation almost 12 years removed from the crime: "if we'd had our capabilities now back then, it would have made the cases extremely easier for us. Hindsight—you always want to be able to go back with what you know now."

Part IV

Two Brothers Investigate a 51-Year- Old Cold Case

Chapter 10: Researching Cold Cases—Our Process

"You want desperately to get these people... You'll do literally everything you have to do to solve the case."
—Sgt. J.R. Emory, 1994

The final section of the book details our investigation into the murder of Virginia Olson. Before we begin, we want to point out that you, the reader, now know no more about this case than everyone except the current law enforcement officers assigned to it. For years, stories about the murder of Virginia Olson have been passed down at UNCA and within the local Buncombe County community, almost like a rite of passage; most of the specific details surrounding the investigation are not known by contemporary audiences. Even worse, much of what publicly circulates is based on half-truths, rumors, gossip, and theories that imagine connections between the Olson case and other unsolved murders. In the interest of thoroughness, our investigation has made every effort to look at some of these theories—even the ones that might seem absurd—and then engage them on their merits based on our experiences as a professor or law enforcement official.

The Cold Case Years

Our previous chapter ended with Will Annarino's ill-fated trip to Santa Fe, NM, to question the Asheville Police Department's primary suspect. This individual was the focus of a search warrant that was served on his place of residence on the night of April 29, 1973, exactly two weeks after Olson's murder. This detail was repeated to the general public during the initial frenzy of press coverage that passed along updates to a shocked Asheville community on the status of the investigation. For 13 years, task forces and Asheville Police detectives hinted at an "imminent" arrest and boasted of knowledge of the murderer's identity. Their confidence level in their assessment is nowhere more present than in their press conversations just before leaving for New Mexico.

One notable feature of the New Mexico coverage was the consistent interviews and press releases for two years (83-84) during the second and final major investigative push to solve the case. When detectives returned from Santa Fe, they only made one public statement about the investigation: "We gave it our best shot, but the trip wasn't successful." During our first conversation with Detective Kevin Taylor, the Asheville Police Department's current cold case detective assigned to the Olson case, we inquired about this significant shift. We directly asked whether this meant that the blood tests performed on Olson's jeans—which Annarino publicly alluded to during these years—returned an unfavorable result. Taylor hesitated to address this question directly and didn't offer any details or elaboration in response to our question. Still, he provided a kind of confirmation when he said, "Well...you didn't see an arrest, right?"

Following the failure of the New Mexico trip, the Olson case officially goes "cold." Current investigators would likely dispute this characterization. On more than one occasion, they impressed upon us that they are "doing work" and that this case remains "open and active." When you hear statements like this from law enforcement, they are accurate and misleading. In the most literal reading possible, the Olson case is still "active and open." This part is genuine, but the average member of the general public might not completely understand this phrase. To the layperson, "active and open" might sound like someone is getting up each day thinking about the case—making phone calls, interviewing witnesses, reviewing evidence, etc. This is far from the truth, and this is a point worth reiterating: all *unsolved* murder cases remain "active and open" indefinitely.

This is not a special designation given to Olson that somehow represents an extraordinary commitment by a group of investigators. There is no statute of limitations on murder and a few other "major crimes." Without a statute of limitations, the case will only be "closed" once solved. Even when police are nearly sure of the identity of a deceased perpetrator, it is still an involved process to formally close a murder case that didn't go to trial.

We want to be generous in our assessment; in this case, we pinpoint the case as going completely cold around 1994. The case likely went "cold" the day Asheville Police received the S.B.I. lab results from the Santa Fe suspect in New Mexico. After investing so much time and energy into a single suspect, investigators hadn't many obvious routes to begin anew. That said, we tend to say 1994 because this year marks the last public coverage of the Asheville Police Department's association with the case.

On December 4, 1994, the *Asheville Citizen-Times* ran an article titled, "8 Buncombe murder cases still open." The Virginia Olson case was featured in this article. The optimism that characterized prior coverage and hinted at new leads is absent. Instead, in two brief paragraphs, the article only sums up the investigation's initial focus and the failure of this focus to lead to an arrest: "A prime suspect was questioned and released two weeks after the slaying, and was questioned again in 1984 when Asheville police reactivated the case and flew to his home in New Mexico. There was insufficient evidence to take to a grand jury."

After this article, no significant coverage of the case was penned in the city's flagship newspaper between 1994 and today. This is especially unusual given the close relationship between past investigators and the press. The logical conclusion is that there is nothing significant to share. Current Asheville investigators will claim that they continue to test materials associated with the case, but they also concede that no primary suspect exists.

Current Asheville cold case detectives also confirmed that the suspect Asheville Police honed in on between 1973 and 1984 is no longer considered a prime suspect. To ensure we correctly understood this startling admission, we asked, "Is this your opinion about the previous suspect, or is this view representative of the Asheville Police Department's shared consensus?" They unambiguously confirmed that this view is shared by all of the current investigators tied to the case. So, while the case is admittedly "open," it is most certainly "cold."

Before we proceed to our analysis of the historical investigation of Olson's murder, along with our theories about this case, we think it's important to talk about how we went about this entire process. Our research into this case, partly due to the age (a crime 51 years ago), presented many unanticipated challenges that we will highlight. We hope understanding cold case processes and our process will help shed light on the complexities of reinvestigations. Aside from the original investigators in 1973, virtually all work done on this case in 1974, 1977, and 1984-86 presented the challenges associated with cold cases.

The Body: Cold Case Detectives vs True Crime Writers

All cold case investigations begin with the body. The victim's body is where most investigations begin, and since 1972, when crime scene protocols started to appear, protecting the integrity of the body and the crime scene has taken on increased levels of importance. Today, most departments have statewide standards concerning crime scene preservation, and investigating officers are bound to follow them strictly. Audiences for forensic-focused police procedural shows like *C.S.I.* often glamorize depictions of the work done by crime scene investigators. Still, the role of chemistry, physics, biology, and geology in contemporary criminal investigations cannot be overstated.

Forensic technologies have advanced considerably since Olson's murder in the early 1970s, when things like fingerprints, geological scrapings under fingernails, blood type, plaster molds of footprints, and the presence of semen were often the extent of the scientific work that most departments were able to perform. To provide some additional historical perspective: at the time of Olson's death, rape kits had not yet become part of law enforcement investigations. The first documented use of a rape kit in a criminal investigation would not occur until 1978, a year after the 1977 task force. Several vital advancements developed by the time of the second major Olson investigation in 1984. The same month that Will Annarino and members of the Asheville Police Department traveled to New Mexico to interview their prime suspect, they also moved the Asheville Police Department to computerized case management for the first time.

In the 70s, most forensic blood tests focused on an individual's blood type and "secretor status." A secretor test is based on the idea that, for some individuals, blood cells aren't the only cells in the body that contain genetic markers of blood type (A, B, AB, or O). Some individuals also "secrete" these markers in their saliva, mucus, and other body fluids. Blood type and secretor status are independent of one another, which means knowing an individual's status as a secretor or non-secretor *can* be a way for investigators to eliminate a suspect since these markers exist based on a single genetic mutation.

Let's think about the practical application here. Suppose police in the 70s are investigating Prime Suspect X. Investigators believe this individual had the motive and opportunity to commit the crime. Forensics determined that there were two blood types at the crime scene. The victim is type A, and another type B blood type was found on the victim's body. There is clear physical evidence of a struggle, and the presumption is that this second blood type is from the individual responsible. When blood is taken from Prime Suspect X, it is determined that he is also type B. When detectives test the type B sample, they discover the individual is a secretor. However, when they test Prime Suspect X, he is determined to be a non-secretor. This new test would exonerate Prime Suspect X since a genetic mutation in one blood sample does not align with prime suspect x's genetic composition. Secretor status can correlate with other health conditions, but health conditions cannot cause a change in secretor status.

Cold case detectives start with the literal body of the victim. For *true crime* researchers, the work with the body begins with public records, business records, and nonphysical evidence that analyzes the body of the victim in social relationships. The focus on the nonphysical is different, but the principle is still the same: the investigation moves from the body outward. During one of our conversations with veteran true crime author Mark Pinsky, he described public records associated with the victim as the "bones of case research." He explained that murder cases often involve many "moving parts," but the public records attached to the case are the anchor points. They are the unchanging parts that don't move and are merely recovered and interpreted by investigators.

Our public record search started with four simple requests: a FOIA request to the FBI and the U.S. Justice Department to determine the scope of the Olson investigation, a request for a non-certified copy of Virginia Olson's death certificate from the Vital Records Office of Buncombe County, a request with the City of Asheville for a copy of the initial incident report, and a request with the NC Medical Examiner's Office for a copy of the autopsy report and narrative. Both federal and state agencies have rules and laws regarding open records requests. When starting a new investigation, looking into particular local processes is a good idea.

Public record requests tend to be the "easy" part of research. As a writer, you are looking to these records to get lists of names associated with the case and essential information to investigate further. For example, we received a copy of Virginia Olson's death certificate from Buncombe County when we filed our request. While this document might look simple, it contains some critical information. First, it provided the victim's full name, date of birth, estimated time of death, the names of her parents (and their address), the location of her death, the name of the doctor who certified her death, and the cause of death. In this case, the death certificate described Olson's immediate cause of death as a "stab wound in left chest." It described a "laceration left neck" as "contributing to death but not the cause of death."

The medical examiner's report is the next logical step since it will provide more insight into the findings listed on the death certificate. This report is generally easy to obtain since many jurisdictions now have websites that allow anyone to fill out a brief form to submit their request for processing. The turnaround time varies, but in our experience, the people in the medical examiner's office were incredibly helpful.

Retrieving the medical examiner's report of Virginia Olson's autopsy proved to be a logistically complicated ordeal due to several colliding factors. First, a fire in 1975 destroyed most of the files at the NC Medical Examiner's Office. For this reason, their office only directly fulfilled requests for investigations that began after 1976. When our initial request was denied, we were referred to the North Carolina Archives with the note that the remains of the files that were damaged in the 1975 fire were subsequently transported to and stored at this location. Therefore, we filed a request with the NC Archives for a copy of the medical examiner's report, but their response was unexpected. The Archives informed us that they could not locate a copy of the file and that it was likely destroyed in the fire. They advised us to file a request with the Buncombe County Clerk of Court's office. This whole process had already become more involved than prior research experiences, but we went ahead and filed a record request with the clerk's office. More accurately, Brian focused on gaining further clarification from the NC Archives, while Cameron began the process with the Buncombe County Clerk's Office.

The absurdity of finding this report took another turn when the clerk's office suggested we contact the NC Archives for the Medical Examiner's report, and the NC Archives explained we would have to get the report from the Asheville Police Department. When we first began work on this case, we reached out to members of the Asheville Police Department to introduce ourselves and our book. This was a courtesy, but we also wanted to establish lines of communication with those currently tied to the case. The Asheville Police Department initially proved to be very supportive and gracious. In this case, Cameron's status as a former law enforcement officer worked to our advantage.

There is a professional courtesy that law enforcement tends to extend to their own, which worked to our advantage here. Cameron reached out to Capt. Silberman, the current head of the Criminal Investigations Division (CID, which was formerly the Detective Bureau), to explain our situation.

While Asheville Police acknowledged that a copy of the M.E. report resided in their master case file and had no problem with us having a copy of this public record, they initially denied our request for help because they believed it set a potentially bad precedent. Police departments and journalists often have a complicated relationship. They both need each other for different reasons, but their interests can differ enough that each is wary of requests outside the normal scope of the "rules" that govern most of their official interactions.

In this case, a variety of originating agencies, like the NC Medical Examiner's Office, have entire staff that process and fulfill public records requests. Individual departments might be forced to process "some" records requests, but unless they are legally bound to do so, some understandable trepidation greets any attempt to ask more of them. This is understandable since taken to the extreme, the police do not want a situation in which reporters can "expect" to get public records directly from them. Processing a significant number of these requests could negatively impact their ability to do day-to-day work.

In this instance, we decided to contact the public information staff of the NC DHHS (Division of Health and Human Services), which is the state government area that the medical examiner's office works within, and we explained our situation and formally requested their assistance. We found this office to be incredibly helpful and apologetic about the difficulties we experienced. Ultimately, they offered to help mediate contact with Asheville by requesting a copy of the report. Once obtained, this copy would be subject to our original records request. Creative solutions won out that day, and we think the larger lesson to true crime writers is the need to be persistent when obstacles emerge.

We encountered similar issues obtaining the search warrant the SBI served on April 29, 1973. We will discuss this issue in more depth in Chapter 12, but it is worth noting that obtaining this document took months and required the assistance of many outside individuals. During our early conversations with the current cold case squad, they were able to definitively confirm for us that the suspect who entered police radar during the first two weeks after Olson's murder was the *same* individual that Annarino referenced during the final push to solve the case in the 80s and the same person that the Asheville P.D. delegation went out to interview in Santa Fe, New Mexico, in 1984.

Once this information was confirmed, we decided to obtain this search warrant to discover his identity. Doing so would open up new research avenues and allow us to publicly name the individual who has inspired community gossip and speculation for the last 51 years.

We were also interested in why this individual's name had never publicly leaked. Between 1973 and 1976, the Asheville Police Department released the names of many individuals tied to this case (like the Florida suspect). If this suspect had been definitively ruled out, then why was he exempt from this same treatment? The notion that this was simply a matter of "discretion" seemed inconsistent with other releases. For example, the names of the two underage boys who discovered Olson's body were provided to the press. Papers even printed their home addresses, the names of their parents, and where they attended junior high school.

Obtaining this search warrant proved tricky. The Asheville PD initially denied our request for the document and seemed sheepish in interviews whenever the conversation turned to this suspect. While "gaslighting" is probably too strong of a term, there was an effort to distance themselves from this suspect and downplay the significance of the investigation's emphasis on this single individual. When we requested the search warrant, we were told we must go through the Buncombe County Clerk's Office.

Cameron took the lead in handling this part of the research and had numerous conversations with staff in the clerk's office who liked to sigh and lament the difficulties in finding such an old record. At one point, one staff member even described our search as a "needle in a haystack" given the document's age and hinted that it might have been destroyed.

Cameron often left these conversations incredulous that an investigative agency could stress that they were "actively working" on the Olson case while hinting that official documents tied to it might not exist. Cameron repeatedly reminded the clerk's office that what they suggested amounted to the potential destruction of essential records related to a major crime. For context, it is highly irregular to destroy documents tied to an unsolved murder case.

I was equally baffled since my background as a PhD researcher means I'm relatively comfortable navigating materials in library archives and special collections. In my experience, "archive" signals some form of coherent, systematic organization. Things like finding guides containing lists of documents and the corresponding boxes and folders that house them are expected at manuscript libraries like the Library of Congress, the New York Public Library, and many others. In the case of the NC Archives, we discovered that "archive" is a generous and potentially misleading term since most of our conversations with the Archives staff suggested that fulfilling public record requests is more closely aligned with spending weeks rummaging through unorganized boxes kept in a warehouse until the searcher either gets lucky or returns the request as unfulfillable.

In contrast, the FBI FOIA system is highly organized and efficient. During the pandemic, the FOIA request system moved almost entirely online, and these electronic tools have only improved since that transition. As mentioned earlier, we tend to file an FBI and Justice Department FOIA request to understand the scope of each investigation we research. A response that "no records exist" is an easy way to focus all future requests toward state-level agencies. Sometimes, these requests can turn up interesting insights. For instance, one group of students in my "Writing True Crime" class researched the 1999 mysterious death of Ricky McCormick in Missouri, and their FOIA request resulted in copies of correspondence between the F.B.I. Crime Lab and the Sheriff's Department with investigative jurisdiction. These results provided insights into the types of materials and tests a smaller jurisdiction sought the FBI's guidance on. In our case, the FBI returned our FOIA request with a letter stating that they have no records related to Virginia Marie Olson's death. In this case, "nothing" was something. For better or worse, this investigation was conducted "in-house."

All of the above documents, from the death certificate to the M.E. report, are ways we engaged the "body" of the victim, but the other significant way involves what we can call "the body in motion." Here, we are thinking about relationships with family and associates, routines the victim followed, and any other traceable objects the victim carried, utilized, or possessed. Police sometimes use the phrase "victimology" to reference a similar process. This meant interviewing those close to Olson, from fellow cast members in the shows she performed at UNCA to romantic interests, teachers, and casual acquaintances. Collectively, patterns start to emerge that provide some insight into the victim.

Media Coverage and "The Muscles"

We will follow through with bodily analogies concerning the research process further. In the above discussion, we addressed how police and true crime investigations often begin with the body and then move outward. According to Pinsky's explanation, the public records are the "non-moving parts." They will never change, and you must understand them as an anchor point for all that follows. If public records are the body and the "bones," then media coverage comprises the "muscles" for the researcher. These pieces are alive and in movement, which is another way of saying they can change.

Media coverage was helpful to us for two primary reasons: it provided insight into how the community and law enforcement attempted to narrate the tragedy. Comparing details within media coverage also offered the possibility of identifying overlapping patterns between the Olson case and other related events.

It is important to note that not all media coverage is "equal." Some reporters consistently had access to more significant details concerning the Olson investigation than others. For instance, in the 1970s, Billy Pritchard was highly respected by the Asheville community and law enforcement. He was a seasoned reporter with a reputation for fair coverage. Over time, he gained the trust of law enforcement, reflecting the depth of some of his stories concerning the Olson case. Between 1973 and 1978, he was the primary reporter to provide the public with updates, and some of his details fall outside the normal scope of public records.

Media coverage also aided us in thinking about similarities between the Olson case and other reported cases throughout North Carolina. This is a vantage point that detectives in the early 1970s did not possess. During the 70s, even county-level communications between jurisdictions were not always consistent. It is important to remember that systems like CODIS, which connects federal and local jurisdictions to streamline information sharing, did not emerge until the 1990s. This is why if you ever watch a true crime documentary that focuses on an older case, you might shake your head in disbelief that someone like Ted Bundy or some other infamous murderer with a distinct modus operandi (M.O.) was able to evade detection for so long. There are many occasions in which a lack of an arrest did not indicate negligence on the part of investigators but instead merely revealed the limitations of the systems they worked within.

While law enforcement was not connected in 1973, the news media did have an infrastructure through their wire system that brought news from one county or state to another. Stories were often reprinted or written with the exact quotes from the original authors. At one point in our media research, Cameron remarked that many newspapers, whether in North Carolina, Tennessee, or elsewhere, were using the exact quotes and sources. Of course, this structure does have downsides—especially when an original story is given so much prominence and is recirculated in so many different ways that it might give the casual observer the appearance of a shared uniform belief or attitude. However, sharing information did have its upsides. It was the media, for instance, that first raised possible connections between the Olson case and other murders from different parts of North Carolina. While law enforcement ultimately followed up on these leads, they resulted from an established information infrastructure.

In this dimension of research, our goal was to locate whether or not Olson's murder fell into a clear pattern of crime. Were there similarities between her body and other crimes? We looked for victims or circumstances comparable in age, sex, race, physical characteristics, wounds, bindings, or how the body was left. It is also possible to conclude the socio-economic status of the victims based on their reported clothing, shoes, jewelry, or personal effects. For instance, police in 1978 were initially interested in possible connections between the Olson case and the murder of Mary Burdette. In some ways, the comparison makes sense. As we discussed in an earlier chapter, both women were murdered in a similar part of the Botanical Garden, both women were sexually assaulted, and both women appeared to have lacerations on their throats. However, the M.E.'s report in this case would ultimately conclude that the damage done to Burdette's throat was related to decomposition and not a laceration from a weapon. Other differences in age and the body's appearance would ultimately exclude any connection between the two.

Newspaper coverage can also provide insight into the profile of the possible offender. One of the confusing aspects of this case is the competing witness statements reported between 1973 and 1977. The fact that investigators released these statements tells us they were far less confident about their original suspect, far earlier than they conceded to the public. The changing coverage of how the "prime suspect" was described in the papers offered insights into the evolution of the investigation.

The Social Dynamics of Crime Research

Another aspect of the "body" we paid particular attention to involves Olson's social dynamics. This includes how she tended to think and relate to people and the world, her day-to-day life, and the people she interacted with.

In this case, we explored very early on whether or not Olson's decision to visit the Botanical Gardens adhered to her routine. If not, we would have explored what factors caused her to change her everyday activities. We discovered through statements given by Jane Nicholson, her roommate, and Jeff Doyle, one of the people closest to her, that she often went into the Botanical Gardens alone for a quiet space to read, write, or study. The fact that her school textbooks were found close to her body reflects her adherence to this larger pattern.

Knowing that Olson "often," according to Nicholson, went into these same woods also sets up other questions that are harder to address in 2024. For instance, how many people knew of this routine? The pool of possible suspects would have expanded quite a bit if it were widely known. After all, some predators target those who have predictable routines.

The two main choices we had to confront in this case are the ones investigators addressed in 1973: is someone close to her responsible, or was it merely random? To consider whether it was someone close to her, we would need to explore what stressors existed in Olson's life at the time of her death. For instance, were there conflicts with family members, intimate partners, or others at school that impacted her behavior?

These ideas will be explored more in the chapter dealing with our theories about the crime, but it is worth noting that Olson was experiencing some stressors at the time of her death. She had discovered success at UNCA in the Drama Department and was making friends, but she was also homesick. This is why she was considering transferring to UNC-Greensboro. She was also navigating close friendships with *two men* who both adored her. None of these stressors are particularly abnormal for a 19-year-old college student. Still, they point to a complex internal life that is easy to overlook if one only focuses on her achievements during this period.

The notion that a stranger might have been responsible seems to make sense when the victim had no known enemies, but statistics complicate any easy endorsement of this theory. Yes, random "stranger danger" crimes do occur in the world each day. As we have discovered from the horrific abduction and assault of Karen McDonald in 1974, it is entirely possible that Olson's death came at the hands of someone with no prior knowledge of her. However, before we easily assume it was a stranger, let us consider this by the numbers. According to the FBI's Uniform Crime Reporting Program Database, around 9.7% of all homicide victims in the United States are murdered by someone who is a total stranger. This means that around 9 out of every 10 murders do not fall within this category.

This number is a 20-year average, and it doesn't stretch back to 1973, but let's consider this long-term trend with known data from Buncombe County at the time of Olson's death. There were less than 38 people in Buncombe County aged 15-24 who died in 1973. This number from the 1973 NC Vital Statistics Report encompasses those who died from natural causes like illness, those who were killed in accidents, and also those who were murdered. In a population that was close to 200,000 people, it is clear that random violent murders are not plaguing young people in this area.

Whether or not it is more likely that Olson's murder involved someone with *some* level of familiarity or whether it was a crime committed by a pure stranger is something we can't definitively know. Still, these numbers suggest that we seriously consider those around her.

To speculate about the person responsible, some knowledge of Olson's family and her known associates is essential. In an investigation in 2024, investigators have many more tools than those examining a 51-year-old cold case. In a digital world, investigators typically explore devices or computers owned by the individual and can learn much about the victim's mindset. For instance, in the recent murder investigation in Delphi, Indiana, police were able to learn a great deal about the social world and mindset of victims Abigail Williams and Liberty German based on their social media interactions. In that case, the girls even captured video and audio of their killer during the period immediately before their deaths. Technology allowed the authorities to broadcast the face and the voice of the killer while also exploring what level of interaction or familiarity (if any) the two victims had with him beforehand.

Without the benefit of such technologies, we were left to interview those who knew Olson and to depend on their memories. Memories are tricky because, after such a significant amount of time, they can be lost, changed, or impacted by a myriad of outside factors. In her famous true-crime podcast *Serial*, Sarah Koenig showed that it's challenging to remember many details accurately from an event a few weeks ago, much less one that happened years ago. Therefore, we had to look for consistent patterns in the interview responses.

There were sometimes anomalies in interview responses, and we took these with a grain of salt. For instance, virtually everyone we spoke with described Olson as shy, soft-spoken, thoughtful, and introverted. Different words were used, of course, with some describing her as socially awkward, while others used phrases like "quietly thoughtful." However, from our perspective, most of these descriptions amounted to a variation of the same personality type. These descriptions go with her behavior patterns—especially her desire for quiet time in nature to journal or study by herself. It also aligned with activities we could confirm that she engaged in when she wasn't at school—whether it was her parent's neighbor in Lexington, NC, or her friends from Northern Virginia, they all, unprompted, described her love for being out in nature.

The other commonality about Olson that emerged from our interviews was her steadfast religious devotion. We learned from people who knew her that she attended nearly daily Bible study sessions at UNCA. We also heard from other former classmates that her religious testimonies turned them to Christianity.

The combination of Olson's religious devotion and observed life patterns means she was not at a higher risk of being a victim of a violent crime. To be clear, no one, regardless of their life choices, deserves to be a victim of a violent crime. We don't want this point to be misinterpreted as victim blaming. What we are suggesting is that some lifestyle choices, from being involved in the drug trade to prostitution, do correlate with a greater statistical probability of being a victim of a violent crime.

That is not what happened here; her quiet nature meant her "orbit" was reasonably small. We all have what we can call an "orbit" of people who circulate our lives. Some are close, and others might be acquaintances or coworkers, but being in someone's orbit means they are not strangers. On the one hand, Olson was a drama major and performer. She interacted with groups of students who worked on shows she performed in, and she likely came into contact with members of the audience who attended her shows. She also attended a near-daily Bible study group. However, as someone who was relatively shy and introverted, most of these people exist somewhere in her outer orbit. We interviewed people who worked with her on plays, including her dance partner Rob Storrs, who appeared with her in her final public performance, but none claimed to really "know her."

Our conversations with the many people who interacted with her only emphasized how few seemed to be close to her. Those who were friendly with her and lived near her could describe her routines and personality traits. They often had stories that emphasized many of her best qualities, but few knew details about her life. This means that despite the many people she encountered, Olson's orbit was relatively small. The individuals who were close to her described her as a transformative force in their lives, but this gregariousness was something that the majority of people did not see.

It was the unknowability of Olson—her quiet gentleness and kindness, coupled with her introverted qualities that kept most people at arm's length—that made her death so shocking and tragic to the campus community. The tragedy wasn't just that she was well loved and known, but more that her shy and reserved qualities made her death and the manner of her death seem so disproportionate to the kind of emotional response she inspired in people.

Chapter 11: Reflections and Reactions to the Initial Investigations

In the previous chapter, we discussed our broader methodologies and assumptions as we investigated the Olson case, and in this chapter, we will take things in a slightly different direction. Up to this point, much of this book has been written in a unified voice. The practical reason for this is that we shared research duties like tracking down public records and interviewing people related to this case. We have no substantial disagreements or significantly different takes on the facts of the historical investigations in 1973, 1974, 1977, or the 1980s. We agreed on what happened, and whenever we encountered a new piece of evidence that added additional (or different) understanding, we adjusted our historical narrative accordingly. We realized that most contemporary readers, even those currently residing in Asheville, have little knowledge of what happened within the Olson investigation. We worked hard to get this part right.

Our differences surrounding this case revolve around our evaluations of aspects of the investigations and some differences in theories that have emerged over the years about the crime. We talk about these theories in later chapters. There are some places we disagree, others we agree, instances in which we agree in part but reach a different conclusion, and times when we agree in part and disagree in other parts.

These last chapters are a dialogue in which we have intentionally separated our perspectives in a way that we hope will inspire the late-night discussions and debates we had while researching this case.

In the book's first section, we began with a description of how we were each exposed to the true crime genre and we also introduced our different relationships with crime and police investigation. Cameron has worked as a law enforcement officer for over 18 years and has accumulated experiences and sensibilities shaping how he relates to the case, evidence, suspects, and investigators. Brian has no experience in law enforcement, but as a professor and professional researcher who teaches true crime writing, he has become familiar with navigating research related to criminal cases and the complex moral and ethical questions they raise.

We counterbalance each other and deeply trust and respect each other's views. The dialogue below represents our differing responses to the initial Olson investigations. Since our backgrounds have shaped our perspectives, we have decided to label ourselves accordingly.

The Professor's Take on the Initial Investigations

When I first began researching the historical investigation into Virginia Olson's murder, I was baffled that it remained unsolved. After all, Olson seemed to have everything going for her. She came from an upwardly mobile, upper-middle-class household. She was white at a time when resources were not always evenly distributed to investigate crimes, and she was murdered at a university.

This last point might not sound significant to some, but as a professor, I can attest that universities care about their public perception and will go to great lengths to protect it. In 1973, Asheville prided itself on its low crime rate, and its campus community claimed that virtually no crimes occurred on their actual property. At the time of Olson's death, the university did not even have a campus police force! As someone who teaches at a small liberal arts college, which until recently was in the same consortium of small liberal arts colleges as UNCA, I can tell you that a sales pitch that schools like this make to parents is that their kids are safer on campus than they would be at the larger public universities in the same system.

The fact that this case occurred during the height of the Vietnam War accentuated the idea that UNCA was a shelter from the outside world. Some students during this era went to college specifically to avoid having their numbers drawn in the selective service lottery. Full-time student status protected students from the bodily harm of war. Nationally, politicians like Richard Nixon criticized the "draft dodgers" who attended universities to avoid service and encouraged people to imagine the university as an insulated bubble from the "real world." Of course, in Nixon's worldview, this explanation of the university as a place disconnected from the rest of the world became a convenient way to explain the prevalence of war protests that originated on college campuses during this era that were rarely friendly toward White House foreign policy objectives.

For President Nixon, parents, and college students- for vastly different reasons -the college campus was safe from the "real" world dangers.

Of course, the popular image and the reality of university life during this era are two different things. Contrary to its popular image as a safe shelter, many schools of this era underreported or failed to report campus violence—especially violence directed toward women. Still, the general idea that the school was a safe haven was a powerful one, and the visible and undeniable murder of a student is something that challenges that entrenched narrative.

This is why some of the first statements to come out of the university were attempts to distance the campus from the crime by stressing the location of the murder. That the murder was on "unimproved land" that might have been frequented by students but was government property is now moot since the current chancellor's mansion resides on the site of the murder. Still, that original qualifier and the pressure this murder placed on the administration likely led to lots of additional admonitions for the local police to solve the crime.

By the time Gov. Holshouser got involved by offering additional reward money and directing SBI resources to support the Asheville Police Department, it was clear that everyone wanted a swift resolution. This goal and assumption were undoubtedly shared by Chancellor Highsmith when he met with members of the university Dean's Council in the days after Olson's death. Following the campus-wide memorial services, students were sent home. Holshouser privately confided to staff his hopeful assumption that the case would be solved when students returned to campus the following week.

Consider a contemporary case like Gabby Petito to approximate the level of resources thrown at this case early on. Close to 1,000 articles were circulated during a 12-month period throughout North Carolina, and the latest investigative developments in Buncombe County were passed along. In 1973, this case was not solved for lack of effort. Law enforcement reported feeling immense amounts of public pressure to bring everything to a speedy resolution.

Highsmith's hope for a quick resolution, even in retrospect, is not entirely unreasonable. The Asheville Police Department of this general era solved cases just as complex as Olson's murder, with fewer resources and far less sympathetic victims. Remember the Mary Burdette case from 1978 that we discussed earlier? Burdette was impoverished, had no close relatives or friends to notice she was missing, and her body had decomposed enough that by the time she was found, the original officers on the scene believed her throat had been cut.

Burdette's death, while it shocked the UNCA community, primarily did so because of its similarities to the still-unsolved Olson case. However, even without significant resources or media attention, Will Annarino and the Asheville Police not only solved the case but linked the perpetrator to several other murders that had a similar M.O.

So, what went wrong in the Olson case?

I think the "blame," if you want to call it that, started with the initial crime scene. The April 16th, 1973 edition of the *Asheville Citizen-Times* shows the only public picture of Olson's body being taken from the crime scene, and it is a bit chaotic. Reporters are taking photos, and police and medical personnel are moving freely. We know from conversations with UNCA students that once news of the tragedy reached campus, many students migrated to the area of the crime scene to observe what was happening.

I don't think this is a matter of the police not doing their job, but I do believe it relates to the less-defined protocols for managing crime scenes in 1973. At the time Olson was killed, the state was still in the early stages of creating uniform law enforcement standards. With all of the movement and commotion, it is possible that trace evidence on the body was lost or ignored. By "trace evidence," I mean fingerprints, bodily fluids, hairs and fibers, shoe impressions or markings, or even residue from cosmetics. Living in 2024, none of this sounds exceptionally high-tech, but remember that this type of evidence was what a forensic investigation looked like in 1973.

Police officers attending the original crime scene collected a lot of evidence, including many samples of the materials listed above. We know this because when investigators questioned their first suspect, the 19-year-old kid who broke into the Greek Center 48 hours after Olson's death, police collected fingernail scrapings from this individual that they tested against material found on Olson.

We also know that the scene was chaotic enough that it was hard to differentiate what materials to collect. For instance, detectives collected what they described as "a fatty piece of tissue" not far from Olson's body, but they were unsure if this material was human or animal. The current cold case squad confirmed that these materials were from an animal. So, let's applaud the due diligence of those first crime scene responders, but this kind of crime scene almost certainly resulted in contaminated evidence.

Contamination was not a known variable to investigators in 1973, but as forensic technologies developed over the next 51 years, these original collection methods would impact subsequent investigations. One only has to look at the few crime scene photos published in April of 1973 to notice that there were many people carrying crime scene materials and no one was wearing gloves. Today, many people affiliated with the original case are either deceased or of advanced age. This means that investigating the case today will rely on forensic technology; it will do so without any of the protocols that protect the integrity of materials in contemporary investigations.

One of the other major issues I see with this investigation is how early investigators hone in on a single suspect linked through circumstantial evidence. On April 29th, 1973, two weeks after Olson's murder, the Asheville Police, working with the SBI, executed a search warrant on 205 Hillside, Apartment #1, which was a unit within the Gordon Apartments complex. Shortly after, the suspect was questioned, and the *Asheville Citizen-Times* leaked that once this individual's neighbors learned of Olson's murder, they reported this individual to the police because of some bizarre behavior that occurred on the same day. According to news reports, this suspect allegedly appeared distraught and asked his neighbor to "pray with him." A different neighbor reported an encounter that was just as strange and allegedly involved this individual. She recounted that he said there was "so much blood," along with other incoherent and nonsensical remarks, that she attributed to the Olson murder. Finally, another individual came forward and said that he gave this suspect a ride home during the window of the murder. He claimed they spotted Olson on the hill as they passed the Botanical Gardens, and the suspect pointed her out.

This sounds pretty good so far, right?

I'm happy to concede that this suspect's behavior sounds disturbing in light of the events that occurred that day. The proximity of his apartment to the Botanical Gardens gave him an opportunity; the fact that he allegedly pointed Olson out as they drove indicates he was aware of her during the two-hour window of her death, and his subsequent statements about blood and wanting to pray don't alleviate any suspicions that justifiably arise.

The trouble is that there has never been any physical evidence definitively linking this suspect to the murder. Yes, the crime scene was not managed well, and yes, in 1973, there was limited forensics, but it is also important to remember that Olson was stabbed in the heart. This would have produced a significant amount of blood. The medical examiner stated that at least 2.4 liters of blood were lost during the initial attack, and this outpouring of blood emerged from a wound a little wider than an inch. Remember that 19-year-old kid taken into custody in the two days after Olson's murder? Investigators found some specks of blood on his shoe and were able to test them against Olson to exclude him. *Specks* of blood. If this April 29th suspect were genuinely responsible for the murder, I suspect there would have been more evidence. Given his close physical proximity to the victim when the fatal blow was struck, it would have been hard to avoid a significant number of blood stains.

Could the suspect have disposed of all the evidence? Possibly, but the main issue with this theory is that police also stressed that this individual had severe mental health issues. We heard the word "crazy" come up a few times in discussions with Asheville Police when we inquired about him. It means the question has less to do with whether a hypothetical person would dispose of their clothes, and it instead becomes whether this mentally unstable person would have the foresight to eliminate all physical traces of Olson.

Police repeatedly tried to link this individual to the crime. When they raided his apartment on April 29th, 1973, they took a handkerchief, a white shirt, a velour shirt, a knife, and a pair of "dingo" boots. We learned that the SBI later claimed these items tested "negative," meaning they did not indicate any direct traceable link to the crime scene. Soil samples on boots and other articles of clothing did not yield any results either.

Shortly after the results came back "negative," the suspect was released from police custody and moved out of state. At that point, who could blame him if he was innocent? In 1974, the SBI attempted to expand the investigation to other states. During these years, I sensed they were looking for some way to move beyond who the Asheville Police perceived as their strongest suspect. They look to Florida, and in September of that year, they named Glen Allen Carlson, a serial rapist who once attended UNCA in the 1960s, as a person of interest. However, within days of arriving in Florida, Carlson's ironclad alibi leads investigators to exclude him, and the case goes cold a few months later.

My general take on this period of 1973-1974 is that police struggled to create a working theory of the case. In some ways, this is understandable since, without a working theory, the case could constantly spin in innumerable directions, tracking down tips and theories in many different places. Settling on a working theory can also be detrimental if it promotes tunnel vision or creates confirmation bias.

After the initial investigative rush, some leads continued coming in, but none felt as plausible or robust as the April 29th suspect. My general suspicion is that police had difficulty moving beyond this person since, by 1984, police were still openly discussing him.

Between the 1973-1974 investigation and the 1984 reopening of the case, a 1977 task force looked into the Olson case. However, the so-called "Homicide Squad" was also charged with investigating many other unsolved North Carolina cases to determine if any connections existed between them.

Having such a broad investigative framework limited the scope of the Olson investigation in 1977, which meant that the original case was primarily reviewed rather than new areas of inquiry opened. I'm not aware of any new tests done in 1977. The significant contribution of this task force relates to the renewed public visibility they brought to the case. After all, the major developments they contributed were not breakthroughs in the actual case but were instead the new release of previously undisclosed information.

The task force informed the public about previously undisclosed witness statements, including a statement from a Hendersonville man who likely spotted Olson sitting together with her killer. The witness statements offered contradictory information about the suspect, with some describing him as old and others as younger. They all seemed to agree on the paratrooper-style boots and military jacket garb he was allegedly wearing.

Not surprisingly, this led investigators to hone all their attention on military vet suspects. There was an officer on active duty leave who was questioned at a Merrimon Avenue hotel, and it was later released that the April 29th suspect had also served time in the U.S. Army as an officer.

Notice how these details, if read in a certain way, suggest the police's preconceived idea concerning the original suspect.

A few significant issues with theories surrounding military ties raise red flags for me. First, in 1973, college campuses were gripped with anti-war protests related to the Vietnam War. The cultural dissonance produced by the war cannot be overstated, and on a progressive campus like UNCA, there were overwhelmingly negative sentiments about America's participation in the conflict. As soldiers returned home from their tours and began attending UNCA in increasingly larger numbers, there was undoubtedly some suspicion and discomfort.

The Vietnam veteran was different; a new vocabulary that didn't always have positive connotations emerged and was often mapped onto the men and women who served in this era. While post-traumatic stress, as an experience, has existed as long as war—in World War II they called it "shell shock"—the term PTSD finally made its way into the diagnostic handbook used by psychologists for the first time during the Vietnam War.

PTSD was associated with the experiences of the common foot soldier in Vietnam, and that had the effect of eliciting sympathy for the soldier who struggled while also crafting a negative image of the soldier as a mentally damaged "loner." In other words, while the antiwar movement expressed an interest in caring for those traumatized by Vietnam, there was also skepticism about the extent to which such individuals were safe to be around after going through the traumatic experiences of war.

The idea of the "damaged loner," who feels misunderstood and marginalized from society and who is prone to violence, dominated popular culture. Think about the Rambo film, *First Blood,* to get an idea of the famous depictions of the Vietnam veteran that began to emerge in the years after Olson's death.

While life can imitate art, I'm generally distrustful of solutions that too closely mirror broader cultural trends. In this case, my initial thought was that it was likely that Olson was murdered by someone her age who happened to be wearing a military jacket, which was the style of the time, rather than by a "loner" veteran who was psychologically damaged and interested in raping and murdering an innocent young girl. Sound familiar? If so, it is because this is also the plot description of Brian De Palma's Vietnam film *Casualties of War*, starring Michael J. Fox and Sean Penn. The 1977 task force released new information, but they essentially came to the same conclusion as the original investigators: they thought it was the April 29th suspect.

When the case was finally reopened in the 80s at the behest of Will Annarino, the layers of confirmation bias thickened, and the possibility of thinking beyond these earlier assumptions became harder. In our conversation with current Olson cold case detective Kevin Taylor, he described Annarino as "very thorough in everything he did" and someone with "a great reputation in the community."

Annarino is no fool; his work in the Mary Burdette case is a textbook example of great detective work. However, it is possible that his work in that case proved correct because he did not come in with many set impressions of a particular suspect. Whenever new information emerged, he tended to pivot. While investigators initially wondered about a possible connection to Olson, Annarino, and company quickly changed their focus once they learned that the Burdette M.O. did not as closely mirror the circumstances of Olson's murder as they initially suspected.

Annarino's flexibility in the Burdette case made him effective, but when the Olson case came up, he seemed unable to move beyond the conclusions of the previous investigations. He convinced the district attorney to reopen the case and requested permission to test Olson's "blood-soaked jeans" using new blood tests available through the SBI Crime Lab. He wanted these tests to confirm his preconceived ideas of who was responsible. In a March 5th, 1985 statement to the *Asheville Citizen-Times,* he tells reporters that the Asheville Police Department knew the identity of the person responsible for Olson's murder. In fact, on this and other occasions, he mentions to the paper that they have known the murderer's identity all along. According to the paper, he even states, "I know where he's living and where he works." Quite frankly, these are not the words of someone with an open mind. Of course, the ironic thing is that as I dug further into this case, I became increasingly convinced that Annarino's instincts in the 1980s were correct. We will address this at the end of the book.

However, when I first examined the whole investigation, I came away with the impression that investigators during this era stretched their prime suspect to support their theory. So, when witnesses emerged that claimed the suspect was in his early 20s, the police dismissed those theories by explaining that their April 29th suspect was in his 40s but looked much younger from a distance.

Unsurprisingly, media coverage of the Olson cases disappeared following the failed Santa Fe trip. The detectives did not secure a confession, and the SBI lab results were unable to link the suspect to the crime. Today, Asheville's cold case team agrees that this suspect was not responsible for Olson's death.

Not responsible.

Let's take a moment to assume they are correct. This means that roughly 13 years of forensic tests and focus between 1973 and 1986 were disproportionally devoted to someone now considered not guilty.

Restarting an investigation so far removed from the original circumstances is challenging. I'm not saying it is impossible, and Cameron might even point to examples of it successfully happening, but in 2024, we are left with few good possibilities. If the killer was a peer at UNCA, then that individual would be between 70 and 74 years old today. If this person was in their 40s, as several witnesses described, then this person would be in their 90s or most likely deceased like the New Mexico suspect.

The cold case team investigating today stressed that they are "actively working on it." They haven't given up. We believe them and admire their commitment to the case, but it is hard to imagine their investigation options beyond possibly engaging in DNA or ancestry-based genetic tests.

The memories of the original witnesses and those close to Olson are no longer reliable after such an extended time. This case is unlikely, therefore, to be solved through the methods used by past investigators. I see it solved only through a confession, which seems doubtful, or a unique combination of new circumstantial evidence and DNA testing.

I have my theory about how this murder occurred and the individual who I think likely committed it. Still, my initial impressions of the first investigations were that investigators settled too early on the individual they believed was responsible, and even when they attempted to look elsewhere, they could never exclude this person entirely. When this person was fully excluded as a viable suspect, it was too far removed from the context needed to start the investigation over again. This is not the fault of one or two people but rather an issue with the collective focus over multiple years and investigations. This is an example of a community acting in good faith but not considering alternatives seriously.

The Cop's Take on the Initial Investigations

One Sunday, while working as a beat cop, I received a call for a 911 hang-up. Raleigh's area code is 919, so this kind of misdialing is somewhat common. Nevertheless, when these calls come in, you must verify that no one needs help. This is generally uneventful: you knock on the door, ask if someone called 911, and then tell little Johnny to stop playing on the phone.

I arrived at the apartment complex where the call originated from and was met by my check-in officer, Kyle. Due to the unknown nature of these calls, two officers are often dispatched. Kyle and I walked up the three flights of exterior stairs to the apartment. I knocked on the door and announced, "Raleigh Police."

I could hear someone walking to the door. I listened to the interior shuffling of door latches. A man finally opened the door, but only a few inches. He stuck his face in the door's crack and said softly, "Are you the police?"

"Yeah, Raleigh Police," I replied. "Did you call 911?"

The man, later identified as Jeremy Beane, opened the door and stepped out. While standing outside, Jeremy started to say, "Um, I called the police because…."

Then Kyle blurted out, "Dude, what the fuck is wrong with your neck!?"

Jeremy was a 6'2 African American male with a large afro and thin build. What made him stand out that day was that his neck looked like a watermelon wedge that was missing a piece. It honestly did not look real, there was no blood on his skin or shirt. His skin was also gray; it looked like a Halloween mask.

Jeremy then took a second and said, "Yeah.. um… I killed my girlfriend last night, and then I tried to kill myself."

I was in shock and confused about how he was still alive, but I managed to get out, "You are under arrest."

I grabbed his wrist and pulled out a pair of handcuffs. When I looked down, I was greeted by another large wedge missing from his wrist. I gave him a quick search and placed him on the ground. I ordered him to extend his legs, cross them at the ankles, and put his hands on his knees before asking, "Where is your girlfriend?"

"In the back bedroom," Jeremy said calmly.

"Are you sure she is dead?" This might sound like a dumb question, but I was still processing what was happening.

Jeremy looked at me with zero emotion and said, "Yeah, I am pretty sure."

I walked into the apartment and was met with a blood trail. I followed the trail to the back bedroom. I could see a figure propped up against the bed with a blue blanket covering it. The blinds were closed, and the lights were off. I painted the figure with my flashlight. I pulled away the blanket to find Jeremy's girlfriend. A flap of neck skin was the only thing keeping her head attached to her body. She had stab wounds all over.

We later learned that Jeremy had just been discharged from a local mental hospital. When he returned to his girlfriend's apartment, they had a heated argument. The result was that Jeremy stabbed her over fifty times. He then decided to kill himself by cutting his neck and wrist. He had done this in the shower, which is why he did not have any blood on him. Jeremy then ate a bowl of cereal and took a nap. When he woke up and realized that he was still alive, he decided to call 911.

Jeremy is now serving a life in prison-sentence and sporting a giant neck tattoo in an attempt to cover up his poor life decisions.

In police work, some cases are easy to solve. You get a lucky break. You find the witness, you get a confession, or the jealous lover of the suspect becomes your best source.

None of these things happened in the Virginia Olsen murder investigation.

When I looked at this case from the beginning, I noticed the year. 1973 was the year that North Carolina Training and Standards was first implemented. These new rules gave all departments standardized training in basic law enforcement. An example would be how to set up a crime scene and how to process it properly. Crime scenes contain valuable material that is fragile and easily overlooked.

I am sure the officers on the scene that day did their best with the resources and training available. Some of the pictures of the scene that day, though, show crowds of people near Olson's body as it was being escorted on a gurney from the scene.

The investigation had many other issues and challenges that would make it complex today. The location was remote and on the border of the UNCA campus. Since the murder occurred on a Sunday afternoon, most of the students went home for the weekend, which would make conducting interviews more challenging.

Police knew the location as an area where "winos" liked to hang out, and they also described it as a "lovers' lane." We know that high school kids also went to this area, and two of them were responsible for finding and reporting the body. The area is 50 acres, with people walking around a half-mile loop throughout the day. According to reports, about 100 people were in the area at the time of the murder. We also know that Olson's friends could walk around the crime scene, showing her picture to officers. Due to the diversity of the population that frequents the area, you are now looking at suspects ranging from teenage boys to adults.

The crime scene itself yields a wide range of unanswered questions. When interviewing Detective Taylor, I asked if the area where Virginia was found was where the rape and murder occurred. I asked this question because two witnesses reported seeing Olson sitting with a man. One witness stated that he could see her sitting on a large rock from the roadway. Even though I am skeptical about the accuracy of some of these statements, they are consistent with the area not being very secluded.

It amazes me that the killer would be bold enough to take her shirt, cut it into strips with a knife, rape her, and then murder her. We can assume some dialogue happened between the two as well. Remember, this happened on a beautiful Asheville spring day in the early afternoon with people walking around.

I think a more likely scenario is that the killer, at some point, threatened Olson with a knife. He used the threat of violence to force her into an area of the woods. I believe this was around 1:45 p.m. when a witness reported seeing the pages of a book flapping in the wind on a rock. Keep in mind that at the crime scene, police documented finding a book with Olson's glasses placed neatly on top. I believe this is the book in question unless there were multiple books at the scene.

If the killer did move her to another area to rape her, the logistical aspects of the rape would make more sense. While the rape could have lasted as little as a minute, it is unclear how long it would take to remove her clothing, cut the clothing into strips, and bind her. I believe that the police may have searched the area for blood, but small pieces of thread from a shirt would have been hard to find in a forest. The only tool that could have located another area would have been a trained police K-9 dog, which we know was not deployed.

We know that she was killed on the rock where she was found. We know this due to the massive amount of blood found at the scene, which resulted from a stab wound that pierced her heart. Olson was found in a pool of blood, bound and gagged. Her notebook was near her, with her glasses folded on top.

I believe that the killer wanted her body exposed. He tried to exert his dominance and humiliate her. I think that he raped her off the path that she was found on, ordered her back to the rock, and stabbed her in the heart. After her heart stopped, he stabbed her in the throat. He then placed her glasses on her notebook and fled.

The other option is that the killer did not fear being seen. It has been reported that Olson was also gagged. Maybe the killer felt that being seen was not an issue. We would also have to conclude that the pages of her book were observable because the killer had already placed her body in a prone position by that point.

Since this is an ongoing investigation, Detective Taylor could not comment on whether the semen sample that the original medical examiner noted and obtained in his report is still viable. In 1973, DNA was not an option, and rape kits were just starting to become utilized by departments nationwide. The investigators at the time would take blood samples. The goal would be to document the victim's blood type and identify the suspect's blood type. The investigators would also find out if the blood donor was a secretor or non-secretor. People who are secretors produce ABO antigens in their plasma. Without going into the science of this test, the National Institute of Health reports that 20-40 percent of the population are non-secretors. The variation changes with the blood type and geographical region.

The reason why this is important is that investigators would be able to use this technology to determine the blood type and secretor status of the killer. An example would be "type A positive non-secretor." Even this information does not rule out other suspects, but in 1973, it would be an excellent way to confirm if the suspect in custody did have the same markers as the killer.

Without the technology of the day, Asheville Police and the State Bureau of Investigations (SBI) began tracking down leads and witnesses. The officers and investigators started with a canvass for witnesses. The officers successfully located people who saw Virginia sitting beside two men. One of the men was described as wearing an army-issued jacket. The other was described as wearing colorful clothing. The officers also responded to citizens who believed they had information about the murder. One of these statements was odd enough to inspire a much closer examination. A witness reported that a man came to her door and made a statement about it being a "bloody mess." The person appeared to match the description of the man with the colorful clothing seen with Olson.

This information led to a search warrant that was executed two weeks after the murder. Investigators seized a pair of boots, a kitchen knife, and other items. On paper, it sounds like the case was going to be solved. The evidence was sent to the SBI for lab testing, which we can assume was for the ABO test described earlier. We can only assume that all the tests were negative because no arrest was made after the warrant.

Throughout the years, other suspects were looked at by the Asheville Police and the SBI. Interviews were conducted in multiple states. When Annarino reopened the case in the 80s, he concluded that the man from the search warrant should be the prime suspect. It is unknown if he received additional information or was basing this on the previous eyewitness accounts.

What puzzles me is why they continued pursuing this suspect for decades. To make matters worse, Annarino made a speech in the 80s announcing that a contingent from the Asheville Police Department was leaving for New Mexico and hoped to come back with Olson's killer. It sounds like a Clint Eastwood movie or maybe a police revision of *Braveheart*. It certainly does not add any value to a case to let a murder suspect know you are coming to interview him via national news.

It should be no shock that this group returned with nothing but a round-trip ticket stub and a few empty promises. Annarino sent a sergeant to do a news conference, letting the public know that no arrest had been made but that the case would remain open.

From all accounts, Annarino was a solid investigator. It intrigues me that he would be so bold but flawed in his thinking. Annarino was known for bringing modern investigative techniques to the Asheville Police Department. He even brought in computer programs to manage case files. Until then, a detective sergeant would not be able to monitor the progress of the cases assigned to detectives.

Annarino also showed through the years that he could lead his investigative team in solving murders. It makes me wonder if the speech was a calculated move. Maybe he knew his case was wholly circumstantial, and this was a bold attempt to intimidate the suspect into a confession. His reasons are unknown, but we all know that according to Detective Kevin Taylor, who is currently assigned the case, the Santa Fe suspect that many investigators focused intense scrutiny on is no longer alive or a suspect.

As of 2024, no other suspect has been named. The case is still under investigation; Detective Taylor utilizes modern policing and technology. The crime scene is now the home of the UNCA Chancellor. To most, Virginia is a mere picture on campus that students pass throughout their day.

Chapter 12:
The Santa Fe Suspect Finally Revealed

One of the persistent mysteries surrounding the investigation into the murder of Virginia Olson involves the identity of the "Santa Fe" suspect that the Asheville Police Department visited in the 80s. When we started researching this case, we immediately became interested in this individual because, for two generations of investigators, he remained their prime suspect. He is the same individual the SBI served a search warrant on during the evening of April 29th, 1973. He is also the same individual that Will Annarino repeatedly references in the 80s when he tells reporters that investigators are close to an arrest.

Beyond the fact that this individual remained a top suspect for the SBI and the Asheville Police Department for close to 13 years of investigation, we were also interested in him because many rumors and gossip have circulated throughout Asheville for over 50 years surrounding his identity. Several story variants exist about this individual. Most of these describe him as a man in his 40s (based on Annarino's 1980s conversations with the press) with mental health issues who was receiving treatment in Asheville in 1973 and who lived close to the crime scene. This individual is also often described as "highly educated" and from an affluent northeastern family who worked to protect him from police scrutiny after he popped up on the original investigators' suspect list. There were also stories circulated in the *Asheville Citizen-Times* about alleged neighbors who called police about a disturbed individual who asked a neighbor to "pray with her" shortly after Olson's murder.

As part of our research, we filed a request with the City of Asheville to obtain a copy of the search warrant that the SBI executed on April 29th, 1973. This event occurred precisely two weeks after Olson's murder, and it was widely reported in regional newspaper coverage. The response to our initial request stated that the case was so old it would likely be challenging to locate the document. One individual with the clerk's office even called the effort to find the search warrant "like searching for a needle in a haystack." However, after a few months of waiting, the search warrant was delivered by the city, and it finally provided us with the identity of the long-suspected murderer and some insights into the investigation that followed Olson's murder.

We want to treat this revelation with the care and respect it deserves. All of the information that follows in this chapter is based on the actual affidavits and search warrant records we received from the city of Asheville. The current cold case investigators attached to the Olson file no longer consider this individual a prime suspect. However, they also refused to explain whether this individual had been excluded as a suspect or if their thinking had merely deviated from the original investigators.

We also want to emphasize that Charles Chambers, who brought the affidavit to the District Court to obtain a search warrant, was a respected and seasoned SBI agent with an impeccable record. In 1983, he was the agent in charge of the Asheville district, and he had already garnered respect from colleagues across the SBI and in Asheville for his intelligence and skill as an investigator. Chambers was used to dealing with unusual cases. In 1966, he was part of the investigation into the triple homicide of two men and one woman: Vernon Shipman, Charles Glass, and Louise Davis Shumate, in Henderson County, North Carolina. That case featured murdered victims who were arranged in a crude semicircle, rumors of voodoo rituals, and a female murder victim who was found with part of a tirejack left in her vagina.

Similarly, years later, Chambers would be associated with the 1981 murder of Rhonda Hinson in Burke County, North Carolina. That case featured a young woman who was shot while driving her car home two days before Christmas. We point these cases out to stress that Chambers was accustomed to working cases with a high profile involving unusual circumstances.

While we concede that current investigators no longer consider the "Santa Fe Suspect" to be the person responsible for Olson's death, it is worth noting that between 1973 and 1985, he was at the top of virtually all suspect lists for all investigative authorities. Some of the few surviving investigators from the original case still believe this person is responsible for the crime. Since there is disagreement among law enforcement concerning this individual's role, we have decided to refrain from any definitive judgment and will present what we discovered instead. You, the reader, can determine whether you find this information compelling.

The Events of April 29th, 1973

The search warrant in question was brought to the Buncombe County District Court Division on April 29th, 1973, by Agent Charles D. Chambers of the North Carolina SBI. To obtain a warrant, Agent Chambers presented a probable cause affidavit that named John Reavis Jr. of 205 Hillside, Apartment #1, Gordon Apartments, as an individual who "on his person or premises" possessed property related to the murder of Virginia M. Olson.

We want to stress that law enforcement officers typically only include enough details in their affidavits to receive a search warrant. These documents are not exhaustive. They provide us, the readers, a snapshot of some evidence against a suspect. It would be unusual and unnecessary to include *all* evidence against a suspect.

Agent Chambers would list the items the SBI requested permission to search for at Reavis's apartment. These items included: "glasses, knife, white shirt with red in it, dark boots, part of a lady's green "T" shirt, woman's garments [sic], clothing of Virginia M. Olson, man's or woman's garment containing blood, rust pants, and a handkerchief." The affidavit alleged that all of these items were related to the "murder of Virginia M. Olson on April 15th, 1973 across the street from the Botanical Garden, Weaver Blvd., Asheville."

Some of these items, like the green shirt, are consistent with what Olson was wearing that day, while others, like dark boots, are related to the description that witnesses provided of the suspect. It is curious that "clothing of Virginia Olson" is listed under the warrant. The only article of clothing the medical examiner noted in his report that appeared to be absent was Olson's underwear. It is, therefore, entirely possible that police believed Reavis had them in his possession.

Since the search warrant requested permission to search the personage of John Reavis, the request also describes his physical appearance. The document lists him as an individual who was 42-45 years old, with "brown mod length hair, and 6 ft tall."

Similarly, the search warrant describes the location of his residence as "on the south side of Hillside, 1st premises on the right traveling east from Merrimon Avenue." The warrant provides even more detailed information about the specific location of the suspect's apartment, stating that "Reavis' apartment is the first on the right as you enter the building as is designated #1."

The location of Reavis's apartment is another factor that interested authorities. It was located roughly 1.3 miles from the Botanical Gardens, where Olson was murdered. The apartments offered a direct route to the crime, and parts of this walk would have provided Reavis with some cover.

After clearly establishing the location of the search (the suspect's personage and place of residence), Agent Chambers was tasked with establishing probable cause for a judge to authorize the search. Agent Chambers offers six reasons for the search request, most of which emerge from statements provided by witnesses who offered affidavits to the court. The reasons listed below have been copied directly from the search warrant:

1. On 4-15-1973 Virginia Olson was murdered at the top of a bank across the street from the Botanical Gardens; part of her clothing was torn and there was blood on the scene, this happened between 12:00 noon and 3:00 p.m.; her textbooks, glasses, and pin were found at or near the rock atop the bank in a clearing & she was found dead 35 feet from the rock.

2. Ray D. Honeycutt told affiant that he saw a dark mod-haired white male, with glasses and dark boots go straight up the bank at 1:05–1:15 p.m.

3. Gerald Echols told affiant that he saw a male & female atop bank about 1:15 p.m. & were gone at 1:45 p.m., 4-15-73, the same date Honeycutt saw a man.

4. Mr. James Goure told affiant he carried Reavis to Botanical Gardens before 1:00 p.m. 4-15-73 and pointed out a girl to him; when questioned 4-29-73 after Miranda rights, Reavis said he saw

a girl sitting from a top bank & is not visible from Gardens or Weaver Blvd.

5. Judy Needles told affiant that at 2:40 p.m., 4-15-73, Reavis came to her 5D Dunbar Apt, was nervous, & wanted someone to pray with him; Dunbar is a 10 min walk from the crime scene.

6. On 4-29-73 Reavis was wearing boots, rust pants, wears glasses, and fits description Honeycutt gave your affiant.

7. The Magistrate, Clerk of the Superior Court, officially signed off on the search at 10:05 p.m. The search warrant was executed that evening, and the SBI seized items taken to the state crime lab for processing.

These initial tests produced no definitive connection between Reavis and Virginia Olson. The justification for the search warrant boils down to three main lines of reason: 1) the similarity in description between Reavis, in both appearance and dress, and the man that witnesses saw in the Botanical Gardens on April 15th; 2) the apparent discrepancy that Agent Chambers believed to exist between Reavis's description of the location he observed Olson and the only place she would have been visible (e.g., far closer to the crime scene itself); and 3) Reavis's alleged strange behavior that witness Judy Needles described to investigators concerning his actions in the immediate period after Olson's murder.

So, after 51 years of gossip and community speculation, this is the individual police suspected.

There are many things this search warrant request cannot tell us: First, it is unclear what the original investigators believed Reavis's motive to be. His location and the witness sightings might place him around the Botanical Gardens on April 15th, but many other people were also circulating in the park that day. What reason would he have to attack Virginia Olson?

Reavis's relationship with James Goure is also not especially clear. At the time, Goure was the founder of a Christian ministry organization that began in Black Mountain in the early 70s. Were he and Reavis friends? We contacted this organization, which still exists today, and aside from this search warrant, we could find no possible connection between the two men. None of the members we spoke with who were part of the group in the early 70s had any recollection of a John Reavis Jr., and the organization only had around 50-60 members in the early days.

What were Reavis and Goure doing at the Botanical Gardens on April 15th? Were they together the whole time, or did Goure drop him off?

The strangest part of the search warrant involves Goure's testimony that he "pointed out a girl to him [Reavis]" while they were in the Botanical Gardens. This cryptic statement is casually dropped in but not explained. Given the context of the document, we assume this "girl" was Virginia Olson. Otherwise, why would it be mentioned that a warrant should be obtained to search Reavis's apartment for clothes and garments worn by Olson? Also, what does it mean to "point out a girl?" What were the two of them doing?

While the temptation might be to assume something sinister, this document inspires more questions than answers. For instance, was James Goure also questioned extensively? Goure is now deceased, but by his affidavit, he was near the Botanical Gardens with Reavis, "pointing" Olson out around half an hour before her murder. Due diligence would require that all people who were known to be in the vicinity of the murder just before it occurred should receive additional scrutiny. In no way does this imply the guilt of any of these individuals.

We found the presence of Goure in this document curious, too, because Olson's religious devotion was the consistent feature of virtually all conversations we had about her with her classmates and friends. We know she attended nearly daily prayer meetings at UNCA and kept a "spiritual journal" to record her thoughts on spiritual matters. This led us to wonder whether Reavis was a member of Goure's religious organization (or Goure was, perhaps, acting as a kind of spiritual advisor) and whether the religion angle might create some link to Olson. In the end, we discovered that this religious group did not have a presence on UNCA's campus in 1973. Similarly, we could find no connection between Olson and any of Goure's groups. As a result, we could not establish any obvious link that might allow us to claim it is reasonable to assume that Olson and Reavis were acquaintances.

We know that on more than one occasion, Will Annarino stressed that Reavis suffered from significant mental health issues that made communication with him challenging. We could not get a copy of the police's interview with Reavis in Santa Fe, NM, in the 80s, and others associated with that trip refused to discuss it. Therefore, it is hard to understand the additional evidence that led the first two generations of investigators to express the certainty of Reavis's guilt, and we are equally unsure whether he was later forensically excluded or if the case theory changed.

Chapter 13: "He Never Sassed His Mother": Terry Hyatt and the Overlooked Connections between North Carolina's Most Famous Serial Killer and the Olson Case

February 1st, 2000, wasn't a good day for Terry Hyatt. He stared ahead with a blank expression on his face that signaled a resignation to his fate and a dissociation from the words of family members who ceremoniously paraded, one-by-one, to the Buncombe County Superior Court speaker's podium to address Judge James Downs and plead for mercy directly. The whole thing felt undignified to Hyatt, who was more accustomed to being the one in control. For more than 20 years, Hyatt had thrived on exerting the power of life and death over his victims.

"He never sassed his mother" and "he taught me what love could be" were among the more tone-deaf statements made by the family of one of North Carolina's most notorious serial killers. There were times when the pleas seemed particularly ironic, especially when a former neighbor stated that Hyatt "never talked trash" about women. Courtroom onlookers rolled their eyes and made barely audible groans following some of these cringe-worthy statements. The Judge, like Hyatt, did his best to maintain a neutral expression.

That day, Hyatt's family offered the court pleasant anecdotes that bore little resemblance to the man authorities charged with viciously kidnapping, raping, and stabbing to death Betty Sue McConnell and Harriet Delaney Simmons four months apart in 1979.

Just three days later, Hyatt would again show no emotion as Judge Downs would formally sentence him to death. The Judge concluded the proceedings with remarks that sounded less like prayerful concern and more like a combination of religious damnation and earthly judgment when he solemnly intoned, "May God have mercy on his soul."

There are many unknowns surrounding Terry Hyatt, but whether or not he was a devoted son and loving uncle or a cold-blooded killer who caused panic in the late 70s in Buncombe County is not debated. Hyatt brutally killed Betty Sue McConnell and Harriet Delaney Simmons. That much is certain, and the court's verdict only confirmed what law enforcement knew to be true. Instead, the central question surrounding Hyatt relates to how many other women he killed that law enforcement doesn't know about.

At the time of his sentencing, Hyatt was a 42-year-old former movie theater janitor and mechanic with an unremarkable but extensive history of petty crimes. Throughout his teenage years, the Asheville Police repeatedly picked up Hyatt on burglary, robbery, and assault charges. In 1975, when he turned 18, his luck ran out when Buncombe County Superior Court Judge Kenneth A. Ferrell revoked Hyatt's probation when he pleaded guilty to stealing a purse from a woman named Mary Carey in Asheville. This early jail sentence was the culmination of repeated run-ins with law enforcement during his teenage years. The Judge handed Hyatt a two-year jail sentence.

When Hyatt got out of prison, his behavior escalated, and in 1979, he abducted a woman named Carolyn Brigman at knifepoint near the West Asheville post office. Brigman, a 40-year-old Asheville native, would later tell police that she was walking home after completing a shift at Krispy Kreme when Hyatt pulled up, grabbed her, put a knife to her throat, and forced her into his pickup truck. Hyatt would eventually let her go, but not before telling her, "I ought to cut your damn throat and throw you in the river." Hyatt would remain in prison until 1987 for the Brigman kidnapping and would stay under parole supervision until 1990.

What happened next is truly shocking. Remember, Hyatt went to prison in 1979 and remained there until 1987. He would next come to the Asheville Police's attention 19 years later, in 1998, when investigators linked him to the abductions and murders of 21-year-old Betty Sue McConnell of Asheville and 40-year-old Harriet Simmons of Franklinton. Yes, you read that last sentence correctly. Throughout the 80s, authorities spent a lot of time and money pursuing the McConnell and Simmons murders, but the man who committed these murders was sitting in jail while they investigated. Those murders happened the same year that police arrested Hyatt for kidnapping Brigman. Still, authorities in 1979 didn't make the connection until eight years after his release from prison and the conclusion of the probationary period. Even worse, Hyatt was only captured because one of his "friends" who witnessed these crimes went to the police and volunteered the entire story about what happened. Without this confession, the Hyatt case might still be unsolved.

When law enforcement officials with the SBI and the Buncombe County Sheriff's Office finally connected Hyatt to these 1979 murders, they acknowledged investigative mistakes. David Barnes, the director of the Western North Carolina division of the SBI, would tell the *Asheville Citizen-Times* that it was hard to understand why Hyatt, who was arrested for committing an abduction at knifepoint just months earlier, could have been overlooked as a possible suspect.

"How he slipped through, I don't think anybody can explain," was the only thing that Barnes could offer when reporters pressed him on how this mistake could happen.

What investigators conceded was that Hyatt was responsible for *three* known abductions in 1979, and two of those abductions resulted in murder. In 1998, the SBI would tell the *Asheville Citizen-Times* that they planned to explore possible connections between Hyatt and other unsolved murders in the region.

The theory: Should Hyatt be considered as a possible suspect in the Virginia Olson case?

The Professor's Take on Terry Hyatt's Possible Connection to Olson

The possible connection between Terry Hyatt and Virginia Olson is worth taking seriously. I'm not suggesting that Hyatt is (or should be) a prime suspect. Still, after studying Hyatt's criminal history and the mismanagement of his prior investigations, I don't think the suggestion should be wholly discarded.

Today, every law enforcement agency in Western North Carolina concedes they screwed up the 1979 Hyatt investigation. The admission from David Barnes that the SBI had no clue why law enforcement overlooked Hyatt as a suspect should give us pause about the level of confidence that authorities voice now when they discount his possible involvement in other crimes from the 70s.

At the time of Olson's 1973 murder, Hyatt was 16 years old and roughly two years into his known criminal career. That same year, he would drop out of Enka High School after completing the 10th grade. Those around him during these years reported how disengaged he seemed. One teacher told the *Asheville Citizen-Times* that Hyatt "didn't seem sad or happy. He always had a blank look on his face. It was hard to connect."

By the time he left school, Hyatt was already engaging in robberies, and I'm highly skeptical that his three known kidnappings in 1979 represent some novel violent turn. Hyatt told Brigman that he "ought to cut her throat," and he also referenced other victims who had experienced this same fate. In light of the 1979 murders he would later be linked with, we know this was not an idle threat. These threats sound like someone who has done this before and that Brigman is the exception to his pattern of rape and murder.

Since investigators failed to consider Hyatt's M.O. in the Brigman case as a possible link to the McConnell and Simmons abductions, let's consider his record in light of the Olson case. First, it is worth pointing out that the Woodfin area in which Betty Sue McConnell was murdered and ultimately discovered is around 3 miles from the campus of UNCA. If we think in geographical terms, the Botanical Gardens is close to the area that Hyatt was known to frequent.

When Hyatt left Enka High School, he undoubtedly had more free time. His father told reporters that in 1979, he worked odd jobs, like construction and working on cars. This means that he lacked steady and consistent employment. It also means he could roam freely. The officers who were originally at the Botanical Gardens crime scene told the press that the area Olson was killed in was known by teenagers as a "lover's lane." Even though Hyatt lacked much of a social life during these years, he was likely familiar with the places his peers discussed.

Based on his behavior in 1979, Hyatt liked to drive around in his pickup truck looking for possible victims. When he accosted victims, he used his knife to force their compliance. Even as a teenager, he drove around looking for potential victims for his robberies. Finding a victim and the right location is not something that happens instantaneously. Instead, we know Hyatt drove to different places and waited for the right opportunity. If the Woodfin area where McConnell was abducted was part of his "hunting grounds," and assuming the boundaries of this area extended over several miles, this places the Botanical Gardens squarely within his sphere of interest.

Thanks to the testimony of Jerry Harmon, who was not only with Hyatt during his 1979 murder spree but also witnessed his crimes and dramatically confessed to the Buncombe County Sheriff's Office, we have a pretty good idea of how Hyatt operated. In a 2002 NC Supreme Court hearing concerning Hyatt, the following testimony from Jerry Harmon about the murder of Harriet Simmons appeared in the official court briefs:

> Helms testified that while he and the defendant were returning from a beach trip in 1979, they encountered a woman with car trouble at a rest stop. The defendant told the woman they could help by driving her to get a part that would fix her car. Helms testified that the woman got into their van, but later stated that defendant "took her unwillingly." They drove up a mountain outside of Candler, North Carolina, and stopped on a dirt road, where defendant had sex with the woman in the back of the van. Helms testified that defendant did not rape the woman because "she was willing" but that she was scared of both of them because defendant was carrying a knife.
>
> Defendant then took the woman into the woods while Helms remained in the van. Helms heard the woman screaming. After approximately thirty minutes, Helms saw defendant emerge from the woods alone, with blood on the bottom of his shirt.

The most significant thing to come out of NC Attorney General Roy Cooper's Supreme Court brief is an acknowledgment that the SBI suspected Hyatt to be responsible for other murders. In fact, in one section of the brief, he discusses the SBI's efforts to link Hyatt to the unsolved 1998 murder of 20-year-old Asheville resident Amber Lundgren:

> The two officers questioned the defendant at his residence in Asheville based on the information they learned from Harmon and Dean Helms. Agent Shook and Detective Benjamin identified themselves as law enforcement officers and informed the defendant they wanted to ask him about the death of Amber Lundgren, a homicide victim whose death occurred in early 1998.

My point in bringing up the Lundgren reference from the NC vs. Hyatt Supreme Court legal briefs is to remind you that investigators have publicly confirmed they are exploring links between Hyatt and other unsolved murders from Western North Carolina. Many other cases match Hyatt's M.O., and Olson's murder is one of them.

The prospect of Hyatt as a suspect is intriguing because he wasn't arrested or associated with rapes and murders until 1998. He wasn't even linked to abductions until 1979. This means he would not have been on the periphery of investigators in the 1973, 1974, or 1977 waves of the Olson investigation.

Law enforcement had no idea that a predator like Hyatt was in the area and becoming increasingly bolder with his criminal activities. Even when he went to jail in 1979, it was for charges related to kidnapping. Law enforcement had not connected that he was also consistently raping and murdering women in the region that same year. In other words, when the SBI's 1977 task force convenes to examine possible connections between Olson's case and others in the area, they do so with incomplete information. Had Hyatt been apprehended earlier, investigators would certainly have explored a possible connection between a known serial killer in the Botanical Gardens area and the Olson case. By the time Hyatt was apprehended in 1998, the Olson case had gone completely cold and there were no main suspects.

Hyatt's escalation can only be observed in retrospect, but now that we have that perspective, let's consider why he might be a plausible name to toss around.

The weather was nice on April 15th, 1973, and students and community members flocked to the Botanical Gardens. There were reportedly 100 people in the Botanical Gardens that day, and many were women in the demographic of Hyatt's known and alleged victims. McConnell was 21 at the time of her death, and Olson was 19. Amber Lundgren, who is a suspected victim of Hyatt, was 20 years old.

The Woodfin area that Hyatt is affiliated with in the McConnell case is a short distance from the Botanical Gardens, and Hyatt was known to frequent some of the camping grounds in that region. These details potentially align with Hyatt's preference for privacy and a willingness to act boldly. Hyatt's other abductions tended to happen during the early morning hours between midnight and 4:00 a.m. The temptation might be to imagine that he prefers to work at night, but I think the isolation of potential victims is the critical detail here. While the Olson murder occurred between 1:30 p.m. and 3:30 p.m., it is worth noting that she had walked off the main trail and secured a more secluded spot away from others. She wanted privacy to study, but this also meant she separated herself from people who might have been able to offer aid or whose presence might have discouraged someone looking for a victim.

Hyatt undertook his crimes with some assistance from others. When the SBI allowed Hyatt to speak with his father before his arrest in 1998, agents overheard him try to explain their visit away as one related to his past experiences running with the "wrong crowd"—when he used to get in trouble. This statement aligns with some of his juvenile arrests. He was arrested with a peer in at least two of those cases. There is a saying that "everyone is the hero of his own life story." I suppose that maxim extends to Hyatt—even though it's hard to reconcile the lack of self-awareness here. Perhaps he never considered himself the "wrong crowd" people should avoid.

If Hyatt were tied to the Olson case, it would likely mean that there was more than one perpetrator. Perhaps Hyatt coerced Olson's compliance with a knife as he did with his other victims, and another accomplice helped tie her up. In the McConnell case, Hyatt's accomplice acknowledged his awareness that Hyatt planned to rape their victims, but he denied any predetermined plan to kill them. He suggested this part of the outcome came solely from Hyatt. This final act typically followed the sexual assault. The proclaimed "innocence" of this friend/witness is difficult to stomach, but remember, investigators don't have enough to convict or even arrest Hyatt without this person.

Perhaps that same pattern of abduction-assault-murder occurred here. Hyatt and an accomplice spotted Olson and imagined her as a vulnerable target. They distracted her with some minor talk and then surprised her with a knife and numbers to force her compliance, and then after the rape, the murder occurred, just like in his other known cases.

Of course, this could be another curious coincidence that has plagued this case. My strongest case *against* Hyatt's involvement is as circumstantial as my theory for his involvement.

Over the years, investigators with ties to both cases have failed to make the connection, and part of me finds it unlikely that they neglected to consider Hyatt once his other crimes were known. SBI Agent Bill Matthews, one of two men placed on the Olson case full-time in 1974, would later work on some cases involving Hyatt in 1979—similarly, Det. Kevin Taylor, the current cold case detective assigned to the Olson case, also has a long history of involvement in investigating Amber Lundgren's murder and others with possible links to Terry Hyatt. As a result, I think it is likely that investigators would have considered a connection if one existed. I struggle to balance that assumption with knowledge of the previous mishandling of the McConnell and Simmons investigations.

The Cop's Take on Terry Hyatt's Possible Connection to Olson

While writing this book, I had to have an awkward conversation with my wife. It was one of those dialogues that I rehearsed in my head and debated even initiating. One part of me thought, "She could learn about it along with everyone else when she reads the book." However, I ultimately decided that this may lead to my own murder, and the best plan would be to come clean and explain my actions.

So, I let her know that I was going to try and become pen pals with serial killer Terry Hyatt.

"Are you sure he isn't getting out? What if he escapes?" she asked.

I was ready for this one. I assured her that he was serving six life sentences plus 99 years.

The goal in writing Terry was not to befriend him. Terry is a piece of shit and does not deserve to continue living. I wanted to know how many women he killed and whether Virginia Olson was an early victim. Finding a way into the conversation was hard, so I asked him about everyday topics. "What sports do you watch? Do you have any hobbies?"

Terry didn't respond to my message; some of this may be related to his learning disability. When he was in elementary school, his teachers were unaware of these issues, and they described him as the kind of kid who spent his day staring off into space. This probably led to Terry dropping out of school in 10th grade.

Police records indicate that Terry's arrest record begins at 16. One thing to remember is that 16 was the minimum age for someone to be charged. Terry likely had other petty crimes that are not public records due to state laws regarding juvenile offenders.

The important part about this time in his life is that he sees women as easy prey. Terry stole women's purses and a few cars. On February 12, 1974, Terry was convicted of motor vehicle theft. Due to his age and lack of criminal history, the judge sentences him to two years' probation. Terry then violates his probation by getting caught stealing a purse. The Buncombe County Judge then revokes his probation and gives him an active sentence of two years. Terry escaped from prison in May the following year. The details of how he escaped are unknown, but he was caught after 24 hours.

After serving two years in prison, Terry remains off law enforcement's radar until 1979. Terry's first significant conviction was in October 1979 for kidnapping Carolyn Brigman. Terry pulled his truck beside her while she was walking home from work. He pulled a knife on her and told her to get inside his vehicle. Terry ended up driving her around and kept making threats that he would "slit her throat." According to the victim, while driving over the French Broad River, Terry also remarked, "I have placed a lot of bodies in that river." Brigman was able to convince Terry that she did not like the police and that if he let her go, she would not tell anyone. Terry let her go, and she went straight to the police station. She gave the police a description of Terry and his truck. Police could track Terry down and take him into custody. Terry was convicted of

Armed Robbery and 2nd Degree Kidnapping on January 24, 1980.

I'm not sure if investigators asked about his prior comments regarding the other bodies he told Brigman he dumped in the French Broad River. Maybe investigators were just happy with the current charges. The kidnapping was Terry's first violent felony, and this may have unduly influenced investigators to believe that Terry used the comments to gain compliance and that his literal statement was not to be taken seriously.

Another factor to consider is that Harriet Simmons's body was not located until March 23, 1980. This means her case started as a missing person's investigation. A missing person's case in 1979 would have relied on some form of public assistance. Due to the amount of investigative time needed for these cases, I'm skeptical that much effort was spent on these cases.

When we look at the cases Terry is involved in, several consistencies are consequential. Harriet Simmons was murdered on April 15, 1979, the sixth anniversary of Virginia Olson's murder. Even though decomposition had removed the flesh and organs, Dr. Tate, with the North Carolina Medical Examiner's Office, found four injuries to Simmons's ribs consistent with being stabbed. Virginia Olson and Terry's other victims also died of stab wounds. In the Simmons case, he disposed of her body in the Pisgah National Forest. Olson was murdered in a 50-acre National Forest that borders UNCA. Another interesting fact about the Simmons crime scene is the items that investigators collected. According to court documents, "A search of the area produced bones, clothing, jewelry, a set of car keys, other personal effects, and a short segment of silver duct tape." We can assume that the "short segment of silver duct tape" would indicate Terry binding the victim's hands. This is another parallel to the Olson case.

On August 25, 1979, Betty McConnell became Terry's next known victim. That day, she left her job at Dunkin Donuts and never returned home. Three hours after being reported missing, she was discovered in a driveway near the French Broad River. The witness, who also owned the property, stated that McConnell advised that she had been stabbed and thrown in the river. EMS was called, but McConnell ultimately succumbed to her injuries: five stab wounds to the chest and stomach. Investigators located a bloody trail that went to the French Broad River. They also identified her vehicle on the bank of the river.

A few notable mistakes were made in this case that later hurt the viability of the investigation. The first investigative anomaly is that McConnell's vehicle was never processed. This vehicle would have possessed Terry's fingerprints, which would have been instrumental in an arrest. Additionally, a rape kit was conducted, and a semen sample was extracted, but the Buncombe County Sheriff's Department lost the sample during a move. The rape kit became noticeably missing when investigators started processing rape kits for DNA, and it was nowhere to be found.

The McConnell and Simmons cases would not have been solved if not for "self-proclaimed drunk" Jerry Harmon coming forward to assist investigators. As stated earlier, Harmon walked investigators through the crime and gave us some insight into Terry's thinking.

Harmon's testimony teaches us a few things that were also noticed in the Olson case. The first insight is that Terry committed crimes with another person present. One of the puzzling questions about the Olson murder is how it could be committed in the daytime and in an area that people frequently pass through. It would make logical sense that if Terry had an accomplice as a lookout, it would resolve this issue. Next, Harmon explained that Terry gained control of his victims through convincing threats of violence.

He consistently used a knife to threaten his victims into compliance. I believe this method was used on Olson, which is why the medical examiner did not find any defensive wounds.

We learn even more about Terry when SBI investigators interview him. When Terry was read his Miranda warnings by SBI Special Agent Shook and Buncombe County Detective Benjamin, he asked investigators to speak with his "daddy." The investigators wrote this exchange down on their Miranda form and then transported him to his father's home. After they return to the interview, investigators ask him again if he would like to speak with them about the murders. Terry responds like a child by telling them, "Daddy wants me to call a lawyer." Detective Benjamin told Terry that he was 41 years old and needed to decide if he wanted a lawyer. Terry then went on and made incriminating statements that led to his arrest for murder.

On February 1, 2000, Terry Hyatt was convicted of the murders of Betty McConnell and Harriet Simmons. On February 5th, Terry received two death sentences, which are scheduled to be carried out via lethal injection. He was also given six consecutive life sentences for the rape, kidnapping, and robbery charges related to both victims.

On January 15, 2005, while in Central Prison (Raleigh, NC), a sample of Terry's DNA was taken and entered into CODIS, the Combined DNA Index System. CODIS is the name commonly used to reference this computer software, which links local, state, and national databases of DNA profiles. Law enforcement officers submit samples from convicted felons, unsolved crime scene evidence, and missing persons. When authorities entered Terry's DNA, it immediately connected him to another unsolved murder of a North Carolina woman named Jerri Jones.

On July 9, 1987, Jerri Jones had finished working her shift at a local Harris Teeter grocery store in Charlotte, North Carolina. She was last seen alive, waiting near the store for a ride home from her boyfriend. She didn't make it, and on July 10, 1987, her naked body was found about a mile away from the store.

When investigators entered Terry's DNA into CODIS, they learned through a hit confirmation that this same DNA was found on a cigarette butt near the body of Jerri Jones. Terry's semen was also located in her mouth. When Terry was interviewed in 2005, he calmly told investigators that he intended to rape her in the back of his trunk. After raping her, he claimed that Jones tried to run. Terry said that he killed her by stabbing her with his knife and then cutting her throat. Terry pleaded guilty to murder and was given another life sentence.

The correlation of these murders to the murder of Virginia Olson cannot go unnoticed. Some people may argue that Terry was only 16 at the time of Olson's murder. I would say that it makes more sense. The witnesses that located her body were 14 and 17 years old. This is an area that high school-age kids and college students like to visit. Terry was a local, so it's a safe bet that he knew about the area. Terry has three known murder convictions, which share too many similarities for him not to be considered a suspect.

It amazes me that the only reason Terry was caught was because of his alcoholic friend stumbling into the Buncombe County Sheriff's office. Until then, no one had any evidence of Terry being a murderer. Law enforcement only received his DNA when he was booked into Central Prison for the first time. A sample of his semen was taken from Betty McConnell, but the sample was lost. Harriett Simmons had decomposed so badly that her flesh was no longer on her body. The medical examiner knew she had been stabbed due to the marks on her rib cage. Again, there is no physical evidence.

We also can see from Terry's other encounters that he doesn't think women have any human value. When he sees a woman that he wants to have sex with, he grabs them, threatens them with a knife, rapes them, and then kills them.

What is his actual body count?

I feel confident saying it is likely more than three. It seems unlikely that for many years, Terry got away with three murders and then abruptly stopped. He had a system that worked. We know he only waited five months between the first two women that he raped and killed. He only stopped because of a prison sentence. The only real question is, how many more bodies are around the French Broad River? Was Virginia Olson one of his early victims?

The only way to confirm that Terry is not responsible for Olson's death is to compare DNA samples. We asked Detective Taylor if they had a viable semen sample from the Olson case. He stated that since Olson's murder is an active investigation, he is not at liberty to comment. I would like to believe that the Asheville Police Department has a semen sample that has been entered into CODIS. However, given that Buncombe County law enforcement agencies have lost other samples from this area, I also feel assuming a viable has been well maintained is not something that can be taken for granted.

So, what does a plausible scenario involving Terry look like? It was Sunday, April 15, 1973. The weather was around 60 degrees by noon. Olson told her friends she would go to a wooded area near the Botanical Gardens on the UNCA campus. The area that she went to is a 50-acre forest. The study spot she ultimately picked featured a rock large enough to be seen from the bottom of the trail. After studying maps of the area, it is perfect for Terry to hunt. There are many trails, and the woods provide a great place to stalk victims.

Terry saw her and noticed that she was all alone. Terry attended high school at Enka High, only 11 miles from UNC Asheville, so he knew the area. From past interviews with people close to Olson, we know her faith in God was important to her. As we can see from Terry's previous cases, he does not accept rejection. If Terry was involved, he likely pulled out his knife and threatened her. He must have been confident that he would not be heard or had a friend with him. Since this occurred during the middle of the day, he used the knife to cut parts of her shirt. He binds her arms and gags her with her shirt. He then rapes her. He sees the tears running down her face and the look of trauma in her eyes. He then realizes that he cannot let her live. He stabs her in the chest multiple times until her body goes limb.

The medical examiner stated that little blood came from Olson's neck wound. This means her heart had stopped when this injury occurred. I believe that was the final measure to ensure death. It is still unclear if the murder happened on the actual rock that she was sitting on or someplace close. It seems daring and too risky, but Terry seems to take this risk throughout his life as a rapist and murderer.

As of this writing, Terry has never been interviewed about the murder of Virginia Olson.

Chapter 14: The Murder of Suellen Evans and a Two-Campus Theory

Suellen Evans was a 21-year-old student who was murdered on Friday, July 30th, 1965, in the arboretum of the University of North Carolina at Chapel Hill. The tragic circumstances of her death occurred a short distance from the steps of William C. Friday's Presidential mansion. The attack started in broad daylight between 12:10 p.m. and 12:25 p.m. Several UNC-CH students and even some nuns walking in the area heard screams. At least five individuals ran to the scene and attempted to help. No weapon was found near Suellen Evans, and those first individuals only caught fleeting glimpses of a man leaving.

Before we jump into a theory that considers connections between Olson and Evans, let's take a moment to chart the last 48 hours of Suellen Evans' life.

As the last weekend of July 1965 approached, Suellen Evans was angry with her boyfriend. She was a serious student and did her best to navigate living away from home for a summer session in Chapel Hill, NC, while maintaining a relationship with her boyfriend. Lately, Evans had begun to question his level of commitment. He hadn't visited her as often as she wanted in Chapel Hill, and this weekend, she was supposed to return home to Mooresville, NC. Under normal circumstances, these reunions were things she would have looked forward to, but on this particular weekend, she was still weighing whether or not to tell him she planned to come home. She had many mixed feelings. Some of her friends advised her to do something to make him jealous, but at 21, she was starting to feel too old for such games. She was ready to get married soon and start a family. She didn't even like dating—despite her friends always trying to set her up on blind dates.

On Thursday, July 29th, Evans discussed these options with friends while she packed her suitcase for the weekend. She wasn't in the best mood. She decided to pack just in case she decided to go, which was still likely despite her annoyance. She decided she wanted to look good if she was going home. This meant a laborious evening doing her hair, but she also had a big sociology quiz to take the following day. She eventually gave up in frustration and decided that only two of the three items on her "must-do" list could be accomplished that evening. She was a woman of priorities, so she chose packing and studying. Her hair would have to wait. She told her roommate she would try to return to her dorm after her quiz to do her hair.

She made a few phone calls that evening, and her plans began to take shape. She would go to class and take her quiz, then rush back to her dorm to meet her cousin Don Gabriel and her friend Dianne Wren by 2:00 p.m. Dianne was her hometown friend and had not seen Evans in a few weeks. She decided the drive back to Mooresville was the perfect time for "girl talk." There were serious discussions to be had concerning the situation with her boyfriend.

Suellen Evans planned a tight schedule for that morning and didn't allow much time to eat. Friends later recalled that this was normal for her ever since she went on a diet to lose weight. A few weeks before her death, she bragged to some classmates that she lost five pounds. She was happy with the results and hoped to lose more weight before the end of the summer session.

On the day of her death, she woke up ready to get dressed. The previous night had been stressful, and her initial agitation with her boyfriend had started to subside for the first time in a while; she looked in the mirror and felt pretty and confident. She chose a blue-striped suit with a large collar piped in red. She put in her favorite silver earrings, which she had purchased recently, and marveled at the dress that hung from her dorm mirror for a few minutes. The dress was her creation.

The new earrings were a favorite because they were also her first pair, and while they were store-bought, the ear-piercing was a homemade job courtesy of her new summer school friends. One of the girls in her dorm hall at UNC-CH had recently convinced her to be "daring" and take the leap. Evans had initially been skeptical but ultimately let her pierce her ears with a needle and an ice cube, and now she adored looking at the earrings. They were reminders of her bravery.

That morning, she didn't have too long to admire herself in the mirror since her sociology quiz started at 9:00 a.m. in Alumni Hall, north of the center of the university's campus. Students had the entire class period to take the quiz, and Evans worked carefully even as other students departed early around her. She had long ago learned that being last was okay if you ultimately got the desired result. Evans was among the last students to turn in papers on this particular day. She placed her quiz on top of the others on her professor's desk and departed by 10:30 a.m.

The quiz had gone well, and she began to allow herself to think that the day would be okay after all. Her next destination was a class in the Education Department in Peabody Hall. As she walked, it felt refreshing, like spring. It would take her less than five minutes to get to Peabody Hall, which meant she had some time to spare, so she intentionally slowed down a little and allowed herself to take a moment to say hello to a few classmates she passed and observe a building in the middle of renovation repairs at the intersection of Old Well and Y-Court.

The class passed quickly and uneventfully and ended just before noon. Suellen Evans exited the building, and a friend and classmate from the same dorm jogged up to greet her. Earlier that summer, they started walking back to Cobb Dormitory after class. It was one of those rituals that many young women of this era adopted on college campuses as a safety precaution as much as a social one. This was the plan on that day because Evans still had to get her hair done before her cousin and hometown friend picked her up to take her back to Mooresville.

As Evans started walking alongside her friend, she abruptly stopped and checked her watch. She seemed to have forgotten something but was trying to gauge her time. Evans explained to her friend that she would like to speak to her sociology professor, Dr. Edgar Butler, before returning to her dorm. Since it was just after noon, she believed she had enough time to take care of this errand and get back to do her hair before her 2:00 p.m. pick-up. She told her friend to go ahead without her and that she would drop by her room when she returned.

When Evan arrived at the sociology building, she could not locate her professor. She hung around this building for 15 minutes, pacing back and forth impatiently, before giving up this errand and starting toward her dorm.

Remembering that she still had time, and even more so since she wouldn't be able to meet with her professor, she decided to take a brief stroll around the university's five-acre arboretum, which was located almost immediately behind the Alumni Building, which housed her sociology professor's office.

At this point, the specific timeline becomes a bit fuzzy, but we know that Evans was walking through the arboretum before 12:25 p.m. As she walked around admiring the flowers, someone grabbed her from behind, pushed her into some bushes, and tried to force her down onto a bed of periwinkles.

Evans fought her attacker- police reports note ample evidence of that struggle in the disrupted quality of the garden bed where she and her attacker went to the ground. She fought for her life and tried to get away. This wasn't a secluded area; she yelled and called for help.

Several children under 50 feet away were riding bicycles as her attack proceeded. Evans made one final attempt to get help by screaming as loud as she could. After these screams, her attacker gave up any attempt to sexually assault her, stabbed her in the heart, and slashed her neck.

Despite the crowded nature of the arboretum, no one saw her attacker- or at least- no one saw the attacker in a way that would allow for an easy identification. One of the first students on the scene who ran towards the sounds of Evans' screams did report seeing "a dark arm—darker than sunburn."

"Are you hurt?" this first student asked as she found Evans.

"No, but I think I'm going to faint. He tried to rape me," responded Evans in a voice that was weak from the rapid blood loss. Her injury was so severe that she didn't seem to comprehend fully the peril she was in.

These were the last words she would speak on this earth.

A nun arrived after Evans lost consciousness and immediately started CPR. Police arrived too, running in from three directions, but it was too late. When it became evident that Evans was dead, police began to turn their attention to sealing off the arboretum. Their suspect couldn't have gotten far. However, in the middle of all this chaos, authorities could not secure the scene entirely. When more reinforcements arrived, the suspect was no longer in the arboretum.

Over 800 people attended the funeral of Suellen Evans on Sunday, August 1st, 1965, at the Vanderburg Methodist

Church in Mooresville, North Carolina. Close to 30 students and the two nuns who attempted to help Evans were in attendance. It was a sad occasion, and following the service, hundreds paraded by Evans' casket before it was buried.

The Investigation Goes Cold

Leads initially poured into the Chapel Hill Police Department, and several suspects were explored and discarded during the early investigation. There was the young man who witnesses spotted near the arboretum with blood on his shirt that would later be attributed to a shaving accident. There was also the rumor of an African American soldier who was in the area after going AWOL and who subsequently stole a car that he discarded a few counties over. The SBI eventually located and questioned this individual, and the *Asheville Times* reported that officers described this person as "a mentally ill negro man, and we couldn't comprehend what he said." Authorities might not have been able to talk to this suspect, but they took samples of his clothing and sent them to the SBI lab for testing. This lab work ultimately excluded him as a suspect.

As other suspects failed to pan out, students grew increasingly concerned and attempted to take matters into their own hands. They put up fliers, held rallies, and even organized a search of the arboretum to find clues that the police might have overlooked. The first of these organized searches turned up several hundred volunteers. The *Winston-Salem Journal* would report that "nothing of consequence" occurred in these efforts.

As the media coverage of the case increased, locals also tried to help, and the police reported they had accumulated a large number of knives turned in by citizens who found them on the side of the road or near their trash.

A persistent question that eluded police during the immediate investigation concerned Evans' precise whereabouts during the 25-30 minutes that seemed unaccounted for in her movements between leaving her sociology professor's office and her attack in the arboretum. In the days that followed, none of the students who were also in the Alumni Building recalled seeing her, and even though her ride to Mooresville was reportedly running late, that information had not been communicated to Evans. Her roommates told police that Evans was unlikely to walk and talk with random boys. She was shy, polite, and kind but "not a hellraiser" and not the type to speak with a boy who complimented her.

Evans' personality led police to scrutinize her sociology professor and her known associates, but these conversations did not produce any leads or connections. That quiz she was so worried about for her sociology class was examined, and it was revealed that it would have received an A- or B+. A small detail that no longer mattered after her death.

The memory of the incident faded as quickly as the police's case. Close to nine suspects had received significant scrutiny from the police but were each excluded with solid alibis. By the fall semester, students barely recognized the name Suellen Evans, and the university had stopped asking students to walk in pairs within the arboretum.

Life moved on until eight years later when Virginia Olson was murdered. North Carolina papers resurrected the story of Suellen Evans and pondered possible connections between these two murders on two different campuses. By April 18th, 1973, three days after Olson's murder, the *Greensboro Daily News* would run a headline that declared, "UNC-A, UNC-CH Killings Similar." And it wasn't just media outlets; our conversations with cold case detectives taught us that the Asheville Police also explored possible connections between these two crimes.

The Professor's Take on the Two-Campus Theory

On the surface, the 1965 murder of Suellen Evans on the campus of UNC-Chapel Hill seems to beg comparisons with the 1973 murder of Virginia Olson at UNCA. The similarities between the two cases are uncanny. Evans and Olson were both introverted individuals who left deep impressions on those who knew them. They also appeared quirky and less knowable to those who only interacted with them casually. Both women died in garden spaces tied to UNC-system universities in the middle of the day with many people present. On the day Olson was murdered, there were reportedly over 100 people walking around the Botanical Gardens adjacent to campus, and on the day Evans died, the arboretum was full of students, family, and community members strolling around the garden pathways. A group of children was less than 50 feet away when the assault on Evans began.

The cause and manner of death are also similar for both women. Olson was raped and stabbed in the heart, while Evans' attacker unsuccessfully attempted to rape her and killed her by stabbing her in the heart. Both women were also at transition points in their lives. Olson contemplated a transfer to UNC-Greensboro to be closer to her family, and her death occurred during the final four weeks at UNCA. Similarly, Evans planned to *return* to UNC-Greensboro to be closer to her family and boyfriend. She was in the final weeks of summer session courses at the UNC-Chapel Hill and planned to leave following their completion.

Another fundamental similarity was that the suspects in both cases were assumed to be veterans. In the Evans case, authorities tracked a military officer with a history of mental health issues to South Carolina, and his AWOL status inspired greater scrutiny. In the Olson case, the second and third suspects were individuals with military ties. One suspect was an army officer on leave staying at a hotel on Merrimon Avenue on April 15th, 1973, while John Reavis Jr., the prime suspect, served as a lieutenant in the U.S. Army during the Korean War. Papers reported that Reavis also fled the Asheville era during the first 48 hours after Olson's death and spent that time in Myrtle Beach, South Carolina.

Finally, a university gardener was, at some point, considered a suspect in both cases. In the Olson case, witnesses described the gardener to the police as a man with "wild eyes," and the police would later describe this individual as having "emotional problems." The gardener in the Olson case worked on the day of her death and was moving around enough that many individuals enjoying the scenery that day reported his presence. A nearly identical situation occurred in the Evans case.

The theory that some reporters in the 1970s raised was the possibility that these murders were somehow connected.

At first glance, the parallels in these cases seem to warrant special attention. Based on our research, law enforcement authorities in Asheville and Chapel Hill compared notes around 1973, when leads in the Olson case began to stall. Since reporters and law enforcement took the possibility of a connection seriously in 1973, I think it's reasonable to explore it.

I've already outlined some similarities between the two cases, and now I want to highlight some of my problems with the so-called "two-campus theory." Yes, there are many overlaps between the circumstances surrounding the deaths of Olson and Evans, but this focus ignores the geographic and temporal distance between these cases. They occurred eight years and more than 200 miles apart from one another. In addition, the emphasis on the "dark arm" that witnesses reported in the Evans case—implying that the main suspect was African American or, at least, non-white- is also a differentiator in this case since all of the witnesses in the

Olson case, despite their divergent testimonies, all described Caucasian suspects.

I suppose the biggest issue I have with this theory is that it presumes this kind of violence towards college-age women was somehow a unique event, so that these events "must" be connected. Cases of attacks and sexual violence on college-age women abound from this era, and other deaths resulted from a stab wound to the heart. Betsy Aardsma was murdered in broad daylight in 1969 in the main library at Penn State after being attacked in the stacks and ultimately stabbed in the heart. In North Carolina, VISTA worker Nancy Morgan was attacked, bound, gagged, raped, and murdered with a knife in Madison County.

My point is that violence toward women was sadly more common around college campuses in the 60s and 70s than we might imagine today. The public only heard about the cases that were impossible for universities to cover up. In the October 31st, 1984 edition of the *Asheville Citizen-Times,* an article by reporter Paul Clark echoed a variation of this point when he noted that sexual violence on the campus of UNCA was far more prevalent than many people realized. The article stated that "if you take any comfort in the figure [those official police reports that show low levels of UNC-A campus assaults], you're making a real mistake."

One of the hardest things about investigating the Olson murder is that there are so many instances of cases that seem like they might be connected or should be connected. There is a temptation to compare the Olson case to others like Suellen Evans, which has similarities in circumstance, or even cases like Karen McDonald and Mary Faye Burdette, which had geographic similarities.

The fact that there have been significant efforts to link the Olson case to others like this one signals to me that few specific leads currently exist. When a case doesn't seem to make sense by looking closer at the details, it is natural to expand the scope of the investigation to make the more minor details mean something in a larger context. In this particular case, the significant similarities between the cases were, sadly, more common than people might imagine. What we are left with is a fascinating but coincidental victimology.

Since no physical evidence or witness statements have connected these two cases, I chalk this one up to another strange coincidence.

The Cop's Take on the Two-Campus Theory

I am not sure why our society has such a fascination with serial killers. When looking into the Virginia Olson murder, many believe that the Suellen Evans murder is linked. While no concrete evidence is available, the theory has gotten much attention. It's not just the public or crime sleuths that noticed the similarities. Asheville Police investigators also looked at the theory as well.

Comparing the two cases raises provocative "what if" questions: If the same person is responsible, are there other victims? What did the killer do in the eight years between the two murders? Did the perpetrator spend this time in prison for an unrelated crime?

While it may be a slight possibility, I think it is worth exploring.

The Chapel Hill Police Department apparently started the investigation using modern patrol techniques. The officers responded from different directions to the crime scene, which increased the chances of engaging the suspect. The department utilized a trained K-9 and attempted to track the suspect. A canvass for witnesses was conducted, and a witness who believed they saw the suspect flee the scene was located. Unlike the Virginia Olsen case, the murder occurred on the UNC-CH campus, which would greatly benefit the officers when creating a perimeter. Like the Olsen case, no immediate suspect was located despite a frenzied initial investigation.

A few other details about this investigation: the Chapel Hill Police reached out for help from the public with this case. They released details of the case and even described the murder weapon. This led to a townwide search that involved everywhere, from the campus to the sides of roads on the outskirts of town. Keep in mind, this is 1965. DNA was not an option. If located, the police could fingerprint the weapon. Regardless, the police were getting complete support from the public.

The North Carolina SBI added more experienced investigators to help pursue the case. Leads were run down, and a detailed timeline of Evans's movements was produced. Since Evans was a student, there were aspects of her day that were easier to document. Investigators could pull her class schedule, ascertain where she was supposed to be at particular times, and then plot the most likely routes students would take moving from building to building. By all accounts, Evans was an average college student who appeared mild-mannered, shy, and kind to those who interacted with her in classes.

So why was she targeted, and who was responsible for her murder?

I believe this was a crime of opportunity. The suspect was looking for a victim. He wanted to find someone alone that he could control. We know that Evans had left her classmate and was walking by herself just before her death. We can assume that she may not have been fully aware of her surroundings due to thinking about school and going home to visit her boyfriend.

Even though many people were in the arboretum on the day of her death, it is worth remembering that this was a summer session. UNC-CH is the flagship public university in the state of North Carolina, and in the 1960s, it also had one of the highest enrollments. However, the area would not be as saturated with students during the summer as during the regular academic year.

I think the killer chose the location with an awareness of all these variables. He would have the option of walking around until he found his victim or picking a perfect spot while waiting for his prey. I believe the second option would give the best opportunity for success. In the years after the murder of Suellen Evans, there would be other sexual assaults and attempted assaults in the arboretum before the university would eventually advise students not to walk through at night.

Since the investigation is over 50 years old, it will most likely only be solved with a deathbed confession. Since Evans proudly fought off her attacker, she was not raped. Some media honed in on this detail and claimed her last words, contrary to initial reports, were, "He did not rape me." For investigators, this means a lack of semen samples, and this absence makes me doubt if any other DNA was preserved.

The only other hope in the case is to link it to a case like Virginia Olson's. The odds are unfavorable, but some similar suspects are named. For example, both cases featured a gardener working at the arboretum, whom the police initially suspected and questioned. It is possible that an employee who committed this crime feared being investigated and thus fled to another UNC campus. However, if police in both cities explored a potential connection between these crimes, then something like overlapping personnel records would be an area they likely considered.

Another similarity is that both cases featured a "former army lieutenant" as a prime suspect. In the Evans case, it was reported that the lieutenant went AWOL shortly after the murder. Is it possible that this same individual fled to Asheville?

We may never know if anything truly bonded these two people together besides the tragic way their lives ended. Both cases are still open; until they are closed, we must not rule out any possibility.

Chapter 15: Highland Hospital, Urban Legends, and Community Gossip

"We tell each other stories, we believe stories. I love watching the slow rise of the urban legend. They're the stories that we use to explain ourselves to ourselves."
—Neil Gaiman

Highland Hospital was a mental health asylum built in Asheville, NC, in 1904 by Dr. Robert S. Carroll. The hospital was initially named after its founder but officially became "Highland Hospital" around 1912. Dr. Carroll ran the facility until 1939, and on more than one occasion, he stated that treating patients with a myriad of "nervous diseases" was the facility's primary specialty. At its founding, Highland Hospital gained a reputation as a progressive treatment facility. According to Duke University's Highland Hospital archives, "the guiding principle of Dr. Carroll's care philosophy was occupational therapy, especially outdoor activity." A nurse affiliated with the facility would explain their mission this way: "Patients were assured of 330 outdoor days in which they could exercise outdoors, thereby augmenting the oxygen supply to their sick brains." In addition, the hospital contained spaces for "hydrotherapy" treatments, provided patients with spacious suites, and offered large porches with sweeping mountain views of Asheville, NC.

In 1939, the hospital's ownership was transferred to Duke University, and within ten years, it became a haven for World War II veterans battling nervous conditions that resulted from combat experiences. This trend continued throughout the Vietnam War. When we consider the rumors that have developed over the years about Highland Hospital, it is recommended to think about the links the hospital had to war veterans and assess the prevalence of suspects who were former military officers and who allegedly received treatment in the area.

Today, Highland Hospital is most famous for its 1948 fire that killed several patients, including the writer Zelda Fitzgerald, who was married to the famous American novelist F. Scott Fitzgerald. The infamous fire started in the hospital's kitchen and became so intense that they travelled up the dumbwaiter shafts to other floors. This helped to spread the fire quickly and ensure that stairways were not easily accessible to patients who tried to flee.

Asheville Fire Chief J.C. Fitzgerald (no relation to the hospital's famous patient) told *The Asheville Times* on March 11, 1948, that the fire had already broken through the facility's roof when fire trucks arrived. Fortunately, many of the patients had already fled by this point, but rescue attempts were complicated for those who remained in the facility.

"It was impossible to get near or in the doors because of the terrific heat," said Patrolman J.C. Wible, who, along with Capt. Enloe were the very first responders to arrive on the scene.

It was a chaotic scene that began at 11:45 p.m. when the first fire alarm reached the station. A second alarm, followed by a general alarm, occurred next and within six minutes of this first event, which emphasized to everyone involved that all personnel were needed at the site.

"It was horrific," was the description that one firefighter would succinctly offer.

The scene of the fire was a strange combination of an awe-inspiring natural spectacle, coupled with the frantic commotion of the personnel on the scene and the peculiar calmness that many of the patients demonstrated as they attempted to help direct firefighters. While some patients screamed in pain and terror, others maintained a stoic calmness and tried to help. *The Asheville Times* reported that some patients "stood at locked windows with flames licking at their backs and calmly directed rescue operations." One of the most startling stories we encountered involved a patient whose room was ablaze, with all her furniture on fire. Even as sparks threatened to catch her dress on fire, she calmly directed officers who placed a ladder near her window. She instructed them to be careful as they opened her window, and once it had been opened, she deliberately lowered herself out of the window and down the ladder.

Every piece of Asheville fire equipment and even a fire truck from nearby Enka was rushed to the scene. More than 40 full-time firefighters participated in the efforts to extinguish the fire that evening. The first bodies were discovered by 8:00 a.m. the following day after an exhausting night and amidst worries of a possible structural collapse.

Zelda Fitzgerald was the most famous victim of the fire, and her death brought the hospital a level of infamy. Still, her presence at the facility is a reminder that it was notoriously private because many of its guests had considerable wealth and resources. Zelda Fitzgerald was initially committed there in 1936, and her presence helped confer a wider reputation on Highland as a space capable of discreetly treating high-profile patients. Following the conclusion of the fire, the Asheville Fire Chief announced that no public inquest concerning the fire or the resulting deaths would occur.

Despite lacking an inquest, the tragic fire in 1948 transformed the hospital's reputation and brought it lots of unwanted publicity. Soon after, ghost stories started circulating about the victims of the hospital, and police would sometimes need to be called to discourage curious onlookers who traveled to the location out of morbid curiosity. Even today, the location of the former hospital is part of several popular Asheville-based "ghost tours."

At the time of Virginia Olson's death, the hospital remained an active private facility. Duke continued to operate the facility as a mental health hospital until the 1980s, when it was sold to a private care group and became a "recovery home" for troubled kids and teenagers.

Shortly after Olson's death, a series of persistent rumors circulated throughout the Asheville community that suggested the murderer was an escaped patient whose identity was protected by the Asheville Police Department due to his family's prominence and financial influence.

The Professor's Take on the Highland Hospital Rumors and Gossip

One of the most colorful and persistent theories of Olson's murder involves Asheville's infamous Highland Hospital. Cameron will provide a more in-depth look at some individuals responsible for circulating this gossip. Still, the general contemporary internet gossip is this: in 1973, a wealthy patient at Highland Hospital who the staff knew to be a sexual predator was able to escape, rape, and murder Olson in the Botanical Gardens, and then shortly afterward, his wealthy family engaged in a community-wide cover-up. Most versions of this story describe the patient's psychiatrist as uncooperative with investigators, which leaves the police with few tangible leads to connect the "known" perpetrator to Olson. This tale has several variations, but most point to how the family used its resources to assist in the perpetrator's escape to the New

England region and its societal influence to discourage law enforcement from pursuing him.

Most urban legends contain some kernel of truth, and the Highland Hospital gossip is no exception to this rule. My take on this theory is that it is a strange cocktail of fiction, of publicly known facts about more than one suspect in the early years of the investigation, and that it draws some inspiration from a popular urban legend circulated in American culture around 1960.

The principal fact this Highland Hospital theory relies on for effect is that the perpetrator has a mental illness—he is a demented and murderous sex fiend who represents a real and present danger to residents of Buncombe County. Newspaper readers in Asheville who followed developments in the Olson investigation from 1973 to 1977 would have noticed a consistent law enforcement emphasis on a variety of different persons of interest and suspects who were all described as mentally ill.

There was the unnamed 19-year-old suspect taken into police custody on "breaking and entering" charges roughly 48 hours after Olson's murder. Police encountered this individual with what appeared to be fresh blood stains on his shoes in a building close to campus. The SBI later determined this blood was not related to the crime scene. Yet this suspect's recent escape from a mental health asylum in Richmond, Virginia, became a central part of this public story.

Other initial suspects with mental illness included a UNCA gardener who witnesses reported seeing in the Botanical Gardens on April 15th. Police later acknowledged that this individual's job required him to work in the Botanical Gardens, but they simultaneously described witness statements to local reporters that originally characterized the individual as having "wild eyes." At the time of his release, police seemed to concede the gardener exhibited some "strange behaviors" on the day of the murder. Still, they explained those behaviors by stressing his "emotional problems."

In 1974, Asheville Police named Glenn Allen Carlson -the serial rapist in Florida that SBI agents Maxey and Matthews brought to the attention of the Asheville PD -as a person of interest in Olson's death. Maxey and Matthews became suspicious of Carlson when they learned that he previously attended UNCA and lived near the Botanical Gardens in 1969. In Florida, authorities accused Carlson of raping at least 40 different women. Matthews and Maxey also noticed that Carlson possessed a lengthy arrest record in Buncombe County, though many of those charges were related to burglaries. The SBI and the members of the Asheville Police went to Florida in 1974 to question Carlson and to confirm his whereabouts and movements at the time of Olson's murder. Police ultimately excluded Carlson after multiple witnesses confirmed his alibi that he was delivering newspapers in Florida on the day of Olson's murder. For our purposes, the most significant detail is that Carlson received a sentence of life in prison but served it at a mental hospital for the "criminally insane."

The most infamous example of a known mentally ill patient in the Olson case is John Reavis, Jr., the notorious Santa Fe suspect. This book is the first to reveal his identity, and local media reported in 1974 described him as an individual who received treatment from a local Asheville psychiatrist who refused to cooperate with the police.

Reavis indeed came from a wealthy family with a father who practiced law. There was initially a lot of reason to be suspicious of this individual. Witnesses would later tell police that he seemed disturbed and "off" on the day of Olson's murder. He even complained about "blood" to one neighbor and asked another neighbor to "pray with him." It is also true that this individual left town within 48 hours of Olson's murder and traveled to Myrtle Beach, South Carolina. When the suspect returned home on April 29th, two weeks after the murder, police and SBI agents were waiting to chat with him, which led to the execution of a search warrant that night; before they departed, they took items from his apartment to the SBI lab for testing.

Other stories about Reavis, without his name, of course, circulated widely in the Asheville community, and I think the media's failure to give this individual an identity, which was not consistent with their handling of other suspects in this case, contributed to the rampant community speculation about his identity.

Not long after SBI Crime Lab failed to forensically connect items seized at Reavis's apartment on April 29th to the murder, he allegedly left the area. He relocated to a mental health facility near Boston, Massachusetts. This individual would remain a suspect for 13 more years as he struggled with mental health issues and attempted to start his life over in different states. He would eventually relocate to Santa Fe, New Mexico. In the 1980s, a delegation of Asheville Police would visit him on a widely publicized trip to New Mexico that unsuccessfully sought to secure a confession. Reavis passed away in 1992 in Santa Fe, New Mexico, and the Olson case once again went cold.

By the 2000s, new detectives assigned to the case excluded Reavis as a suspect, but the legend of the roaming, depraved, and well-resourced sex fiend was already too deeply ingrained.

My take is that the consistent police emphasis on mentally ill suspects eventually collapsed with a rapidly circulating urban legend from his era that would come to be known as "The Legend of the Hook Man." The origins of this urban legend trace back to a June 8, 1960, "Dear Abby" column that was nationally syndicated in newspapers around the country. "Dear Abby" was a highly popular advice column that appeared in most American newspapers in the 20th century. In the June 8th, 1960 column, a reader wrote to Abby with an urgent plea that "if you are interested in teenagers, you will print this story" and a minor disclaimer that "I don't know whether it is true or not."

The following story will likely feel familiar even to those who have never read the original text because some variation has been retold in the media over the past 64 years. The original story describes a young man and his date who "go to their favorite lover's lane to listen to the radio and do a little necking." Shortly before they start kissing, they turn on the radio, and an announcer interrupts with an urgent message that "an escaped convict is on the loose who served time for rape and murder." The announcer mentions that a distinguishing feature of the man is that he has a hook instead of a right hand. The couple understandably becomes unsettled and decides to end their date. The boy takes the girl home, and the original story concludes with a dramatic finale: "When the boy took the girl home, he went around to open the car door for her. Then he saw—a hook on the door handle!"

Most urban legends aim to encourage or discourage specific thoughts, beliefs, or actions. This one is explicitly directed towards "teenagers," and the "lover's lane" setting is vital to the message. The boy and girl plan to "neck," which seems like a harmless activity, but that carefree expression of affection and sexuality contrasts with that of the "escaped convict," who we learn was in jail for rape and murder. The story's point works by asking the reader to compare the boy on the date to the convict, and the implicit warning is one about the dangers of premarital sex. When nothing happens between the boy and girl and they arrive back at her house, they discover the "hook," a symbolic reminder of the dangers of sexual expression. In other words, this is a "near miss." The young man and woman narrowly avoid literal danger, and the moral of the story is about the kinds of hazards that teenagers often fail to grasp as they start to explore relationships and sexual expression. The "near miss" is less about the actual convict, who is never directly depicted in the story, but what he represents: deviant expressions of sex, which in this era includes all forms of premarital sex.

Many substantial differences exist between the original "Dear Abby" story and the other "real" stories of suspects described here. However, it is worth noting that by the 1970s, at the time of Olson's death, this popular urban legend had morphed in revealing ways. The setting was no longer just "a prison" but became a "mental asylum." Similarly, the convict changed from someone who committed "rape and murder" to a "sex fiend looking for his next victim."

My point is that by 1973, urban legends that depicted the world as a dangerous place filled with mentally ill sexual predators who were roaming "lover's lane" locations (which virtually every town possesses) looking for victims were common. Police on the crime scene even told reporters that the secluded section of the Botanical Gardens that became the crime scene was a spot for "lovers and winos." As a result, audiences blurred this popular urban legend with real-life details of actual suspects. The urban legend, in its strange way, helped to legitimize the search for and interest in suspects that were set apart from society—marked as deviants with dangerous sexual perversions.

I'm not suggesting that the person who committed this heinous act did not have any mental health issues. Instead, I assert that these widely circulated stories gave credibility to rumors about possible connections to Highland Hospital that have never been legitimately established.

This Highland Hospital gossip is simply baseless, but the effects of the story are genuine. By focusing so much on mental health patients who are "set apart" from polite society, these stories discourage people from imagining or exploring the potential dangers immediately around them. Readers readily accept that someone who is mentally "deranged" in an asylum could rape and murder a stranger to fulfill their perverse pleasures. We see in this grotesque image a more comforting suggestion than imagining that someone close to us, perhaps even someone who appears to love us and who appears "normal" to others, could be responsible for such a violent act.

Retelling the Highland Hospital rumor is ultimately about reinforcing truths we desperately want to believe, and the prevalence of these rumors and their effects are not only limited to readers but also shape the preconceptions of criminal investigators and how they imagine likely suspects.

The Cop's Take on the Highland Hospital Rumors and Gossip

"For what it's worth…it's never too late, or in my case too early, to be whoever you want to be. There's no time limit. Start whenever you want. You can change or stay the same. There are no rules to this thing…I hope you live a life you're proud of, and if you're not, I hope you have the courage to start all over again." These wise words are from F Scott Fitzgerald, who as my brother pointed out, was responsible for many great literary works. Fitzgerald spent a lot of time writing at the Grove Park Inn in Asheville, North Carolina.

The rumor is that his days at the Grove Park Inn were filled with drinking and writing while his wife Zelda was being treated at Highland Hospital. Zelda was being treated for schizophrenia, even though later reports state she had bipolar disorder. Some people claim that is why her husband drank so much, to deal with her mood swings. Highland Hospital was where the wealthy went for treatment of mental health disorders.

The above quote draws many comparisons to the hospital in an eerie way. It would be a perfect voiceover for a horror movie. Highland promoted itself as a place to relax, play volleyball, nap, and enjoy the therapeutic fresh mountain air. Exercise was used as a form of therapy. From the outside, it sounds more like a county club or all-inclusive resort. If you go online, you will still find original promotional materials used by the hospital that show nurses taking groups for hikes or playing volleyball with them. We have included one of the hospital's postcards in this book, which conveys this general appeal. These kinds of commemorative trinkets were sold in local gift shops.

Still, these relaxing images obscure a darker reality of mental health treatments in the early 20th century. After reading about treatments used at facilities in the 20s and 30s, the images I conjure are less optimistic. I picture a male nurse wearing an all-white uniform telling Zelda, "We can make the best or the worst of it," while he straps her to the bed for electroshock therapy. I can also imagine an attractive nurse injecting Zelda with insulin to put her into an insulin coma. Yes, this was an actual treatment used in the early 20th century. This doesn't sound particularly relaxing anymore, right?

Another fun fact that I think contributes to the darker rumors about the hospital stems from some of the practices put in place by Dr. Carroll, the founder of the hospital, who was known to hire mental health patients who had been "treated." It is no surprise that when a fire was started in 1948, and killed Zelda and others, investigators questioned some of the employees. Willie May Hall was a night shift supervisor, and when police interviewed her a month after the fire, she stated, "There are six places in Oak Lodge (one of the Highland Hospital patient buildings) I have picked out that could be set on fire. I have thought about it so much. I am afraid of what I might do, and I want you to lock me up."

Given the history of the hospital, it is no surprise that after Virginia Olson was murdered, rumors circulated about the "patient from Highland Hospital." One of the popular theories that is still spread on podcasts and online true crime groups is that a patient from a prominent family escaped from the hospital, killed Virginia Olson, and then returned to the hospital's protective enclosure. In most variations of this story, hospital staff observe the patient throwing away his bloody clothes in the dumpster. Others reported that he even had in his hospital chart that he murdered someone in the area.

I want to be clear: I love podcasts, and I appreciate that there are many bizarre and entertaining aspects to the Highland Hospital rumors. However, I found it hard to believe any of these rumors because they seemed to rely on many stereotypes I've encountered in horror films. I'm generally distrustful when a story passed off as "true" starts to sound like a plot I've experienced before.

I decided to take a different route with my investigation into this Highland rumor and gossip: I started looking for the source of the rumor mill. I began with the social media sites and forums that predominately circulated it. This work led me to a forum that contained a link to a podcast for an episode that focused on Virginia Olson's murder. I listened to it and discovered that this host offered the theory that a person from Highland Hill committed the murder in a very "matter-of-fact" presentation. By tracing posts associated with their profile, I finally arrived at a thread that asked for information on the patient at Highland Hills who was suspected of the murder. A member of the group, whom I will call "Sam," responded that he was a former employee and had information about the case. On the surface, it appeared that Sam was confirming the long-circulated theory.

I decided to reach out to Sam and simply started the conversation by asking him for his theories on the murder. He first responds, telling me, "I have no idea of the name of the person who killed Virginia Olsen….I worked as a 'Psychiatric Nursing Assistant' at the Old 'Highland Hospital.'" Sam then goes into a rant that made me question his reliability after reading it. The following is a small exert:

> While working at Highland Hospital I saw some very bizarre things… "exorcist kind of stuff." And I can tell you for certain there are "Negative Energies"….loose and wandering around the earth…As if the Evening News and daily reports from Municipal Police Departments and Federal Investigative Agencies were not already full of "unsolved deaths" among other bizarre occurrences…Not to mention little Tyrants like Vladimer Putin who are in their own little (or large Fiefdoms) all over Plant Earth… Who have been and are all Plant Earth…who have no problem dispatching others who accidently or deliberately get in their way or are opportunities for them to exercise their power or specific lurid bizarre hungers on.

Sam went on to say that while working at the hospital, he befriended an Asheville Police Officer who was also working at the facility on an off-duty basis. Sam claims that the officer told him, "They knew who the murderer was, but they could not prove it to prosecute him." Sam additionally claims that the same officer told him that "they had found his/her bloody clothes in the dumpster at Highland Hospital."

When I looked into Sam further, I discovered he had repeated versions of this story for many years. As I mentioned, he fell into the category of a former patient who eventually found work at the hospital. From what I can tell, he seems to be the source of the Highland Hospital rumors or, at least, primary circulators.

I think it is safe to assume that when Sam started telling people that "bloody clothes were found in the dumpster," they believed Sam was a witness to the event. No credible report points to the story being true. This story, like the "man with the hooked hand," has become entrenched in the investigation of Olson's death. I believe it is because people naturally want answers. They want to believe that the only person capable of such an act had to come from a mental intuition.

Chapter 16: Our Initial Theory and Lingering Questions

At this point, we have discussed the major historical investigations that have taken place in the Virginia Olson case and also explored some popular theories that law enforcement and members of the Asheville community have circulated. We have attempted to thoroughly address the work and theories of others to establish a clear and public discussion for a case that has not received significant media attention in 38 years. While it was common to see weekly coverage of the Olson investigation during the first few years, the coverage dwindled over time. After the Asheville Police Department's ill-fated Santa Fe trip, only a single extended newspaper article addressing this case would appear over the next 38 years. Even then, this article discussed the Olson case with seven other unsolved cases.

In the 1980s, Captain Will Annarino, who was just a few years away from becoming chief in 1993, would describe the necessity of garnering public interest in cold case investigations to justify expending public resources. He argued that cold cases need public support to remain viable. Our book is built on this premise, and throughout this process, we have come to appreciate the work of the Asheville Police and the SBI on this case. This case has not remained unsolved because a single person has failed to do their job. Rather, a number of limitations, many of which couldn't have been anticipated, have placed current investigators in an untenable position. They are trying to make the most of limited and imperfect evidence that was not collected according to contemporary standards, and certainly without an eye towards long-term preservation. They are also navigating the realities that come with an investigation that stretches for close to 51 years. Two of the three original witnesses are now deceased (Ray Honeycutt and Gerald Echols). Most of the original investigators have passed away, one of the teenage boys who found Olson's body has passed away, and those who knew and loved Olson are now, whenever they are interviewed, acting in good faith but are recalling events and details from decades ago. The Asheville Police Department's main suspect of 13 years, John Reavis Jr., died in 1992, and James Goure, the man who was with him near the Botanical Gardens that day, is also deceased.

We don't want to downplay the near- impossible task that the current Asheville Police Department has inherited, and perhaps this is the reason they have stopped working to educate the public about this case. This lack of public messaging surrounding the case has trickled down to other county offices, and many of the publicly available files associated with this case, which writers and podcasters might access to bring more attention to it, require a near Herculean effort to retrieve.

We were consistently surprised by the bureaucratic nightmare that awaited anyone expressing interest in this case. We say "this case" because we have talked with other researchers who didn't experience the same difficulties we encountered with the City of Asheville and the Buncombe County Clerk's Office. In some instances, these other cases were even older than the Olson investigation. As a result, explanations like "well, it is an old case…we might have destroyed the files as part of our retention schedule" do not easily align with a public-facing narrative that the case remains an important priority.

Since some state agencies do not readily have copies of their division's original records related to this case, we were forced to rely on public communications departments from adjacent government agencies to facilitate access to files and on the support of individuals with inside knowledge of local law enforcement. The Asheville Police expressed some interest in our project. Still, they ultimately proved uncooperative with ensuring easy access to public records like the medical examiner's report (which the M.E.'s office didn't even have) or public search warrants associated with this case. The Asheville Police possessed copies of these records but expressed concern that releasing them directly to us would set a bad precedent for how they relate to the media. As a result, we could only get a copy of the medical examiner's report due to the intervention of the Public Communications Office of the NC Division of Health and Human Services. After some discussion, we decided to include copies of some hard-to-find public documents in this book to make them more easily accessible to others who are interested in this case in the future.

Without easy access to publicly available records, the investigation into this case is placed entirely in the hands of a few part-time individuals who work in the current cold case division. This creates a situation in which the case is passed down, much like a rite of passage, to new investigators every decade or so, but these new individuals have less access to people and potential tips than their predecessors. This is not meant to critique the hardworking people affiliated with this case, but we believe we are about to cross a threshold that will make solving this case impossible. Olson's peers are now in their 70s, and many, including some of her closest friends, are now deceased. Once they are gone, the likelihood of solving this case ends.

These issues have broadly plagued Buncombe County recordkeeping over the last ten years. In a June 17th, 2014 issue of the *Carolina Public Press*, reporter David Forbes covered the federal sentencing of the former evidence room manager for the Asheville Police Department. This particular employee was convicted of stealing drugs and money that were confiscated as evidence in criminal proceedings. However, the paper also noted that this prosecution raised significant issues about how Asheville saved and stored case evidence. The City of Asheville responded by hiring a firm to perform an outside audit of the evidence room. According to the paper, this firm's final report "described an evidence room in massive disarray, with items poorly organized and hard to find, and a broken filing system for basic records." The final audit report prompted then-Mayor Terry Bellamy to tell the paper, "This situation was horrendous." This specific pattern of mismanagement, which was admittedly the result of a new reckless individual, did provide us some context and cause us to pause whenever we were told that records "might not exist" any longer.

We appreciate law enforcement and the idea that active and open cases require a degree of discretion. However, at the time of this book, the Virginia Olson investigation is now 51 years old and remains one of Asheville's oldest cold cases. We have reached a point where more information should be available to the general public. If the individual were a contemporary of Olson- and some witnesses described a man who appeared to be in his 20s -that same person, if alive today, would be in his 70s. If the person responsible were in his 40s (or older), like some of the suspects implicated in this case over the years, then they would be dead or close to 100 years old today. If the person responsible was John Reavis Jr., then he is also dead, and the resources needed to confirm his culpability are unlikely to be spent at this point.

We strongly believe that maintaining such a close grip on relevant details of this 51-year- old case no longer serves a beneficial purpose. In 1977, the SBI released new witness statements and case information to garner new leads and inspire renewed public interest. The case is now at a point in which there is significantly less public awareness of specific details and substantially less information being released that might help generate new leads that are still possible. If the 1977 task force released information to keep the story alive to prompt memories from potential witnesses—perhaps details that were not obvious at the time, but are in retrospect—the situation in 2024 is more dire. If John Reavis Jr. is, indeed, not the murderer, which is the current opinion of the Asheville Police Department, then perhaps someone is out there with information that could be helpful.

Family whisperings, like community gossip, are sometimes passed down generationally. Perhaps something a grandfather or uncle said or did might take on new meaning. Perhaps an article of clothing, a journal entry, or a mention in a letter that is found while cleaning out a person's estate didn't make sense at the time, but new information in the case prompts this individual to come forward. All of this is, of course, a long shot, but it is the only one that exists.

Our Initial Theory: The Murder, April 15th, 1973

After spending so much time with this case, and as the only people who have ever written a book about it, we decided it would be best to make our thought process as transparent as possible. About six months before we began the process of revising the book we took a look at the evidence we had accumulated and began putting together a more developed discussion of what we think took place on April 15, 1973, and what might be some reasonable assumptions about the individual responsible. As you will discover in the "Final Revelations" chapter, some new developments occurred at the end of our process that didn't challenge our initial theory so much as they expanded the context of possible suspects and raised additional lingering questions.

April 15th, 1973–Reconstruction and Commentary

We believe the murderer is someone with other victims who preceded Virginia Olson. Their other crimes likely involved rape or some other form of sexual assault, murder, and comparable circumstances. According to the FBI's Crime Statistics, fewer than 9% of all murders are committed by a total stranger. Cases that legitimately fall into this 9% category are challenging to solve because they are often based on opportunity or a very individual rationale, not a specific motive tied to a particular person. In other words, in these rare cases knowing more about the victim and their circle provides little insight into why the crime occurred.

In the Olson case, we are confident that the murderer was someone who possessed familiarity with the Botanical Gardens and the surrounding hills and woods. He was likely moving around the gardens on April 15th looking for a suitable victim. Terry Hyatt would do similar things when driving around different parts of Asheville in his truck without a specific victim in mind, and he would look for someone who seemed vulnerable.

The area adjacent to the Botanical Gardens where Virginia Olson died crisscrossed with paths that led in multiple directions, but it was also slightly removed from the most trafficked areas. Remember, the first officers at the crime scene described the location as an area frequented by "winos and lovers." This description implies that the area was slightly more secluded.

When Virginia Olson said goodbye to her roommate Jane Nicholson around noon on April 15th, 1973, she was looking for privacy. She grabbed her journal, glasses, and Spanish textbook because she had a final exam the following week. As Nicholson and others have told the media and law enforcement many times, it was not unusual for Olson to study alone in the woods.

The weather on Sunday, April 15th, was perfect, and students and community members flocked to the Botanical Gardens and nearby areas for leisurely strolls. For students, the atmosphere was about reconnecting with friends after spring break travels. There was also the anticipation of a summer break that was less than four weeks away and the frenzy of final exams just around the corner.

Olson left Craig Dormitory with her books and spoke briefly with a few other people in her hall about their breaks before going outside. She gave those individuals no indication that she was meeting someone and only stated that she was heading out to study. She exited the dormitory building by 12:15 p.m. and chatted with 3-4 other students, including one fellow drama major, for another 15-20 minutes before excusing herself with remarks about the Spanish exam she dreaded. During this conversation, she mentioned that she would chat with these friends later at the dining hall, but once again did not mention that she was meeting someone. One of these individuals explicitly recalled asking her about her afternoon plans, and while it's possible that Olson had some and chose not to share them, we tend to take her statement that she wanted some quiet study time very literally. She was, by all accounts, a serious student, and she was concerned about a grade in one of her classes. She intended to actually study.

As she left her friends, which was also the last time any UNCA students would see her alive, she strolled toward

Weaver Blvd., which divided the campus from the Biltmore Botanical Gardens. She briefly stopped at the road, fumbled through her books, turned around, waved one last time, and then walked into an area near the gardens. This last acknowledgment occurred between 12:35 and 12:40 p.m.

Olson liked spending her free time walking around the Botanical Gardens and the surrounding hills. From some spots, like the one she was found at, the university campus was visible, and the view was serene. She likely did the same on this day. She was in no hurry. She needed to study but also went to the gardens to enjoy the day and the natural beauty.

As she walked through the garden, she likely thought about the flowers Jeff Doyle was fond of photographing and providing the scientific names for on their many walks as they talked about their plans for the year and beyond. He was going to be a botanist, and since Olson shared a passion for the outdoors, she enjoyed the new language he provided her to describe plants she had long admired. She had just spent part of her spring break with him on similar walks, and this information was fresh in her memory. He vividly recalled taking pictures in similar gardens the week before her death, and even told us that Olson's shadow appeared in some of these pictures. This was part of their routine and a shared passion.

After walking around the garden for 10-15 minutes, Olson decided to look for a more private place. Over 100 people were mingling through the garden that day, and she wanted to stake out her spot.

She felt comfortable walking off the main path because she had done this many times. Besides, it was broad daylight, and she wasn't alone. She had seen the occasional drunk in the gardens before, but she never reported to any of her close friends that she felt unsafe. Quite the opposite, she told people she felt more peaceful in the garden's tranquil spaces.

Around 1:00 p.m., Olson arrived at her usual spot and settled in. She was alone in this spot for around 10 minutes. She had time to open her books and write a few notes in her journal. We know she was still alive at 1:05 p.m. because Ray D. Honeycutt, a witness listed in the SBI's search warrant, offered an affidavit that he passed the lower trail leading up to Olson's spot and glanced up and observed her reading. From his vantage point, he would have been able to see anyone else in her immediate vicinity.

We also know she was alive ten minutes later, at 1:15 p.m., because Gerald Echols, another witness who offered the SBI his affidavit testimony, stated that he passed through the area at approximately 1:15 p.m. and noted a young girl sitting beside a man who appeared to be in his 30s. The two seemed to be conversing, and he didn't notice any obvious signs of distress. He also told Agent Chambers that when he passed back through the area at 1:45 p.m., neither of these two individuals were present.

If these times are accurate, we can narrow the time of the attack to sometime between 1:20 and 1:45 p.m. This timeline gives us roughly five minutes after Olson's last known sighting and the period at 1:45 when she is no longer with the items she brought to the woods.

We believe the perpetrator waited until no one was observable on the trail before the actual assault began. When Gerald Echols passed by the area at 1:45 p.m., he noted that he could see something "flapping" on the rock where Olson had previously been sitting. The original investigators would note that this flapping was from Olson's textbook blowing up in the wind. In other words, Olson had been separated from her reading and possessions by 1:45 p.m. Given her previous insistence that she was going to the park to study for an exam that concerned her, we think it unlikely that she took an extended break just as she settled into her studies.

We think the assault was already over by 1:45 p.m. because unless both were very still and in the prone position, one of their bodies would have been visible from Echols's location on the trail. Asheville Police detectives confirmed to us that Olson's murder happened very close to the spot where she was sitting. Therefore, when Echols only notices the book and no other individuals, it is because Olson's body is prone and just out of his line of sight. The murderer had already departed. Gerald Echols died on May 31st, 2021, so we can't follow up on his statement, but his testimony and description of the suspect were a key part of the early investigation.

Given the witness statements and the FBI's crime statistics, it is tempting to imagine the murderer was a peer at UNCA and perhaps even a personal acquaintance. After all, Olson was spotted chatting with another young person (in his 20s or 30s depending on the particular witness)—and she did not appear to be in immediate distress- in the 30 minutes before her death. The location also bordered UNCA's campus, and many students regularly frequented the area. The age of the average student had steadily increased during the Vietnam War, and during Olson's time at the school, a wave of non-traditional commuter students, had developed. It would not have been unusual for a student to be in their 20s or early 30s at this time. Even Chancellor Highsmith, when he learned about Olson's death, privately conceded to department chairs and deans that every young man on campus without an ironclad alibi was a suspect.

We find the UNCA student scenario less likely for two primary reasons: First, this was an individual with some experience with this kind of assault. This was neither a crime of passion nor the perpetrator's first time. The timeline we highlight above (and include in the book's appendix) is so tight that the murderer would have needed to work efficiently. If this was a crime of passion or was perpetrated by someone familiar with her, it is unlikely that they would have been able to quickly think about cutting her clothes up and tightly binding her body as they carried out their assault. After the assault, which produced a significant amount of blood that certainly covered their clothing and body, they would have needed to have the presence of mind to maneuver through the forest in a way that would avoid the risk of running into others outside that day. The murderer might not have been targeting Olson specifically. Still, he *was aware* that people would be at the Botanical Gardens, and he knew spots that were used but were more private than the most trafficked trails.

We've seen other cases of murderers staking out a location and waiting for the right moment and victim. In the recent Delphi, Indiana case, accused murderer Richard Allen is an excellent example of this kind of predator. He allegedly kept a close eye on the bridge that would ultimately trap his victims and waited for the right person. In his case, authorities alleged that he had already planned out his escape route in advance. This allowed him to avoid significant contact with other people in the park that day.

The same situation happened here, with the murderer likely hanging out around the secluded spot, and Olson happened to be at the wrong place at the wrong time. The demographic of those known to frequent this spot—younger people using the areas as a "lover's lane" and "winos"—are two types of victims that present different kinds of vulnerabilities. Winos would be impaired and less likely to offer intelligent resistance, while people like Olson or the high school students who found her would be younger and more likely to be controlled through threats of violence.

While Olson's circle was small, we noticed that the people in her life were incredibly protective of her—almost protective to the point of raising suspicion. None of the people in Olson's life knew of anyone stalking or harassing her. She also never voiced any concern to those who were closest to her about any man in her life. Olson was a prolific letter writer and kept friends near and far up-to-date on her thoughts, aspirations, and life happenings. Most of her friends still retain her letters, and some of them read us excerpts of these letters to aid in our research. These letters and journals provide a window into her state of mind in the days, weeks, and months leading up to her death, and nothing we initially saw in them offered any hint that she felt concerned about her safety. We fully believe that if another student, or certainly a random community person, had ever threatened her, she would have told someone close to her or noted it in her letters and personal journals.

Since no such concern was ever expressed, we think this was not someone on her radar. The murderer approached her minutes after she had settled down and caught her off guard. At that crucial moment, she likely looked around and realized no one else was immediately in her vicinity. Olson quickly trusted other people but was also a knowledgeable woman attending college in the 1970s. Even though UNCA did not have a high *reported* crime rate, women who attended the school during this era have told us that they were always mindful of the possibility of an assault. For instance, even before Olson's death, women on campus tended to walk in pairs in the evenings; these precautions were second nature to many.

The murderer, from his hiding position, would have seen the occasional person passing by and didn't want to act prematurely. He likely made some friendly overture. He didn't threaten her immediately because he couldn't afford for her to call out for help. He needed time to evaluate her and the surroundings to calculate his risk. We know the assault didn't happen right away, or else Gerald Echols would have noticed something amiss when he passed the pair at 1:15 p.m. We believe it is likely that the individual Echols observed with Olson at 1:15 p.m. is the murderer.

The murderer was aware of his surroundings and realized he didn't have a significant amount of time. After

Echols passed at 1:15 p.m., he knew he had to act. He pulled out a pocketknife and threatened Olson's life unless she complied—much of the thrill he received from this kind of assault involved exercising power over his victims. The point was not just killing them, it was about soliciting their compliance with his commands. Even though he was careful, the semi-public setting of the crime was risky and contained many variables he would be unable to control once the assault started. Part of his gratification is related to the risky element.

This is one of the many reasons the original investigators believed John Reavis Jr. to be an appropriate suspect. Remember, Reavis had been arrested on a "voyeurism" charge in San Francisco before relocating to North Carolina. Part of the thrill of voyeuristic activities is the risk involved in "looking." If Reavis is responsible here, he would have likely been in a position to "watch" Olson's movements, which we know interested him, but this time, he ultimately decided to act. The main issue with Reavis as the suspect is that there has never been any evidence connecting him to an actual assault, especially in a case like this one and much of the evidence suggests an individual with prior experience.

Making his victims appear more vulnerable allowed the murderer to feel even more powerful. He didn't bring any rope or other "murder kit" items with him to the park that day because he knew how to handle these situations. He likely told Olson that no harm would come if she obeyed his commands.

He started by cutting her green shirt into small pieces, and he used the first pieces to gag her mouth. During this time, the threat of violence hung over the interaction and would have garnered quiet compliance. The medical examiner's report describes this gag as "one which pulls the lower jaws" and was "composed of green knit material which is also tied around her neck." She was wearing dungarees that day (e.g., overalls), and these clothes were intact, which means he forced her to partially undress before cutting her shirt. He didn't bother with her bra.

After gagging Olson, he forced her onto her knees, asked her to turn around and bound her hands with the same material. This made their position less evident to potential onlookers on the path below. The medical examiner said this process left her "knees muddy with small gravel marks and small abrasions."

Once Olson was bound, the murderer forced her to the ground. The medical examiner noted that pieces of earth and vegetation were ground into her hair, likely from this movement. The rape occurred next, and the medical examiner pointed out that both pubic hair and semen were found inside the vaginal canal.

Following the rape, we think the suspect likely heard (or thought he heard) some people coming down the trail and decided to act fast to avoid testing Olson's continued compliance. Remember, if the timeline in the witness affidavits was correct, then the murderer had less than 20 minutes remaining before Gerald Echols made his 1:45 p.m. pass by on the trail that led to the murder spot. Did Echols or the dog that was allegedly with him make a sound that was heard?

The murderer stabbed Olson once in the chest in a single blow that was hard enough to directly pierce the left ventricle of her heart and start a significant hemorrhage. The medical examiner would report that she lost 2400 ccs of blood from her heart, which is the equivalent of 2.4 liters of blood in rapid succession. When the knife was removed, the stab wound was only a single inch, but such a small exit space would cause the blood to spray, and it likely would have covered the perpetrator and his clothing.

The loss of blood from the chest rendered Olson unconscious almost immediately. The murderer then dealt one final blow with a slash across her left neck. According to the medical examiner, this wound was 8 cm deep and extended across the thyroid and up to the carotid artery. There was little evidence of much blood passing through this wound, which caused the medical examiner to conclude that "it likely occurred after the stab wound to the chest."

What happened next is the second reason we believe that this murder was carried out by an individual who has committed other crimes. The amount of blood that law enforcement observed at the scene and the amount of blood that the medical examiner claims was lost mean the murderer's clothing was visibly saturated. This is not the kind of situation in which the murderer could take out a handkerchief, wipe his hands, and calmly resume his walk to leave via the main trails of the hills he was in or the nearby Botanical Gardens discreetly. This would have drawn a significant amount of suspicion. It would have been a shocking sight. For proof, one need only look at the murder of Mary Burdette, which occurred in the same spot five years later. In that case, the murderer took a taxi ride to and from the murder scene. It was the taxi driver who first alerted the police because after emerging from the woods, the suspect in the case, which also involved rape and murder, was covered in blood.

The same thing happened here, but this murderer was more experienced and organized and was not going to call a cab. Instead, he likely had a car parked somewhere along an adjacent road on Weaver Blvd and used one of the more secluded paths to navigate directly to it and avoid the Botanical Garden crowds. The other possibility is that the murderer lived close to the crime scene and was able to move back toward his place of residence before Olson's body was discovered.

The familiarity with the terrain is another reason why John Reavis Jr. was a prime suspect for the original investigators. He lived a mile from the Botanical Gardens, and cutting through to Weaver Blvd would have given him a direct path home. He could have remained shrouded in the woods for a significant part of this walk if he chose to do so. Regardless of the murderer's identity, he likely knew the topography and the spaces where people congregated. He avoided those, and no witness observed any person with blood on their clothing during the immediate period surrounding the murder.

We think the event was likely over in 10 minutes between 1:30 and 1:40 p.m. Gerald Echols passes back through the crime area again at 1:45 p.m. At this point, Olson was in the middle of the trail on her side, but from the vantage point of the trail below, he would not have been able to see her. He noticed a "flapping on one of the rocks" elevated off the ground. He didn't overthink her absence and continued on a trail that led out of the woods. Police later confirmed that this book belonged to Olson, but it was still flapping when police arrived.

Olson's body would sit on the trail for 1 hour and 45 minutes before the two high school students, Thomas Guthrie, age 14, and Larry O'Kelley, age 17, would discover her body as they passed through the area after leaving a picnic.

Our Initial Theory: Why This Case Remains Unsolved

We have already discussed our separate thoughts on the initial investigation in earlier chapters, but the question remains: why hasn't this murder been solved 51 years later?

When we started working on this case, we wondered whether DNA evidence remained. After so many years, it appeared unlikely that this case would be solved unless there was a deathbed confession or the identity was revealed through DNA technologies. In our conversations with Asheville Police detectives, they repeatedly pushed back against any insinuations that they weren't continuing to work the case. While they would never confirm what this "work" entailed, they eventually conceded that they have periodically sent evidence to the SBI Crime Lab for unspecified tests.

When we finally got the medical examiner's report, we noted that semen was collected from the crime scene and prepared on slides for storage. The medical examiner noted there were "abundant spermatozoa, some of which are still motile in the wet preparation." It is reasonable to assume that such samples, even from an older case, could still be useful. Since viable sperm samples exist for older cases like the Nancy Morgan murder in Madison County in 1970 and others that preceded Olson, there is no reason to believe that no viable genetic profile can be extracted from such an "abundant" sample. Of course, we assumed that this evidence had not been lost—this understanding would be challenged towards the end of our research.

When the Asheville Police claim that they are still investigating this case, there are a few possible ways to interpret this statement. In the most optimistic scenario, they have viable DNA from the original crime scene and they have entered the perpetrator's genetic profile into the CODIS system. This DNA information system is shared by law enforcement and will show matches whenever the same DNA pops up again. All individuals arrested for felonies have their DNA placed within the system.

The FBI's "CODIS and NDIS Fact Sheet" explains how DNA databases using CODIS work:

> In the case of a sexual assault where an evidence kit is collected from the victim, a DNA profile of the suspected perpetrator is developed from the swabs in the kit. The forensic unknown profile attributed to the suspected perpetrator is searched against their state database of convicted offender and arrestee profiles (contained within the Convicted Offend-

er and Arrestee Indices, if that state is authorized to collect and database DNA samples from arrestees). If there is a candidate match in the Convicted Offender or Arrestee Index, the laboratory will go through procedures to confirm the match and, if confirmed, will obtain the identity of the suspected perpetrator. The DNA profile from the evidence is also searched against the state's database of crime scene DNA profiles called the Forensic Index. If there is a candidate match in the Forensic Index, the laboratory goes through the confirmation procedures and, if confirmed, the match will have linked two or more crimes together. The law enforcement agencies involved in these cases are then able to share the information obtained on each of the cases and possibly develop additional leads.

The FBI began its pilot program for CODIS in 1990, but the index was not widely used until 1994. Coincidentally, the last major article about detective efforts in the Olson case occurred in 1994, just months after the FBI formally received permission from Congress to widely implement their new data collection system through the DNA Identification Act of 1994.

If DNA from the suspected murderer exists, we assume that cold case detectives who admit they have "submitted material for testing" likely placed the DNA profile of Olson's murderer into the CODIS system between 1994 and 2005. Virtually every law enforcement agency in the country was connected to it by this latter date.

Asheville likely adopted this system before 2005 because Will Annarino was police chief until 1993. As we have already stressed, he was responsible for modernizing the Asheville Police Department in the 1980s with a computer system, allowing better case management and supervision. In addition, North Carolina agencies like the SBI have always been among the early adopters of new efforts to use computer technologies in investigative settings. In countless interviews from the 1980s, Annarino stressed the need to separate "old detective work" from the "new detective work" that technology allowed. Given his embrace of technology, we find it highly unlikely that he didn't use this system during the final three years of his time leading the department.

For a moment, let's continue to assume that Asheville has a viable DNA profile of Olson's killer. In this hypothetical, what reasons might explain why the case has not been solved? In this hypothetical that they have an active profile, we are left with only two options to explain why this case remains unsolved:

1. The individual responsible is dead and perhaps committed other crimes, but he did so during an era before his DNA samples would have been collected and put into CODIS.
2. The individual is still alive and has no other known criminal record—so there would be no connection to any existing DNA in the database. In this case, some ancestry/genealogical genetic work indicating a more extensive family tree or association is likely the only way this person's identity is revealed.

We believe the first option is far more likely than the second one. The second one would make sense if this were a crime of passion and not representative of how the individual has generally lived the rest of their life. However, as we have already discussed, the murderer in this case acted strategically and carefully orchestrated both his attack and escape without detection. This was not a chaotic murder scene or crime. Therefore, it is likely that the Olson murder is not his only victim. Our earlier chapter on Terry Hyatt offers a cautionary tale about the sheer volume of outside victims that might exist when evidence is not carefully managed or people slip through the cracks.

Virginia Olson's murder was tragic and brutal, and the tendency might be to imagine that there was something singularly different about this particular crime. Sadly, violence on college campuses was widespread in the 70s and underreported. There was the 1969 murder of Jane Britton on the campus of Harvard and the murder of Betsy Aardsma on the campus of Penn State that same year. Just within North Carolina, there was the murder of Suellen Evans on the campus of UNC-Chapel Hill, the rape and murder of Nancy Morgan in 1970 in Madison County, the abduction and rape of Karen McDonald at UNCA in 1974, the rape and murder of Mary Burdette in 1978, and sadly many others.

The sheer volume of rapes and murders against women, including ones with similar profiles to the Olson case, is more extensive than contemporary readers can fathom. This means it is highly probable that this individual went undetected. However, even if her murderer were caught and arrested and went to jail for a different crime, it would have been before an era in which his DNA profile would have existed within the CODIS system.

In the 70s, before the advent of nationally connected databases, criminals only needed to move states or counties to avoid police detection. Think about the infamous example of Ted Bundy, who would commit heinous crimes, move to a different state, and continue to commit new crimes. At the same time, authorities scratched their heads and desperately looked for local suspects. The exact sequence of events likely happened here as well.

We believe that when the SBI jumped in to assist the Asheville Police in 1974 and began expanding their investigation to places like Florida, Georgia, and Alabama, this was a recognition that the perpetrator had likely left the area. Still, there were few good options for communication between agencies in different parts of the country—even when investigators worked to look for them. This makes the efforts to connect with suspects in these states who had some ties to Asheville all the more impressive. This was not easy work.

The Asheville Police Department assured us they are not experiencing any budgetary issues hindering their ability to conduct forensic testing in the Olson case. We offered the services of several non-profit organizations that could have assisted with testing if money was the issue. Det. Taylor told us on two occasions that resources for testing are not an issue in this case. These kinds of concessions only confirm our original theory about the DNA database. The trouble isn't getting a profile if DNA exists; it is the improbable set of circumstances that would need to take place to bring a killer into the system.

The lack of any public commentary surrounding this case, combined with the main obstacles facing detectives currently assigned, is why the public is unlikely to hear much more about it. This is a shame and a missed opportunity because time is running out.

After completing our initial research, we were left with many lingering questions and few definitive answers. Each new revelation we encountered led to more questions. We have organized some questions for anyone interested in continuing work on this case.

Lingering Questions

1. The connection between the murder of Virginia Olson and the murder of Suellen Evans seems unlikely. Still, if we accept our CODIS theory about the possible difficulties of closing this case, the issues with the distance between these

universities seem less critical. The distance could be what protected the killer. Police acknowledge they have looked into a possible connection several times, but little public commentary has been offered. Is it possible these two cases are connected? The primary rationale for excluding a connection relates to some unreliable witness statements in the Chapel Hill case that seem to emerge from racial prejudice. If we discount these statements as untrustworthy, the similarities between the two cases are pretty eerie.

2. Is it possible that a young Terry Hyatt could be connected to this case? The main issue with this theory is the lingering question about viable semen-based DNA. We know that Hyatt's DNA is in the CODIS system. This means if law enforcement does have a DNA clean genetic profile of Olson's murderer, Hyatt could be easily excluded. However, it is not clear that the semen sample that the medical examiner collected and prepared on a slide was stored correctly. We know for a fact that an "abundance" of semen was observed during Olson's autopsy, and we can also state as a fact that the examiner took several samples and placed them on slides. We don't know if these samples were stored adequately for over 30 years until DNA testing became widely used. If no viable DNA profile of the murderer exists, then Hyatt must be at least considered for this crime. If a viable DNA sample exists, we can take him out of consideration. The uncertainty about the status of the sample is a topic that the police refused to address with us. That leaves us with few definite

ways to argue for Hyatt's inclusion or exclusion. It is all contingent on their DNA evidence.

3. Is it possible that someone in Olson's circle was responsible for her death? Given our theory concerning how her murder took place, we believe this is *highly* unlikely, but we can't completely rule it out. During our investigation, we talked with many people who were close to Olson, and there were occasions when some casual acquaintances who saw Olson during the last week of her life provided us with information we knew to be untrue. For instance, at least three individuals told us that law enforcement never interviewed them, even after we observed case files that confirmed this information was false. These inconsistencies should not automatically raise undue suspicion given the age of some of the people we interviewed; close to 51 years have passed since the murder. We passed along one such inconsistency to Det. Taylor and he explained that this "happens all the time"—people will claim they have not talked with the police even though they might have given multiple interviews. It might be the case that these individuals forgot, or it could be that they wanted to avoid any insinuation of suspicion in a book about a murder. It is hard to say, but it's fair to say that conflicting statements about alibis and other case elements raise potential questions. Those who knew Olson at UNCA all agree that it was common for her to study at the Botanical Gardens, and she did so frequently during preparations for midterms and finals. If her routine was well known, it could open up other persons of interest on campus. We still

believe it is most likely that the murderer was a stranger who committed other crimes before and after Olson. We also think some individuals close to her deserved extra scrutiny, particularly since the murderer's DNA has never been matched in the CODIS system. As we discussed earlier, this means that our murderer either committed felonies and crimes before DNA collection existed or is someone who did not commit any other crimes after the practice went into effect.

4. Have police *definitively* ruled out John Reavis Jr. as a suspect? In our conversation with Asheville's cold case detectives, they confirmed that Reavis, who is now deceased, is no longer considered a suspect. They further assured us that the entire staff shares this view. Nevertheless, they wouldn't explain whether he had been forensically and definitively *excluded* or whether their investigative thinking departed from the original teams that worked the case. We think the difference is essential. Police investigators allegedly turned their attention away from Reavis after the New Mexico trip, but this would have been before the advent of DNA testing. In other words, it wouldn't have been possible to definitively exclude him at that time. We think it is likely that they lacked any linking forensic evidence by 1980s standards and made the decision to move on. Their case at that time was entirely circumstantial. Then, Reavis died in Santa Fe, New Mexico, in 1992, just as DNA testing was first making its way into criminal investigations. Has DNA from Reavis ever been tested against existing samples from the perpetrator? No one will answer that question

for us. The original investigators honed in on Reavis because of his prior voyeurism arrest, his inconsistent statements to investigators, his bizarre and seemingly incriminating statements to individuals who lived near him, and a statement from a friend who placed him close to the crime scene at 1:05 p.m. The one aspect missing from the Reavis scenario is a motive. We know he was under the care of an Asheville psychiatrist at the time of Olson's death, but this individual refused to cooperate with investigators and died several years later.

5. Many of our case theories hinge on whether or not a viable DNA sample from semen exists. We have received contradictory information concerning the existence of this specimen. On one hand, the Asheville police vaguely insist they have "plenty of materials" that are still in their possession for this Olson case. However, whenever we asked whether the semen sample that the medical examiner collected on April 15th, 1973, is still viable today, we encountered silence. Then, in 2023, on the 50th anniversary of Olson's death, UNCA's student newspaper *The Blue Banner* ran a story titled "The 50th anniversary of UNCA's cold case murder" by the paper's editor-chief Hayden Bailey. In this article, Bailey interviewed Capt. Silberman, who currently leads Asheville's CID unit (formerly the Detective Bureau). He seemed to imply that the way evidence was originally collected makes genetic testing less of an option in the Olson case. Bailey quotes Silberman as saying, "certain criteria [in the Olson case] does not make this practical."

6. What is the connection between John Reavis, Jr. and James Goure? Goure was a well-respected religious leader in Buncombe County. Was he acting as Reavis's spiritual advisor as he sought mental health treatment in Asheville? If so, given Olson's reputation as a devout Christian who attended daily Bible studies, might this provide a possible connection between Olson and the SBI's main suspect? We realize this is entirely circumstantial, but if we want to go down this route, it isn't hard to imagine some form of connection. Numerous people told us that Olson always carried a spiritual journal and liked to go into the woods to record her thoughts and poetry. Much of this poetry had religious connotations. Next, Goure led a religious movement that was centered on the notion of going out into nature to pray multiple times a day. We know that Goure and Reavis were close enough that he gave him rides in his car back home. We also know that they stopped off near the Botanical Gardens on the day Olson was murdered and, by their admission, they not only saw her but made an effort to point her out roughly 45 minutes before she was killed. Reavis might not be the killer, but this is a compelling set of circumstantial evidence that makes Reavis an appealing suspect. His prior voyeurism charge certainly doesn't dissuade further suspicion. The Reavis scenario is not a wild hypothetical; it is also a theory held by a majority of the original investigators associated with this case and continued to be the main working theory for 13 years.

7. As we began editing the manuscript for an earlier version of this book, we received a tip

via email from a close friend of Virginia Olson. This individual mentioned a "nagging" concern. They explained that something that took place a few months before Olson's death might be helpful. We have already discussed that Olson was a talented actress who was always looking for new work opportunities that would allow her to do what she loved for a living. She auditioned for summer stock shows, she recorded literature on tape for the blind, and according to this individual, she was attempting to get work in print advertising. Shortly before her death, she sent this individual some pictures that they considered very risqué—at least, risqué for Olson. The images captured Olson wearing the equivalent of a bikini, and her friend couldn't help but feel a little creeped out by the pictures because they seemed so out of character for her. However, they decided not to say anything because Olson "seemed very proud" of the pictures. She allegedly voiced some pride in the fact that people might be interested in hiring her. This individual told us that Olson's description of the shoot made it sound like it was a "test" for possible work. She also mentioned that the individual she sent the pictures to was based in Asheville and had connections in the world of advertising. We know that in the 50s, Reavis worked as a programmer for NBC affiliates. In fact, in a November 15, 1956 article titled "TV Executive Injured in Auto Crash" that appeared in *The Independent* newspaper, which was based out of Richmond, California, Reavis is described as a "TV executive" who specializes in "merchandising and advertising management" for stations like KRON-TV. Is it possible that this lead is another connection to Reavis? Olson's friend mentioned that they believed the proposed work was tied to an "advertising agency in Asheville," but we were unable to find any specific firm that did this kind of work near the university in 1973. We forwarded this lead to the Asheville Police for further consideration. This may be yet another strange coincidence, but it is a coincidence worthy of further exploration.

Our investigation did not solve the murder of Virginia Olson, but we believe we have significantly narrowed the possibilities. We leave the rest to you, the reader, to decide. Let us know, or better yet, let the Asheville Police know if you have any information that might be pertinent to this investigation.

Remembering Virginia Olson

In 2013, UNCA finally acknowledged Virginia Olson's place in school history. Universities often struggle to navigate tragedy, and the trauma of Virginia Olson's unsolved murder has been a long and complicated road for the school to reconcile. Many schools opt to avoid discussing violence directed towards their students out of fear that the narrative might spawn something that harms the school's reputation. UNCA is not unique in this way. As a result, they say nothing, which is just as bad, and memory starts to fade.

UNCA's efforts to remember Olson consist of three memorial plaques fixed to three benches in what has been nicknamed "Ginger's Garden." This memorial resides behind Whitesides Hall and also features a rock that has "Ginger's Rock" emblazoned on it. It is an area to sit and study outside, as she has famously enjoyed doing throughout her life.

The actual site of her murder is now the current location of the UNCA Chancellor's residence. The house covers the actual crime scene, and the campus memorial generically remembers Olson in a way that does not contextualize or narrate the circumstances of her death or their historical impact on the campus community.

Just as the Asheville police moved Ginger Olson's picture from their detective bureau wall to the inside of a folder with barely legible print, UNCA has distanced the person from the crime in a way that absolves the institution from accusations of callous forgetting while also not simultaneously encouraging specific remembrance.

Until this memory is directly confronted, the ghost of Virginia Olson and the three generations of investigations that followed the tragedy of April 15th, 1973, will continue to reduce this once-solvable murder to one that "got away" and the type of case that is best left in the past.

Chapter 17: Final Startling Revelations, Conclusions, and Epilogue

When we started this book, we hoped to discover the real Virginia Olson and the story of the investigation behind her murder; as we finished our work, we realized that the truth in this case is messy and incoherent. Our research excavated information not previously known to the general public, but these revelations simultaneously unlocked new questions, and many of these questions seemed impossible to answer definitively. For instance, what was the relationship between John Reavis and James Goure? Why were they in the Botanical Gardens around the time of Olson's death? Was this outing prearranged or spontaneous? What did Goure mean when he told SBI Agent Charles Chambers that he "pointed out a girl?" Was "this girl" Olson? Were they ever shown pictures of Olson to confirm? Did Reavis participate in the murder of Virginia Olson, or was he potentially a witness to a crime? His voyeurism charge from his time in California demonstrates that he has a history of watching women without their knowledge. If he saw something, is this what made him so agitated and unsettled when he talked to Judy Needles in her apartment complex an hour after the murder? What happened to the semen that the medical examiner collected in 1973 and placed on slides?

The troubles that plagued the investigation into this case were not a unique experience for some law enforcement officers who worked on it. Seven years before Olson's murder, SBI Agent Charles Chambers was an investigator on a July 17th, 1966 triple homicide that occurred in Hendersonville, North Carolina. That case involved the brutal murders of Vernon Shipman, Charles Glass, and Louise Davis Shumate, whose bodies were found "staged" in a grassy open area near Lake Summit by two men who initially mistook the bodies to be mannequins. Like the Olson case, this one sparked fear and outrage within the community and inspired an initial investigation that paired multiple investigative agencies. There are other similarities between the two cases. There were sexual assaults and strange community rumors that circulated about the person(s) responsible in both cases. Like the Olson investigation, this one was also handled by a police force that struggled to preserve the integrity of the initial crime scene. Reporter Derek Lacey's 2016 article for the North Carolina website *GoUpstate*, titled "1966 triple murder still sends shock waves through Hendersonville," quotes the Buncombe County Sheriff's description of the initial crime scene: "It was like a circus out there…They didn't preserve the crime scene. We had never had anything like that around here. Everybody and his grandmother went down there." Such descriptions mirror the atmosphere near the Olson crime scene on April 15th, 1973, as described by UNCA students who were in the area at the time.

More disturbing similarities extend beyond the actual crime scene and involve evidence handling. In the Hendersonville case, law enforcement officials lost *all* physical evidence associated with the case. News reports from the 60s indicated that an SBI Agent named Gary Satterfield personally drove the evidence collected at the crime scene to the central SBI crime lab in Raleigh, North Carolina. The SBI kept it until July 14th, 1969, and then the evidence was returned to the Buncombe County Sheriff's Department. In 2006, the *Asheville Citizen-Times* reported that Agent Chambers transported the evidence to the Sheriff's Department, and official records indicate their acceptance of the boxes containing the crime scene materials. After this acceptance, the materials vanished, and today, law enforcement authorities readily concede that they have no idea where it all went.

In the final months of our research, a source close to the Asheville Police Department told us that the police are no longer in possession of the semen sample that was collected during the April 15th, 1973 autopsy by the North Carolina Medical Examiner's Office. The Asheville Police have not officially confirmed that finding to us, and they refuse to entertain any discussion that concedes the mere existence of the semen evidence that public records from the 1970s openly reference. In a June 23rd, 2024, email communication with a current member of the Asheville Police Department cold case team about the existence of semen and possible DNA testing of it, we were told, "I cannot comment on either question."

The trouble is that Asheville investigators readily concede the existence of DNA in far more recent cases that are also under the investigative authority of the cold case team. For instance, in a 2021 article by reporter Andrea Cavallier for an NBC-affiliated news station, Asheville Police tell the media outlet that they have collected viable samples from a rape kit related to the unsolved murder of Amber Lundgren and continue to submit this DNA for new testing as technological advancements open up new possibilities.

When we read this article, we were initially perplexed because it seems illogical to imagine such a basic concession would not impact the investigation of a case from 1997, but the same level of disclosure is not available for a case that occurred in 1973.

One Final Startling Revelation

This reluctance made much more sense when we finally learned that a viable semen-based DNA sample does not exist. We were told this information by a source close to the Asheville Police Department who professed to possess knowledge of the investigation. We don't think this fact reflects poorly on the original or contemporary investigators. The original investigators worked in an era without DNA knowledge and can't be expected to preserve crime scenes or lab evidence with an awareness of modern needs. Similarly, we don't think the degradation and loss of evidence reflect poorly on contemporary investigators doing their best with materials that cannot benefit from the most advanced testing that might help shed light on the perpetrator's identity. We only fault current investigators for not working harder over the last 20 years to bring more media attention to this case.

The lack of a semen-based DNA sample means this case is unlikely to be definitively solved. The Asheville Police have repeatedly cited the abundance of physical evidence they collected in this case, and the inability of this evidence to produce any meaningful movement reflects some basic facts regarding the crime scene. First, the medical examiner's report indicates that Olson's hands, arms, and body did not show any defensive wounds. This is because the perpetrator forced her compliance through the threat of violence with a knife. As a result, the attacker was not "harmed" during his assault. The police were able to collect many articles that Olson wore on April 15th. Many of these items contained blood since we know she lost close to 3 liters of blood very quickly, but since this blood was hers, it offers no hope of shedding light on the identity of the individual who attacked her. In the 80s, when Will Annarino told the *Asheville Citizen-Times* that a pair of "blood-soaked jeans" had been sent to the SBI Lab for analysis, there might have been some misplaced hope that traces of perpetrator were left behind, but the "negative" result that the lab reported indicated that no material that could be traced to the perpetrator exists.

After 51 years, the only hopes for viable DNA exist in the gag that was placed around Olson's mouth and semen-based DNA left by her attacker. There is a tiny possibility that touch DNA existed inside the knots of the gag near the areas it was tied. A current member of the NC Medical Examiner's Office who is not directly affiliated with this case theorized this is the most likely place to investigate. However, it is safe to assume that this advanced contemporary test is unlikely to be a viable option in the Olson investigation due to the careful collection and preservation methods needed to make it even a possibility. In a July 2023 article titled "Touch DNA: Revolutionizing Evidentiary DNA Forensics" that appeared in the *International Journal of Forensics*, the study's authors describe touch DNA this way:

> Since dead cells are not really visible to the naked eye, successfully locating and recovering them can be challenging. Performing DNA profiling from the samples that are just touched is quite difficult, hence, requires a highly sensitive approach to its proper recovery, extraction, and amplification of the segment. The methods which are used for the collection, sampling procedure, preservation, removal of contaminants, quantification of DNA, the amplifying of the genetic material, and the subsequent analysis and interpretation of the findings all play a role in how well touch DNA analysis works.

Without any touch DNA that might be extracted from the gag, it leaves us with only semen as a viable option. We know that John McLeod, the medical examiner who performed Olson's autopsy, observed semen during his examination. We also know that he collected an "abundance" of this semen and prepared slides that allowed him to see "motile" sperm under a microscope. Less clear is what happened to the semen sample after the autopsy. Was it somehow discarded, carelessly lost, or stored in a way that caused it to degrade? The sample would have been returned to the Asheville Police Department, but what happened next is uncertain. However, there is a historical precedent for the loss of significant case evidence by law enforcement officials within the county.

Without a DNA sample, fewer suspects can be definitively excluded. This means that Terry Hyatt, John Reavis Jr., and others who have been considered over the years by various investigators are back in the mix as possible suspects unless some other confirmable alibi makes their participation in the crime impossible. Terry Hyatt, as we have already discussed, is an excellent example of someone who benefitted from the police "losing" a rape kit associated with one of his crimes. Without this evidence, eyewitness testimony from a less-than-innocent associate became the only way prosecutors could ultimately convict him. Is it possible that something like that happened here? Similarly, the case against John Reavis is largely circumstantial but also compelling.

Masterminds do not commit most crimes, and the "Occam's razor" principle of deduction reminds us that the simplest explanation is often the best one. James Goure's affidavit connected Reavis to the Botanical Gardens in the half hour before Olson's attack, and he also told the SBI that he pointed out "a girl" to Reavis. The original investigators presumed this girl to be Olson. Two witnesses reported a man matching Reavis's description walking up the bank towards the girl and conversing with her. Then, an hour after the murder, Judy Needles claims Reavis showed up at her apartment visibly agitated and asked her to "pray with him." Further, Reavis had a history of sex-based "voyeurism" crimes that traced back to his time living in San Francisco, California. Finally, we were told by a friend of Olson that she appeared in some "test" bikini photo shoots they believed to be "risqué" and that these images were allegedly sent to an Asheville-based man who claimed to have entertainment industry connections. Reavis was directly tied to the world of advertising and filmmaking.

Is it possible that Reavis had terrible luck and was the victim of many different unfortunate and unrelated circumstances that unfairly collided and brought him to the attention of the SBI? Yes, it's possible but it seems infinitely more plausible that he was either directly responsible for Olson's death, played an accessory role in her death, or witnessed her death.

When the *Asheville Citizen-Times* announced that an "arrest was imminent" in the 80s, law enforcement believed the circumstantial case against Reavis was sufficient to take to a grand jury. Buncombe County District Attorney Ron Brown ultimately disagreed and wanted a more direct traceable connection to prosecute Reavis. The methods they attempted between 1973 and 1984 involved secretor tests for blood samples and new "laser identification of fingerprints." For all of the reasons we have outlined, neither of these tests are routes to connect Reavis or anyone else to the crime directly. Reavis died in 1992 and is buried in Santa Fe, New Mexico, but collecting evidence from his body or even a close relative cannot yield a traceable result if there is not a crime scene sample to compare it with.

In addition to the revelations we learned about the case, we also came to see Virginia Olson as a complicated person whose life ended right as she navigated several adult crossroads. She was still trying to figure out who she was and who she wanted to be, even as many around her assumed they knew the "real" version. For some people, she was the devout religious girl who attended daily devotionals, wrote spiritual musings in her journals, and exuded warmth and kindness to everyone she encountered. This is the Olson who volunteered to help the less fortunate and recorded audiobooks for people who are blind. To others, she was shy and quiet—almost to the point of being socially awkward. To still others, she was playful, carefree, and slightly aloof—someone who trusted people quickly and liked spending time in nature. Yet, the shy, socially reserved, hyper-religious girl image doesn't fully align with the ambitious aspiring artist who dreamed of finding work as an actress and was even willing to take what some might view as revealing photographs to be considered for advertising and entertainment work.

Which one of these images was the real Virginia Olson? We've come to see all of them as part of her—parts of a whole that was not yet coherent. All of these seemingly contradictory pieces are representative of someone still in the process of becoming.

The passage of time has a way of replacing everyday memories with more idealized ones. Memory becomes less about the actual person and more about what they represent for the living. For some of Olson's high school friends, her death represented their first experience with actual loss. In interviews with these individuals, we were struck by how remembering Olson tended to morph into reminisces about the interviewee's youth. It was almost as if remembering Olson's story as a tragic one—of someone innocent and kind and highly moral- became a language for them to express something they lost during these formative years in their lives as they transitioned to adulthood.

For others, Virginia Olson's name neatly aligns with the ghost stories circulating within virtually every theater. Students playfully say "good morning" and "goodnight" to "Ginger" as they start or end their day in the theater. Some current UNCA students and faculty were surprised to learn that Olson's murder was an actual event.

As an institution, UNCA struggles to know what to do with Olson's story. On one hand, the "Ginger's Garden" memorial was formally unveiled in 2013, but it is worth noting that it did not emerge from the university, but from those who knew and cared about her. The school is, admittedly, in a difficult position. The school prides itself on its safety and close-knit community. Within this context, Olson's murder is a strange and painful anomaly that reminds us of past violence and the potential for future violence toward women on their campus.

On the other hand, we believe the school genuinely does want to find some way to commemorate Olson, but it simply doesn't know how to do so. The tension between the desire to remember and the pain that such a recollection can evoke emerged in our brief email communications with Michael Strysick, the current Chief Communication and Marketing Officer for UNCA. When we reached out to Strysick's office for an official comment about how the school, in 2024, relates to the case, we received this official statement:

> Because the tragic death of Virginia Olson is the first and only homicide in its jurisdiction, UNC Asheville takes this murder case very seriously. Though the case officially resides with the Asheville Police Department, it remains an active investigation by our University Police. In addition to "Ginger's Garden" created in 2013 near Owen Hall, which includes memorial plaques on three adjacent benches as well as a sitting rock, the University continues to consider other ways to preserve her memory.

Notice how the statement begins by noting that Olson's case "is the first and only homicide" to occur on campus. This language echoes the statements the university officially released following news of Olson's death in 1973. The statement stresses that the university "continues to consider other ways to preserve her memory." Still, the fact that the idea for this memorial didn't originate from the university calls into question the extent to which they are actively looking for ways to remember. It is also worth noting that the first memorial built to commemorate the only homicide that has ever occurred on campus emerged 40 years after the murder. And it only came about after the case had gone completely cold for over 20 years.

Beyond these issues, it isn't clear what remembering Olson and the tragic events of April 15, 1973, means to the institution. Those who knew and loved Olson lament that she has become a ghost story to the UNCA community. Her spirit allegedly "haunts" the land surrounding the Chancellor's House, which was built on the site of her murder. Her spirit resides in Carol Belk Theater, where drama students playfully use her name to connect to larger theatrical traditions; her spirit resides in Ginger's Garden as a general reminder to current students of a life from the past that was not fully realized. In all of these narratives, the actual Olson becomes lost.

As we concluded work on this project during the summer of 2024, another unexpected development occurred: UNCA announced that the Drama Department and major would be phased out due to deficit issues, which totaled around 6 million dollars. Then, on July 24th, 2024, the UNC Board of Governors made the proposed phase-out official and approved it. The decision sparked fierce pushback from the Asheville community. It resulted in a grassroots campaign titled "Keep Theater at UNCA" that led to more than 1,200 letters from community members being delivered to the Board of Governors to protest the decision and ask them to reconsider.

At the time of this writing, the university is planning a "teach out" plan to ensure the 25 remaining drama majors can still finish their degrees. After they graduate, the department and the major will no longer exist. In an August 8th, 2024 article published by the Asheville-based *Mountain Xpress*, Drama Department Chair Lise Kloeppel lamented the loss of the program and struggled to express what it means for the program to cease to exist when she observed that, "For over 50 years, the department has produced exceptional graduates and consistently contributed to the intellectual and creative life of the campus and Asheville communities…I'm extremely proud of our work and saddened by this tremendous loss."

As traces of Olson continue to disappear, it feels sadly poetic that the major that emerged during her time at UNCA is now set to be discontinued as her story finally emerges in a book. We wrote this book because we believe Olson's story matters and we think she deserves justice. Her murder never received significant news coverage outside of Western North Carolina and surrounding regions because the early events of the investigations occurred against the political turmoil of the start of the Watergate scandals. The case also undoubtedly suffered because the main suspect had resources that complicated the investigation for early Asheville PD and SBI investigators. Today, as the Drama Department sadly becomes a footnote in UNCA's longer history, there is the danger that the story of Virginia "Ginger" Olson's murder becomes associated with the past even more.

Our investigation has led us to conclude that this case will not be solved, but we believe it is important for Olson's story and the history of this investigation to be publicly and transparently available. This case remains one of Western North Carolina's oldest and most notorious unsolved cases and is also one of the least understood. Understanding it is the best way we can honor Olson's memory because in telling it we assert that her life and her death mattered. In telling the story openly, we also acknowledge all members of law enforcement, from the past and present, who tried their best to find justice for and speak for Virginia Olson.

Pictures

See high resolution versions of these files at: https://wbp.bz/campusgallery

Figure 1: Virginia Olson's Grave, New Prospect Church Cemetery, Decatur County, Tennessee

Figure 2: McLean High School Thespians, Spring 1971 (Virginia Olson pictured in the far right, wearing a white hat), Photo Courtesy of: Virginia Room, Fairfax County Public Library

Figure 3: Virginia Olson and Jeff Doyle, McLean High School, Spring 1971, Photo Courtesy of: Virginia Room, Fairfax County Public Library

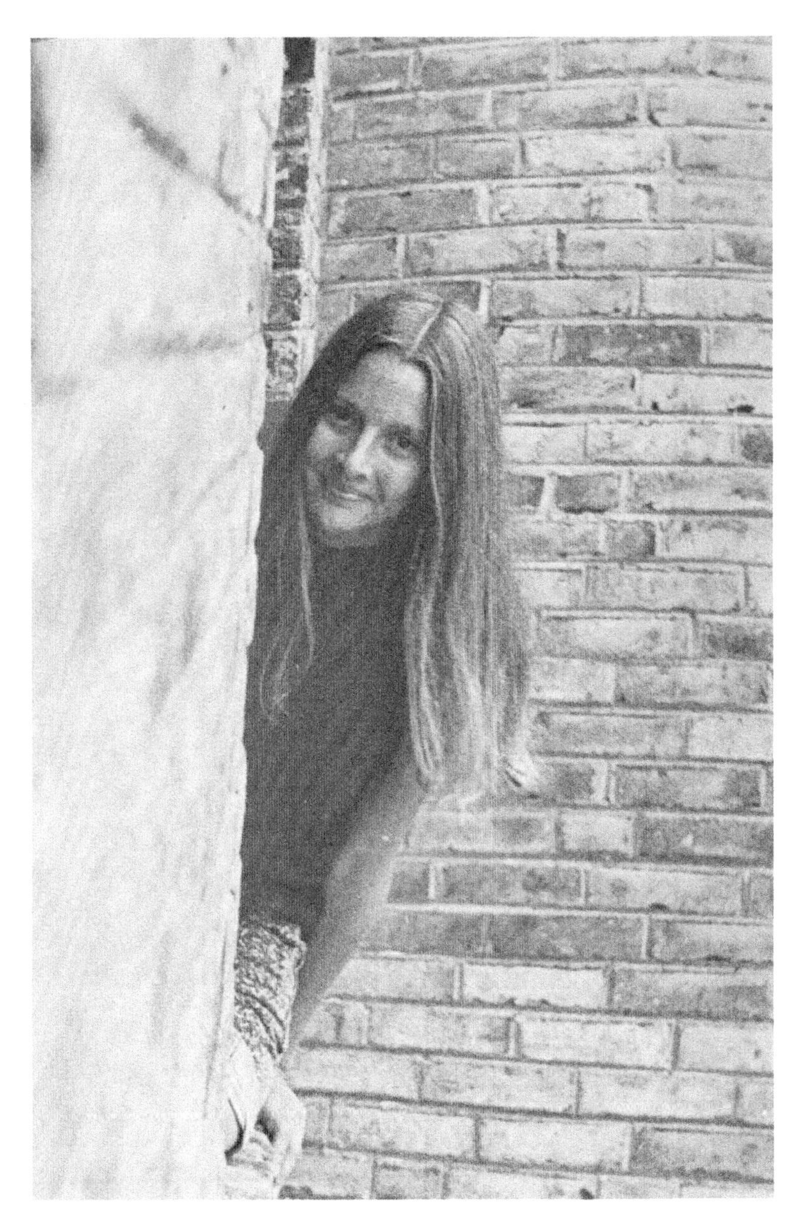

Figure 4: Virginia Olson, circa 1971, McLean High School, Photo Courtesy of: Virginia Room, Fairfax County Public Library

Figure 5: Virginia Olson, 1970, Photo Courtesy of: Virginia Room, Fairfax County Public Library

Figure 6: Virginia Olson, 1971 "Informal McLean High School Yearbook Picture," Photo Courtesy of: Virginia Room, Fairfax County Public Library

Figure 7: Aerial view of UNCA Campus circa 1973, Photo Courtesy of: D.H. Ramsey Library Special Collections, UNC Asheville, 28804

Figure 8: Students Moving in, August 1972, Photo Courtesy of: D.H. Ramsey Library Special Collections, UNC Asheville, 28804

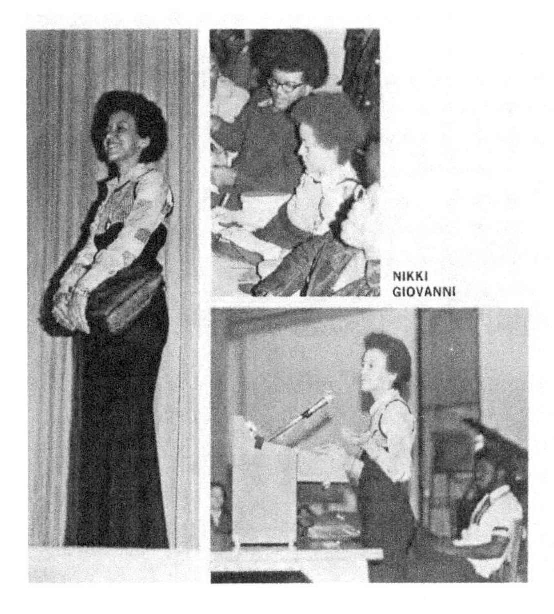

Figure 9: Poet Nikki Giovanni Visits UNC Asheville during 1972-1973 year, Photo Courtesy of: D.H. Ramsey Library Special Collections, UNC Asheville, 28804

Figure 10: UNC Asheville Students Attend Campus Assembly, Photo Courtesy of: D.H. Ramsey Library Special Collections, UNC Asheville, 28804

Figure 11: Winter, 1972-1973, at UNC Asheville, Photo Courtesy of: D.H. Ramsey Library Special Collections, UNC Asheville, 28804

Figure 12: Prof. Arnold Wengrow, who directed Virginia Olson in U.S.A during the Fall 1972 semester. This would be her final production, Photo Courtesy of: D.H. Ramsey Library Special Collections, UNC Asheville, 28804

Theatre of the University of North Carolina at Asheville
presents
John Dos Passos'

U.S.A.

Adapted by Paul Shyre
Directed by Arnold Wengrow

Setting by Dutch Folckemer — Costumes by Sharon Lyons
Lighting by Joe Smith and Dutch Folckemer
Choreography by Lynn Hyde

Lipinsky Auditorium — October 12, 13, 14, 1972

Cast

Fran Adams	Lachie MacLachlan
Kim English	Ginger Olson
Donna Glick	Gail P. Steinbauer
Lynn Hyde	Rob Storrs
Mary Ann Lampley	Jeffrey Sumeral
Dennis Lewter	Gregory Vines

The Young Man........Rob Storrs
J. Ward Moorehouse........Dennis Lewter
Mrs. Moorehouse........Gail P. Steinbauer
Marie O'Higgins........Donna Glick
Gertrude Staple........Mary Ann Lampley
Orville Wright........Gregory Vines
Wilbur Wright........Kim English
Mr. McGill........Jeffrey Sumeral
Ollie Taylor........Lachie MacLachlan
Eugene V. Debs........Jeffrey Sumeral
Janey Williams........Ginger Olson
Joe Williams........Lachie MacLachlan
Mrs. Williams........Gail P. Steinbauer
Alec McPherson........Kim English
Eleanor Stoddard........Fran Adams
Richard Ellsworth Savage........Rob Storrs
Colonel Edgecomb........Gregory Vines
Rudolph Valentino........Kim English
Henry Ford........Lachie MacLachlan
Isadora Duncan........Donna Glick
Mr. Bingham........Lachie MacLachlan

There will be one fifteen-minute intermission

Figure 13: Playbill from U.S.A, October 1972. Virginia Olson played "Janey Williams," Photo Courtesy of: D.H. Ramsey Library Special Collections, UNC Asheville, 28804

Figure 14: Botanical Gardens Walking Trail, 1973, Photo Courtesy of: D.H. Ramsey Library Special Collections, UNC Asheville, 28804

Figure 15: The last public image of Virginia Olson, Photo Courtesy of: D.H. Ramsey Library Special Collections, UNC Asheville, 28804

Figure 16: The UNCA Drama Department performed Tartuffe the same month Virginia Olson was killed, Photo Courtesy of: D.H. Ramsey Library Special Collections, UNC Asheville, 28804

Figure 17: Summer, 1973. Students departed campus with no resolution in the Olson case. Photo Courtesy of: D.H. Ramsey Library Special Collections, UNC Asheville, 28804

The Ridgerunner

Voice of the Students

Vol. 9, No. 5 — The University of North Carolina at Asheville — Sept. 21, 1973

Police Baffled in Olson Slaying

Financial Aid Still Available For Students

Although fall registration has been completed, funds are still available for students needing financial aid for the upcoming academic year, according to Jim Aiken, director of financial aid.

Presently, there are funds available through the National Direct Student Loan Program and the Federal College Work Study Program.

The following work study jobs are available for students: Ramsey Library, one position; foreign language lab, one position; and two positions in the maintenance building. The jobs are for 15 hours

Incoming chief of security, Eugene J. Ray, (center) demonstrates the workings of a walkie-talkie to William H. Pott, Vice Chancellor for Finance, (left) and to P. Thomas Deason, Dean of Students, (right) (Staff Photo by Sam Ferguson)

Ray Named Security Chief

By [illegible]
Staff Writer

The recent appointment of Eugene L. Ray as chief of security for the UNC-A campus marks the latest move by university officials to insure the safety [illegible] al guard to bring the total security force to six men.

In a recent interview, Ray pointed to new measures being taken this year by the UNC-A security force to protect students and [illegible] year security guards have access to an unmarked state car to use when patrolling the campus.

A two-way radio communications system has been installed in Vance Hall for use by the new security

Search Widens, But Assailant Remains Free

After more than five months of intense investigations, the Asheville Police Department and the State Bureau of Investigation remain baffled in the April 15 slaying of UNC-A co-ed Miss Virginia Marie Olson.

Miss Olson, known to her friends as Ginger, was found brutally raped and murdered at 3:30 p.m. Sunday April 15, on a hill across from the University Gardens on campus grounds.

"We're no further along in the investigation today than we were the first day," said Capt. W. H. Wall, chief of detectives for the APD.

Figure 18: Student-led newspapers continued to provide updates on the Olson investigation well into the 1973-1974 academic year, Photo Courtesy of: D.H. Ramsey Library Special Collections, UNC Asheville, 28804

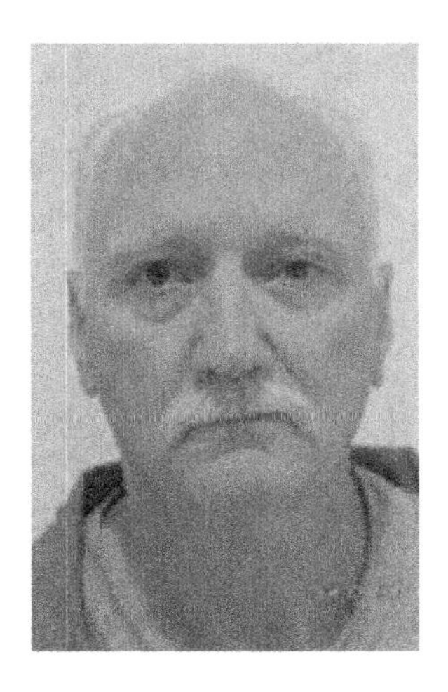

Figure 19: Terry Hyatt, one of North Carolina's most notorious serial killers, is currently on death row in Central Prison in Raleigh, NC, Photo Courtesy of NC Department of Corrections

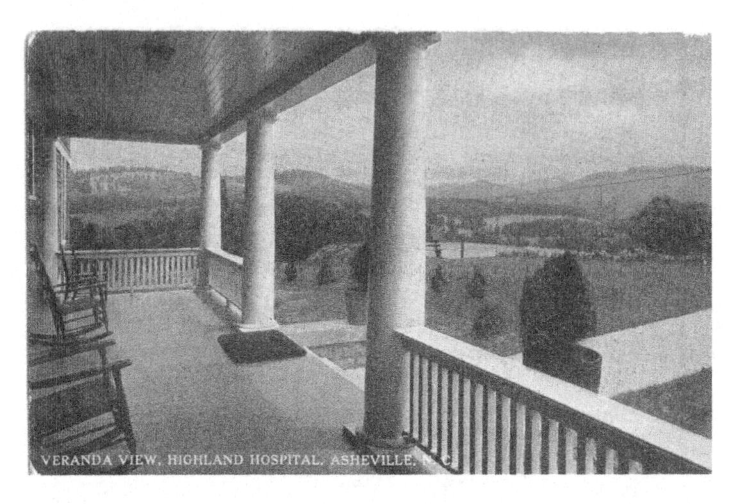

Figure 20: Highland Hospital Postcard, mid-20th century. Highland Hospital's marketing emphasized an atmosphere of ease and leisure. Photo Courtesy of: D.H. Ramsey Library Special Collections, UNC Asheville, 28804

Figure 21: Graduation Day, 1976. Olson would have graduated in this class. Photo Courtesy of: D.H. Ramsey Library Special Collections, UNC Asheville, 28804

Appendix of Select Public Records

See high resolution versions of these files at: https://wbp.bz/campusgallery

Appendix A:

Timeline of April 15, 2024

12:00-12:15 p.m.: Virginia Olson chats with her roommate Jane Nicholson in Craig Dormitory. She tells her that she plans to go to the Botanical Gardens to study for a Spanish final. She leaves by 12:15 and takes her glasses and books.

12:15-12:30 p.m.: Olson walks through the halls of Craig Dormitory and chats with a few friends who just arrived back in town from break.

12:30- 12:45 p.m.: Olson exists Craig Dormitory and chats in the parking lot with a few friends about Tartuffe, the latest UNC-A Theatre production, and about shared upcoming final exams. By 12:45 p.m. Olson excuses herself and walks towards the Botanical Gardens. She stops at Weaver Blvd and waves goodbye and then crosses the street and then goes through the entrance.

1:00 p.m.: James Goure tells Agent Charles Chambers that he brings John Reavis, Jr. to the botanical gardens and "pointed a girl to him."

1:05-1:15 p.m.: Ray D. Honeycutt observes a "dark, mod hair, white male with glasses and dark boots" walking up the bank towards Virginia Olson.

1:15 p.m.: Gerald Echols tells Agent Chambers that he observes a male and female sitting at the top of the bank.

1:15-1:45 [unaccounted for time]

1:45 p.m.: Gerald Echols passes by the area again on his way out of the park. He notices a something "flapping" (which we later learn was Olson's books), and also notes that the man and woman are no longer sitting on the bank.

2:45 p.m.: Judy Needles states that John Reavis Jr. approached her at her apartment and asked her to "pray with him."

3:30 p.m.: Thomas Guthrie (14 years old) and Larry O'Kelly (17 years old) find Olson's body in the middle of a well-worn path. They exit the Gardens and immediately make an effort to notify the Asheville Police.

4:00 p.m.: Multiple Asheville Police Department cruisers arrive. Two ambulances also arrive. Students and those who were walking in the park begin to walk towards the crime scene to see what is happening.

4:30 p.m.: Jane Nicholson becomes concerned by the commotion in the Botanical Gardens and asks some friends to take pictures of Olson down to the crime scene. Shortly after, police use these photos to make a positive identification. The SBI is notified of the incident shortly after the identification.

4:45 p.m.: Dr. Ray Hampton, the Buncombe County Medical Examiner officially arrives at the crime scene. He quickly determines he is dealing with a homicide and files a request for an autopsy.

8:00 p.m.: Dr. John McLeod performs Virginia Olson's autopsy.

Appendix B: Virginia Olson's Death Certificate

NORTH CAROLINA STATE BOARD OF HEALTH
OFFICE OF VITAL STATISTICS – RALEIGH

REGISTRATION DISTRICT NO. 11-95 LOCAL NO. ______ **MEDICAL EXAMINER'S CERTIFICATE OF DEATH** 681

DECEASED

1. NAME OF DECEASED (FIRST) Virginia (MIDDLE) Marie (LAST) Olson
2. DATE OF DEATH (MONTH, DAY, YEAR) April 15, 1973
3. SEX Female
4. COLOR or RACE White
5. STATE OF BIRTH (IF NOT IN U.S.A. NAME COUNTRY) D.C.
6. DATE OF BIRTH 9-13-53
7. AGE (IN YEARS LAST BIRTHDAY) 19 | IF UNDER 1 YEAR: MONTHS, DAYS | IF UNDER 24 HOURS: HOURS, MIN.

8a. PLACE OF DEATH COUNTY Buncombe
8b. CITY OR TOWN Asheville
8c. NAME OF HOSPITAL OR INSTITUTION (IF NOT IN EITHER, GIVE STREET AND NUMBER) UNCA Campus
8d. INSIDE CITY LIMITS (SPECIFY YES OR NO) Yes

USUAL RESIDENCE (WHERE DECEASED LIVED, IF INSTITUTION, RESIDENCE BEFORE ADMISSION)
9a. STATE N.C.
9b. COUNTY Davidson
9c. CITY OR TOWN Lexington
9d. STREET ADDRESS OR R.F.D. NO. 700 Carinal Drive
9e. INSIDE CITY LIMITS (SPECIFY YES OR NO) Yes

10. MARRIED, NEVER MARRIED, WIDOWED, DIVORCED (SPECIFY) Never married
11. SURVIVING SPOUSE (IF WIFE, GIVE MAIDEN NAME)
12. CITIZEN OF WHAT COUNTRY? USA
13. SOCIAL SECURITY NUMBER
14a. USUAL OCCUPATION (KIND OF WORK DONE DURING MOST OF WORKING LIFE, EVEN IF RETIRED) Student - UNCA
14b. KIND OF BUSINESS OR INDUSTRY

15. FATHER'S NAME C.Doswell Olson
16. MOTHER'S MAIDEN NAME Lurodine Woods
17a. INFORMANT'S NAME AND ADDRESS Mr C.D. Olson, 700 Cardinal Dr., Lexington, N.C.
17b. RELATION TO DECEASED Father

CAUSE

18. PART I. DEATH CAUSED BY: ENTER ONLY ONE CAUSE PER LINE FOR (a), (b), (c) | APPROXIMATE INTERVAL BETWEEN ONSET AND DEATH

(a) IMMEDIATE CAUSE: Stab wound left chest

CONDITIONS, IF ANY, WHICH GAVE RISE TO IMMEDIATE CAUSE(a), STATING THE UNDERLYING CAUSE LAST
(b) DUE TO, OR AS A CONSEQUENCE OF:
(c) DUE TO, OR AS A CONSEQUENCE OF:

19. PART II. OTHER SIGNIFICANT CONDITIONS CONTRIBUTING TO DEATH BUT NOT RELATED TO CAUSE GIVEN IN PART I (a) Laceration left neck
20a. AUTOPSY (SPECIFY) YES OR NO
20b. M.E. OR OTHER
20c. IF YES WERE FINDINGS CONSIDERED IN DETERMINING CAUSE OF DEATH

21a. ACCIDENT, SUICIDE, HOMICIDE, UNDETERMINED, NATURAL CAUSES, OR PENDING (SPECIFY) Homicide
21b. DESCRIBE HOW INJURY OCCURRED (ENTER NATURE OF INJURY IN PART I OR PART II, ITEM 18) stab wound by unknown person
21c. TIME OF INJURY MONTH 4 DAY 15 YEAR 73 HOUR 1P M
21d. INJURY AT WORK (SPECIFY YES OR NO) No
21e. PLACE OF INJURY AT HOME, FARM, STREET, FACTORY, OFFICE BLDG., ETC. (SPECIFY) Campus UNCA
21f. CITY OR R.F.D., COUNTY, STATE Asheville, Buncombe, N.C.

CERTIFIER

MEDICAL EXAMINER CERTIFICATION: ON THE BASIS OF THE EXAMINATION OF THE BODY AND/OR THE INVESTIGATION, IN MY OPINION, DEATH OCCURRED ON THE DATE AND DUE TO THE CAUSE(S) STATED.

22a. DEATH OCCURRED (HOUR) 1 P M.
22b. THE DECEDENT WAS PRONOUNCED DEAD MONTH 4 DAY 15 YEAR 73 HOUR 5:30 P M.
22c. DATE SIGNED (MONTH, DAY, YEAR) 4-15-73
23a. SIGNATURE Ray Hampton, M.D.
23b. ADDRESS Asheville, N.C.
23c. MEDICAL EXAMINER OF (SPECIFY COUNTY) Buncombe

BURIAL

24a. BURIAL, CREMATION, OTHER (SPECIFY) Burial
24b. DATE 4-19-73
24c. NAME OF CEMETERY OR CREMATORY New Prospect Bap.Ch.Cem.
24d. LOCATION (CITY, TOWN, OR COUNTY) (STATE) Parson, Tenn.
25. FUNERAL HOME NAME ADDRESS Anders-Rice, Asheville, N.C.
26. SIGNATURE OF FUNERAL DIRECTOR J.T. Rice
LICENSE NO. 373
27. DATE REC'D BY LOCAL REG. 5-2-73
28. SIGNATURE OF REGISTRAR H.W. Stevens, M.D.
29. SIGNATURE OF EMBALMER (IF EMBALMED) J. .Rice
LICENSE NO. 857

Appendix C: North Carolina Medical Examiner's File on Virginia Olson, April 15, 1973

2873 North Carolina State Board of Health 28
OFFICE OF THE CHIEF MEDICAL EXAMINER
CHAPEL HILL, NORTH CAROLINA 27514
MAY 02 1973

☐ Resident
☐ Nonresident

REPORT OF INVESTIGATION BY MEDICAL EXAMINER

DECEDENT Virginia (First name) Marie (Middle name) Olson 425 (Last name) AGE: 19 SEX: F RACE: W

ADDRESS 700 Cardinal Drive (Number and Street) - Lexington (City) - Davidson (County) M W (S) D OCCUPATION: student

TYPE OF DEATH: (Check one only)
Sudden in apparent health ☐
Unattended by a physician ☐
In police custody ☐
Violent or Unnatural ☑
Suspicious ☐
Unnusual ☐
Operating Room or Operative Death ☐
Means: (Agency or Object

	LAST SEEN ALIVE	INJURY OR ILLNESS	DEATH	MEDICAL EXAMINER NOTIFIED	VIEW OF BODY	POLICE NOTIFIED
DATE	4/15/73	4/15/73	4-15-73	4/15/73	4/15/73	4/15/73
TIME	12:15 PM	1 Pm	1 Pm	4:45 P	5:30 PM	3:38 P

IF MOTOR VEHICLE ACCIDENT CHECK ONE OF THE FOLLOWING: DRIVER ☐ PASSENGER ☐ PEDESTRIAN ☐

M.E. NOTIFIED BY: ADDRESS

	LOCATION	COUNTY	TYPE OF PREMISES (E. G., HOSPITAL, HOTEL, HIGHWAY, ETC.)
INJURY OR ONSET OF ILLNESS	UNCA Campus	Buncombe	University
DEATH	"	"	"
VIEWING OF BODY BY MEDICAL EXAMINER	"	"	"

DESCRIPTION OF BODY: CLOTHED ☐ UNCLOTHED ☐ PARTLY CLOTHED ☑ HAIR ___ BEARD ___ MUSTACHE ___ CIRCUMCISED ☐ PUPILS: R ___ L ___ EYES Color ___ OPACITIES, ETC.

	NOSE	MOUTH	EARS
BLOOD	No	No	No
FROTH	No	No	no
OTHER (Sand, dirt, water, etc.)	no	no	no

WEIGHT ___ LENGTH ___ BODY HEAT:

NON FATAL WOUNDS: ABRASION ☐ BURN ☐ CONTUSION ☐ STAB ☑ GUNSHOT ☐ INCISED ☐ LACERATION ☑ FRACTURE ☐
DISTRIBUTION: SCALP ☐ FACE ☐ NECK ☑ CHEST ☑ BACK ☐ ABDOMEN ☐ ARMS ☐ LEGS ☐

RIGOR: JAW ☐ ARMS ☐ NECK ☑ CHEST ☐ BACK ☐ ABDOMEN ☐ LEGS ☐ (none)

LIVOR: ANTERIOR ☐ POSTERIOR ☐ LATERAL ☐ REGIONAL ___

FATAL WOUNDS Blood EtOH Neg

TYPE (GUNSHOT, INCISED, STAB, ETC.)	SIZE	SHAPE	LOCATION	PLANE, LINE OR DIRECTION
Stab	1 in	Straight	Left chest ant.	
Laceration	4 in	"	Left neck	Horizontal

Probable cause of death: Massive blood loss, left chest

Manner of death: (Check one only) Accident ☐ Suicide ☐ Homicide ☑ Natural ☐ Unknown ☐ Pending ☐

ME Autopsy Authorized: Yes ☐ No ☑
Non-ME Autopsy Done: Yes ☐ No ☐
Pathologist Dr. John McLeod 35

I hereby certify that after receiving notice of the death described herein I took charge of the body and made inquiries regarding the cause of death in accordance with Art. 21, Chapter 130 of the General Statutes of North Carolina and the information contained herein regarding such death is true and correct to the best of my knowledge and belief.

4-30-73 (Date) Buncombe (County of Appointment) Ray Hampton (Signature of Medical Examiner) RJV

NORTH CAROLINA STATE BOARD OF HEALTH
OFFICE OF THE CHIEF MEDICAL EXAMINER
P. O. BOX 2488 - TEL. (919) 966-2027
CHAPEL HILL, NORTH CAROLINA 27514

V. Olson
Buncombe
4-15-73

TOXICOLOGY LABORATORY REPORT

DATE: April 17, 1973

FILE NUMBER: T-73-1697

NAME: Virginia Olson

MATERIAL SUBMITTED:

SUBMITTED BY: John A. McLeod, Jr., M.D.

DATE RECEIVED:

RESULTS:

Blood:
Ethanol: Negative

Other Volatiles: Negative

REPORTED BY Arthur J. McBay

SBH Form 1189 (Rev. 3/70)
Medical Examiner

Name: Virginia Olson
Age: 19 year old white female

A-92-73 MAY 17 1973
28
Paid

Source: Medical Examiner

Expired: April 15, 1973
Autopsy: April 15, 1973 8:00 P.M.

2873

Prosector: Dr. John A. McLeod, Jr.

Authority: Autopsy ordered by Dr. Ray Hampton, Medical Examiner of Buncombe Co.

DIAGNOSES

1. Stab wound, left anterior chest, penetrating: skin and subcutaneous tissue; 4th intercostal space, 2 cm. to the left of the sternum; pericardium; left ventricle of heart; and anterior portion of left upper lobe.

2. Intrapericardial hemorrhage ; massive.

3. Intrapleural hemorrhage, massive, left and moderate, right.

4. Intrapulmonary hemorrhage, slight, left upper lobe.

5. Cutaneous lacerations, deep, left neck, involving: skin and subcutaneous tissue; sterno-cliedo mastoideus muscle, left; external jugular vein; internal jugular vein; thyroid gland, left lobe; deep cervical muscle, left.

6. Small cutaneous petechiae, left forehead, periorbital region (not involving conjunctivae).

COMMENT: Death is attributed to the stab wound in the left chest which penetrated the left ventricle of the heart with massive intrapericardial, intrapleural hemorrhage and some external hemorrhage. The wound in the neck, though in itself lethal in nature, probably occurred after the stab wound of chest with minimal bleeding from the neck wound being evident. The external and internal genitalia showed no evidence of trauma but there were inactive and active spermatoza evident within the vaginal canal. The anal canal was negative.

ASSOCIATE CHIEF MEDICAL EXAMINER RJV

35

John A. McLeod, Jr., M.D./lb
Pathologist

GENERAL DESCRIPTION: The body is that of a well developed, moderately well nourished white female who appears the approximate age of 18-20. The body heat is absent. There is no rigor mortis evident. The body is clothed in a pair of faded blue denim dungrees and a brassiere. There are no underpants. There is blood on the brassiere, blood over the face, in the hair, around the neck. There is fecal and mud staining of the dungrees externally. The head is normocephalic. There is some straw and vegetable material around the hair. The pupils are .6 cm. bilateral and equal. Around the eyes, the skin around the left forehead present small petechiae. There is a gag in the mouth which pulls the lower jaws composed of green knit material which also is tied around the neck. In the left neck region is an 8 cm. deep laceration devoid of any cavitation marks which extends through the external cutaneous fat and facia to the sterno-clavial mastoidian muscle to the external jugular vein through the deep fascia, through the nuclear through the external jugular vein extending down to the carotid artery. The carotid artery is intact. There is incision through the left lobe of the thyroid extending through the trachea with involvement of the fascia of the trachea. The incision also includes the cervical muscles with extention into the superficial portions of the cervical muscle. There is a gold chain with a small fish madilion. The hands are tied behind the body with green shirt material. There are some small gravel abrasions in the elbows bilaterally. The nailbeds are markedly cyanotic. In the left chest in the 5th intercostal space 2 cm. to the left of the lateral sternal line is a 2.2 cm. laceration through which is bulging breast parenchyma and liquid clotted blood. The breasts are unremarkable. The axilla are free of adenopathy. The abdomen is soft. The external genitalia are unremarkable. The knees are muddy with small gravel marks and small abrasions .2 to .3 cm. in the left knee. The legs are bound together by the green material described. The feet are dirty on the soles of the feet and heels and around the toes. There is minimal excretment around the anus.

A primary Y-shaped incision is made. The body panniculus is scant. On opening the abdominal cavity the organ arrangement is not remarkable. There is no free blood nor fluid. In the area of the previously described stab wound in the left anterior chest there is discoloration of the adipose tissue of the underlying breast tissue which is red-purple. The puncture wound extends through the 4th intercostal space into the chest cavity. On removal of the chest plate the pericardium is distended with a laceration wound and there is approximately 50 ml. of liquid-clotted blood in the pericardial space. In the anterior left ventricle is a 2.4 cm. laceration which enters into the ventricular cavity. There is a small irregular laceration of the anterior surfac of the left upper lobe. The left lung is totally collapsed and there is approximately 2400 cc. of liquid-clotted blood in the left pleural space and approximately 500 cc. of similar blood in the righ pleural space. The heart otherwise is unremarkable as is the great vessels. The lung otherwise is unremarkable except for the laceration described.

There is extension of blood into the adipose tissue in the high 1st portion of the aorta. The trachea and larynx are intact. External laceration of the thyroid have been described. There is blood in the tracheo-bronchial tree.

DIGESTIVE: The esophagus, stomach, duodenum, jejunum and colon are unremarkable. The gallbladder contains 30 ml. of bile which is removed. The liver is a normal size. Portions are taken.

GENITO-URINARY: The kidneys bilaterally are unremarkable. The pelves and ureters are unremarkable. The bladder is devoid of urine. The internal female genitalia are unremarkable. The cervix is glistening, gray-white. There are some pubic hairs noted inside the vaginal cavity. Specimens are taken from the area of the cervix and the posterior vaginal vault. Combings of the pubic hair were made for hair comparision.

ENDOCRINE: The adrenal glands are not remarkable.

The pancreas is not remarkable.

HEMATOLYTOPOIETIC: The spleen and lymph nodes are not remarkable.

MICROSCOPIC EXAMINATION

CARDIOVASCULAR: The pericardium and epicardium focally contain extravasated erythrocytes. The coronary arteries contain minimal thickening by fibroconnective tissue. The lumens are patent. There is a transmural irregular laceration described grossly around which are extravasated erythrocytes in the anterior left ventricle of the heart. The pulmonary arteries, pulmonary veins and aorta are essentially unremarkable.

RESPIRATORY: Focally within the lungs are areas of extravasated erythrocytes with collapse of alveolar spaces in apposition of alveolar septa. There is minimal engorgement of the septal veins and capillaries by erythrocytes. There is focal disruption of the parenchyma in areas of extravasated erythrocytes.

DIGESTIVE: The esophagus, stomach, duodenum, jejunum and colon are all unremarkable. The gallbladder and liver are essentially unremarkable. There is moderate engorgement of the centrolobular vein portion of the liver by erythrocytes.

GENITO-URINARY: The kidneys, ureters and bladder are not remarkable.

Sections of uterus show the endometrium to be in the late proliferative and early secretory phase. The ovaries, Fallopian tubes, myometrium and cervix are essentially unremarkable.

ENDOCRINE: The adrenal glands are not remarkable.

The pancreas is not remarkable.

HEMATOLYTOPOIETIC: The splenic sinusoids are markedly engorged with erythrocytes. Lymph nodes are essentially unremarkable.

TOXICOLOGY

Negative.

COMMENT: Smears from the vagina and fornices show abundant spermatoza, some of which are still motile in the wet preparation.

Appendix D: NC SBI Affidavit to Obtain a Search Warrant, April 29, 1973

STATE OF NORTH CAROLINA
County of Buncombe

In The General Court of Justice
District Court Division

STATE

v.

JOHN REAVIS, JR.
205 Hillside, Apartment # 1
~~Gordon Apartments~~

AFFIDAVIT TO OBTAIN A SEARCH WARRANT

Charles D. Chambers, Agent, State Bureau of Investigation, Asheville, N. C.;
(Insert name and address; or if a law officer, then insert name, rank and agency)

being duly sworn and examined under oath, says under oath that he has probable cause to

believe that JOHN REAVIS, JR. has on his person, on his premises
(Insert name of Possessor) (Insert one or more of these phrases: on his premises; in his vehicle; on his person)

certain property, to wit: knife, white shirt with red in it, dark boots, eye glasses, part of a ladies' green "T" shirt, woman's garmets, college textbooks (UNC-Asheville), clothing of Virginia M. Olson; man's or woman's garmet containing blood, rust pants, hankerchie
(Describe the property sought)

~~(Insert one of these phrases: the possession of which is;~~ which were used in the commission of, and constitutes evidence of a crime, to wit: murder of Virginia M. Olson
~~stolen; which constitutes evidence of)~~ (Insert name of crime; and

April 15, 1973 across the street from Botanical Garden, Weaver Blvd, Asheville,
date, location ----- if known)

The property described above is located on the person of John Reavis, Jr., white, male 42-45, brown mod length hair, 6 feet tall, and on his premises, 205 Hillside, Apt. # 1
(Insert one or more of these phrases: on the premises; in the vehicle; on the person)

described as follows: red brick apartment, on the south side of Hillside, 1st premises on the right traveling east from Merrimon Avenue, Reavis' apartment 1st apartment on right as you enter building, and is designated #1
(Unmistakably describe the building, premises, vehicle, or person -- or combination - to be searched)

. The facts which establish probable cause for the issuance of a search warrant are as follows: (1) On 4-15-73 Virginia Olson was murdered at the top of a bank across the street from Botanical Gardens; part of her clothing was torn and there was blood at the scene, this happened between 12:00 Noon and 3:30 P.M.; her textbooks, glasses, and pin were found at or near a rock atop the bank in a clearing she was found dead 35 feet from the rock; (2) Ray D. Honeycutt told affiant that he saw a dark mod-haired white male, with glasses and dark boots go straight up the bank 1:05-1:15 P. M. (3) Gerald Echols told affiant that he saw a male & female atop bank about 1:15 PM & were gone at 1:45PM, 4-15-73, the same date Honeycutt saw a male (4)Mr. James Goure told affiant he carried Reavis to Botanical Gardens before 1:00 4-15-73 and pointed out a girl to him; when questioned 4-29-73 after Miranda rights Reavis said he saw a girl sitting on a rock atop the bank; the rock is only visible from atop bank & is not visible from Gardens or Weaver Blvd.; (5) Judy Needles told affiant that at 2;40PM, 4-15-73, Reavis came to her 5D Dunbar Apt, was nervous, & wanted someone to pray with him; Dunbar is 10 minute walk from crime scene, (6) on 4-29-73 Reavis was wearing boots, rust pants, wears glasses, and fits description Honeycutt gave your affiant.
(Continue if necessary)*

Sworn and subscribed to before me

this 29 day of April, 19 73.
10 o'clock Am.

Mary C. Lunsford
Magistrate, ~~Clerk of Superior Court~~

[Signature] Charles D. Chambers
Signature of Affiant

NOTE: The issuing official should swear the affiant twice, once to the affidavit and once before beginning the oral examination of the affiant.

*If a continuation is necessary, continue the statement on an attached sheet of paper with a notation saying "see attachment". Date the continuation and include on it the signatures of affiant and issuing official.

AOC-L Form 104

File # 73CR9415

Film # ______

In The General Court of Justice
District Court Division

STATE OF NORTH CAROLINA
County of Buncombe

SEARCH WARRANT

To Any Lawful Official Empowered to Conduct the Search Authorized by this Warrant -- GREETING:

Whereas information has been furnished me by the affiant named in the affidavit on the reverse hereof, who stated under oath that John Reavis, Jr. (Name of Possessor) has property described in said affidavit, related in the manner described in the affidavit with the commission of a crime, also described in the said affidavit, that such property is located as described in the affidavit. And whereas I have examined under oath the affiant and am satisfied that there is probable cause to believe that the named person has such property on his person, and on his premises (Insert one or more of these phrases: on his premises; in his vehicle; on his person) described in the aforesaid affidavit, you are commanded to search the premises described in the aforesaid affidavit, and John Reavis, Jr. (Insert one or more of these phrases: the premises; the vehicle, name of person) for the property in question. If this property is found, seize it and keep it subject to court order.

Herein fail not and of this warrant make due return.

Issued this 29 day of April, 1973, at 10:05 o'clock (~~A.M~~) (P.M) upon information furnished under oath by the affiant, named below:

Charles D Chambers
(Name of Affiant)
Charles D. Chambers, S. B. I. Agent

Mary C. Lunsford
Magistrate, ~~Clerk of Superior Court~~, Judge

______
(Type or print name of issuing official)

File No. 73CR 9415

THE STATE

vs.

John Reavis, Jr.

SEARCH WARRANT

Issued: April 29, 1973, 19__

at 10:05 (~~A.M.~~)(P.M.)

RETURN

I hereby certify that on April 29,

1973 at 10:05 (~~A.M.~~)(P.M)

this Search Warrant came into my hands, and

that on April 29, 1973 at

10:30 (~~A.M~~) (P.M), I

made search of 205 Hillside Apt #1

and John Reavis

as therein commanded. I took into my custody the following: 1 pr Brown Dingo Boots, 1 white shirt, 1 yellow shirt, 1 kitchen knife, 1 white handkerchief, 1 yellow shirt

which is held subject to further court orders.

This 29 day of April, 1973

at 11:10 (~~A.M.~~)(P.M.)

Carlos D. [illegible]
(Signature)

N.C.S.B.I.
(Title and Agency)

This executed search warrant was returned to me on ~~[illegible]~~ April 29, 1973 at

11:48 (~~A.M.~~)(P.M.)

Mary C. Lunsford
Signature of officer of General Court of Justice

For More News About Brian Santana and Cameron Santana, Signup For Our Newsletter:

http://wbp.bz/newsletter

Word-of-mouth is critical to an author's long-term success. If you appreciated this book please leave a review on the Amazon sales page:

https://wbp.bz/amoc

ALSO AVAILABLE FROM WILDBLUE PRESS

http://wbp.bz/obsessed

ALSO AVAILABLE FROM WILDBLUE PRESS

http://wbp.bz/cb

Made in the USA
Monee, IL
25 January 2025